DRINK AND DEMOCRACY

INTOXICATING HISTORIES

Series Editors: Virginia Berridge and Erika Dyck

Whether on the street, off the shelf, or over the pharmacy counter, interactions with drugs and alcohol are shaped by contested ideas about addiction, healing, pleasure, and vice and their social dimensions. Books in this series explore how people around the world have consumed, created, traded, and regulated psychoactive substances throughout history. The series connects research on legal and illegal drugs and alcohol with diverse areas of historical inquiry, including the histories of medicine, pharmacy, consumption, trade, law, social policy, and popular culture. Its reach is global and includes scholarship on all periods. Intoxicating Histories aims to link these different pasts as well as to inform the present by providing a firmer grasp on contemporary debates and policy issues. We welcome books, whether scholarly monographs or shorter texts for a broad audience focusing on a particular phenomenon or substance, that alter the state of knowledge.

1 *Taming Cannabis*
Drugs and Empire in Nineteenth-Century France
DAVID A. GUBA, JR

2 *Cigarette Nation*
Business, Health, and Canadian Smokers, 1930–1975
DANIEL J. ROBINSON

3 *Remedicalising Cannabis*
Science, Industry, and Drug Policy
SUZANNE TAYLOR

4 *Mixing Medicines*
The Global Drug Trade and Early Modern Russia
CLARE GRIFFIN

5 *Drugging France*
Mind-Altering Medicine in the Long Nineteenth Century
SARA E. BLACK

6 *Psychedelic New York*
A History of LSD in the City
CHRIS ELCOCK

7 *Disparate Remedies*
Making Medicines in Modern India
NANDINI BHATTACHARYA

8 *Art, Medicine, and Femininity*
Visualising the Morphine Addict in Paris, 1870–1914
HANNAH HALLIWELL

9 *A Thirst for Wine and War*
The Intoxication of French Soldiers on the Western Front
ADAM D. ZIENTEK

10 *Pharmacopoeias, Drug Regulation, and Empires*
Making Medicines Official in Britain's Imperial World, 1618–1968
STUART ANDERSON

11 *The Hour of Absinthe*
A Cultural History of France's Most Notorious Drink
NINA S. STUDER

12 *Drink and Democracy*
Alcohol and the Political Imaginary in Colonial Australia
MATTHEW ALLEN

MATTHEW ALLEN

DRINK AND DEMOCRACY

Alcohol and the Political Imaginary in Colonial Australia

McGill-Queen's University Press
Montreal & Kingston · London · Chicago

ISBN 978-0-2280-2474-3 (paper)
ISBN 978-0-2280-2500-9 (ePDF)
ISBN 978-0-2280-2501-6 (ePUB)

Legal deposit second quarter 2025
Bibliothèque et Archives nationales
du Québec

Printed in Canada on acid-free paper that is 100% ancient-forest-free, containing 100% sustainable, recycled fibre, and processed chlorine-free.

McGill-Queen's University Press in Montreal is on land which long served as a site of meeting and exchange amongst Indigenous Peoples, including the Haudenosaunee and Anishinabeg nations. In Kingston it is situated on the territory of the Haudenosaunee and Anishinaabek. We acknowledge and thank the diverse Indigenous Peoples whose footsteps have marked these territories on which peoples of the world now gather.

This book was designed and typeset by Garet Markvoort, zijn digital, in 10/14.5 Range Serif with Range Sans and Trade Gothic Std. Copyediting by Ryan Perks.

LIBRARY AND ARCHIVES CANADA CATALOGUING IN PUBLICATION

Title: Drink and democracy : alcohol and the political imaginary in colonial Australia / Matthew Allen.
Names: Allen, Matthew (Historian and criminologist), author.
Series: Intoxicating histories ; 12.
Description: Series statement: Intoxicating histories ; 12 | Includes bibliographical references and index.
Identifiers: Canadiana (print) 2024052358X | Canadiana (ebook) 20240523644 | ISBN 9780228024743 (paper) | ISBN 9780228025009 (ePDF) | ISBN 9780228025016 (ePUB)
Subjects: LCSH: Drinking of alcoholic beverages—Political aspects—Australia—New South Wales—History—19th century. | LCSH: Drinking of alcoholic beverages—Social aspects—Australia—New South Wales—History—19th century. | LCSH: Intoxication—Australia—New South Wales—History—19th century. | LCSH: Temperance—Australia—New South Wales—History—19th century. | LCSH: Democracy—Australia—New South Wales—History—19th century. | LCSH: New South Wales—Social life and customs—19th century.
Classification: LCC GT2883.A8 .A45 2025 | DDC 394.1/30994409034—dc23

McGill-Queen's University Press
Suite 1720, 1010 Sherbrooke St West,
Montreal, QC, H3A 2R7

Authorized safety representative in the EU: Mare Nostrum Group BV, Mauritskade 21D, 1091 GC Amsterdam, the Netherlands, gpsr@mare-nostrum.co.uk

For Christina and Pierre: democracy also begins at home …

CONTENTS

Figures ix

Acknowledgments xi

Introduction
Drinking and the Democratic Political Imaginary 3

1 A Necessary Evil
Alcohol in Eighteenth-Century Britain 24

2 Politics in Colonial New South Wales, 1788–1860 44

3 Drunken Freedom and Fraternity
The Political Meaning of Popular Drinking 63

4 Toasting and Dining
The Politics of Public Drinking in the British World 85

5 Public Dinners and the Political Imaginary in New South Wales 105

6 The Temperance Movement
Persuasion and Compulsion 123

7 Imagining a Sober Public
Temperance as a Democratic Ideal 136

8 Drinking as a Gendered Performance 154

9 Drunken Savagery
Imagining Aboriginal Drunkenness 181

Conclusion
Toasting Democracy: The National Banquet 204

Notes 215

Bibliography 247

Index 281

FIGURES

1.1 William Hogarth, *Beer Street* and *Gin Lane* (1751). Source: Metropolitan Museum of Art. 32.35 (123–4). 38–9

4.1 Unknown artist, frontispiece in Robert Pocock, *Pocock's Everlasting Songster …* (London: R. Pocock, 1804). 89

5.1 Thomas Rowlandson, *The Brilliants* (1801). Source: Metropolitan Museum of Art. 59.533.1155. 109

7.1 George Cruickshank, *Fearful Quarrels and Brutal Violence …* (1847). Source: Plate 6 in *The Bottle, a Series of Temperance Themed Illustrations by George Cruikshank, with Poetry by Charles Mackay* (London: D. Bogue, 1847). Wellcome Collection. 149

9.1 Augustus Earle, *Natives of N.S. Wales as Seen in the Streets of Sydney* (London: C. Hullmadel, 1830). Source: Dixson Library, State Library of NSW. DL Pe 21. 194

9.2 Unknown artist, *Real Life in Sydney* (ca 1838). Source: Mitchell Library, State Library of NSW. B 1106. 195

10.1 Samuel T. Gill, *Old Colonists' Festival* (Melbourne: J.S. Campbell and Co., 1853). Source: State Library of Victoria. PCLTFBOX, Gill Large Lithographs. 207

10.2 Samuel T. Gill, *Old Colonists' Festival Dinner …* (Adelaide: Penman and Galbraith, 1851). Source: Dixson Library, State Library of NSW. DG V*/Sp Coll/Gill/1. 208

10.3 Samuel T. Gill, *Digger's Wedding in Melbourne* (1852). Source: *Australian Diggers*, ed. D.S. Mitchell (Melbourne, n.d.), 48. Mitchell Library, State Library of NSW. DSM/741/G. 209

ACKNOWLEDGMENTS

My interest in the history of alcohol had its origins in my PhD thesis, "The Temperance Shift: Drunkenness, Responsibility and the Regulation of Alcohol in NSW, 1788–1856," and I need first and foremost to thank my supervisor, Professor Richard Waterhouse. That thesis, however, was largely concerned with alcohol regulation, a subject I barely touch on here. Over the following decade, I have remained interested in alcohol but have increasingly focused on drinking culture and ritual, and their political meanings, and this book is the result.

During the long evolution of this project, I was based at the University of New England, and my colleagues in the School of Humanities, Arts and Social Sciences (under all its many administrative labels) have been a constant and essential support. Their collective patience, wisdom, and empathy was the foundation of my development as a scholar, and this book is a testament to the intellectual culture of Australia's oldest regional university. I especially want to thank Nathan Wise, Richard Scully, David Roberts, and Hamish Maxwell-Stewart from the Discipline of History, as well as the members of the Heteropessimists: Felicity Jospeh, Christina Kenny, and Jennifer Hamilton. I also need to thank the Faculty of Humanities, Arts, Social Sciences and Education for helping subsidize this publication.

The staff at the Mitchell Library, State Library of New South Wales, the Dixson Library at the University of New England, and the New South Wales State Records were uniformly helpful, not least in digitizing resources. My debt to the Trove database, facilitated by the National Library of Australia, will be obvious to everyone familiar with this wonderful resource.

I also need to acknowledge permission to reproduce artworks from the collections of the Mitchell and Dixson Libraries, State Library of New South Wales, the State Library of Victoria, and the National Library of Australia.

DRINK AND DEMOCRACY

INTRODUCTION

Drinking and the Democratic Political Imaginary

On Friday, 9 November 1827, the members of the Sydney Turf Club gathered at the Sydney Hotel on Macquarie Place, in the city's centre, "for discussing a most important subject in the eyes of every Englishman, viz. a good dinner."[1] This "public" dinner was a celebration in honour of the club's late patron and the former governor of New South Wales, Sir Thomas Brisbane, who had donated a cup and a medal to the club as prizes shortly before leaving the colony in 1825. Advertisements in the press notified the reading public of the event, and four "stewards" were chosen in advance: John Mackaness, the Sydney sheriff, George Savage and Edward Aspinall, both merchants, and William Wentworth, a barrister and the leading figure in the nascent democratic movement within the colony. The current governor, Ralph Darling, had also succeeded Brisbane as patron of the Turf Club and was invited to the dinner but declined to attend.[2]

On the day itself about forty men, a "numerous assemblage of naval, military, civil, and law officers, with many private gentlemen," gathered around the giant table, "unanimously" elected Wentworth to serve as chairman and Mackaness as vice-chair, and at six o'clock sat down to dine.[3] Dinner concluded, the cloth was removed from the table, champagne circulated, and the main event commenced: a series of formal toasts, delivered by the chairman, all given "three times three" – with three cheers – accompanied by patriotic music from the band of the 57th Regiment.[4]

As tradition demanded, Wentworth began by toasting the King (accompanied by "God Save the King"), then "The Lord High Admiral" ("Rule Britannia"), and the Army ("George the Fourth's Grand March"). He then proposed the former Governor Brisbane in a longer – and published – speech celebrating him as "the father of Australia ... who mixed among the people, who came into our views, was present at our dinners, assemblies, and meetings ... who fondly cherished every infantile attempt at advancement ... not only by his countenance and interest, but ... [by] private as well as public pecuniary aids. He was the earliest political friend of which the Colony had to boast." The health of Sir Thomas Brisbane "was drunk with the most unbounded enthusiasm, the shouts of applause lasting for several minutes" over the strains of "Auld Lang Syne."[5]

Following this panegyric, Wentworth proposed a series of shorter toasts appropriate to the occasion: the governor and the colony ("Over the Hills and Far Away"); the ladies of the colony ("Queen Caroline's Waltz"); "the Turf with all its consequences" ("Gallop"); "the Jockey Club of England with all the fun and frolic attendant on it" ("Sydney Lasses"); success to the Sydney races ("Black Joke"); and Colonel Shadford and the 57th Regiment ("Rond de Leon"). Dr Douglass, a surgeon and commissioner of the Court of Requests, then proposed Wentworth's health ("Australian Troop"); and Mr Garling, a solicitor and clerk of the peace, celebrated the judges of the colony. Further toasts were not reported, with the exception of a second celebration of "Sir Australia Thomas Brisbane [*sic*], a Native of the Colony, and honorary Member of the Turf Club." The evening concluded with "a few excellent songs," and the whole dinner was reportedly marked by "the utmost harmony and conviviality."[6]

Such public dinners among gentlemen were common in the British colony of New South Wales, but this particular dinner was unusual for being explicitly politicized. The song chosen to honour Governor Darling, "Over the Hills and Far Away," was intended, and immediately perceived, as a deliberate insult that reflected growing public hostility toward him. E.S. Hall, the editor of *The Monitor*, a paper dedicated to the political interests of former convicts (known as emancipists) and highly critical of the governor, claimed that the meeting was "a tolerable representation of public feeling in matters of politics." Though not in attendance himself, he argued that the message the diners intended to convey to Darling and his British superiors was "to testify, by our toasts as well as by our tunes ... our dislike, aversion to, and hatred of [their] aggressions on our properties, liberties, and personal comforts."[7] Robert Wardell, a fellow barrister and ally of Wentworth's, was the editor of *The Australian* (which they co-owned), another, more Whiggish paper that regularly criticized Darling and his administration. His account of the dinner pointedly contrasted the sociability of the former and current governors and linked this to the state of colonial society. Brisbane's "respect for the people's wishes ... and frequent intercourse with individuals and with public bodies, kept society together"; while Darling "has been nearly two years in the Colony, and he has not once condescended to dine either with a gentleman of the Colony, or with the members of any public body," a fact that Wardell linked to the current atmosphere of "suspicion and dislike."[8]

Darling's governorship was defined by his conflict with a growing movement for colonial democracy and its campaign for emancipist rights, elected representatives, jury trial, and a free press, a movement in which Wentworth, Hall, and Wardell were key players. In this context, he saw the dinner as a calculated insult and accordingly resigned as patron of the club and dismissed the members of his administration who had attended the dinner – notably Mackaness and Douglass – from their positions. However, Darling's superiors in London were unimpressed by this petulance, and reprimanded him for allowing his personal opinions and feelings to interfere in the government of the colony.[9] The incident itself subsequently became a political symbol in New South Wales and was mockingly recalled when Darling departed the colony in 1831, an event celebrated with a drunken public festival, held at Wentworth's harbour-side villa, Vaucluse, at which the song was probably performed once more.[10] The insulting toasting of Governor Darling is thus a minor but emblematic moment in the history of democracy in New South Wales.

But this dinner – and more broadly, public dining and the drinking rituals that accompanied it – can tell us a great deal more about colonial politics and the intellectual world in which it operated. Leaving aside the specific insult to Governor Darling, the dinner embodied a tradition that is highly revealing of the British political imaginary, the major focus of this book. This was more than a meeting of a social club over a meal. In the context of colonial politics, and in the light of British traditions, it was also a patriotic celebration of empire, an affirmation of the political hierarchy, the cementing of a fraternal network through public sociability, the performance of a ritual of government, and a subversive argument for democracy.

First, it is worth drawing attention to the *public* elements of the occasion. As noted above, the dinner was announced in advance in the press and reported in all three Sydney papers. The official *Gazette* confined itself to a brief notice, but *The Australian* recorded the toasts, gave a shorter version of Wentworth's speech, and published the editorial cited above, and the radical *Monitor* gave the most extensive account and inspired the subsequent controversy with Hall's interpretation of the song.[11] Such published reports of men dining, drinking, and toasting together, and often of the speeches they gave, were common even when there was no controversy. Indeed, they constitute a significant proportion of colonial literature: at least one such dinner was reported in the press every week in 1827, usually in all three papers. In this explicitly public context, and in a society with no elected political representation, the toasts and accompanying speeches (and songs) at public dinners were an important form of public speech, and their reporting an influential discourse. But the limited nature of the sociably dining public was also telling. Diners were exclusively male, ethnically British, and came from a limited social elite of wealthier emigrants, so-called natives – locally born colonists – and sometimes emancipists. No women, Aboriginal people, or convicts under sentence were present, symbolizing the limits of this emerging public.

Just as importantly, the formal elements of public dinners, notably the appointment of stewards and a chairman, and the protocols of public speaking, echoed a parliament.[12] While the dinner was dominated by the wealthiest and most important guests, and centred on a celebration of the monarch, his senior officials, and the social elite, it was also democratic and rule-bound. The chair was elected (by universal affirmation) and his authority came from a well-understood but unstated code of conduct; indeed, much of the subsequent controversy centred on whether Wentworth and Wardell had breached this unwritten code. As with British politics more broadly, the dinner honoured and reaffirmed the elite of the traditional social order through the endorsement of a wider (but still limited) constituency of gentlemen. Also echoing a parliament, these traditional forms offered the potential to challenge and even subvert hierarchical authority. By insisting on and celebrating the right of assembly, public dinners helped expand the political category of gentlemen – a form of proto-citizenship – and affirmed a kind of fraternal solidarity among them. Gentlemen toasted loyally, but also noisily and publicly, asserting a powerful kind of political voice.

Finally, this public political performance was conducted with alcohol – and copious quantities of it. Based on what was reported, the guests drank wines with dinner and then performed at least twelve separate toasts, each of which required them to drain their glass. No one who participated fully left such dinners sober. The influence of alcohol mattered for the politics of this drinking ritual because drunkenness granted a degree of licence for breaching conventional norms. It probably encouraged the reckless taunting of the governor; indeed, justifying events, Wardell later stressed that the song had been chosen in the heat of the moment, amid a "very convivial party ... the extreme of joviality – and at moments rather noisy mirth."[13] At the same time, public drinking was also a test of civility, one that Wardell insisted they had passed. Gentlemen were expected to display self-control, constraining their behaviour within acceptable norms – performing what I term restrained drinking. The successful performance of such self-control was politically powerful, a demonstration of responsibility as a citizen, one entitled to a say in government. Toasting gentlemen also expressed a kind of homosociality that was implicitly egalitarian: by getting drunk together they demonstrated a collective trust and equality that was at once inclusive as well as exclusive (most obviously of women).[14] The expansion of this masculine ritual embodies the story of democracy in colonial New South Wales and the broader British Empire: growing numbers of white men were politically empowered, but simultaneously the boundaries of this expanding public sphere were strictly drawn to exclude outsiders, notably women and Aboriginal people.

Drinking also had other political meanings. Drunkenness was a powerful symbol of deviance in British discourse about idleness, disorder, and immorality, especially in the context of a convict society in the process of transforming into a settler colony. To this end, the praiseworthy harmony and conviviality of the gentlemen at their public dinner may be usefully contrasted with a police report published on the same day. On Sunday, 11 November, Mary Burt, a convict who had recently fled from her husband, was arrested by a constable, charged with "drunken and disorderly behaviour … upon the street," and sentenced by the acting magistrate to one month in the Third Class of the Female Factory, a workhouse for recalcitrant female convicts.[15] The reporter described Burt's arrest within a literary tradition of humorous public shaming of drunkards (especially women) and employed a series of classic tropes, describing her as "a woman after the flesh – as frail a rib as any son of Adam was ever troubled with" and her behaviour as "most uproarious."[16] We know little more of Burt herself, but her drinking was obviously public and visible in a very different sense to that of the dining gentlemen, although she is unlikely to have consumed more alcohol than they did. Drinking comportment was subjective, a performance that was judged by the social audience and shaped by the discursive symbolism of drunkenness. Restraint and drunkenness were not simply agentive choices, they were perceptions. When someone like Mary Burt drank in public, they were almost invariably read as drunken, and condemned – if not policed – accordingly. Only gentlemen could perform the kind of sociability that made drinking convivial and restrained, rather than drunken.

Thus I argue that the history of public drinking in colonial New South Wales reveals the British political imaginary as it became increasingly democratic. Public toasting enacted a vision of a political order, and this vision was fundamentally egalitarian for those with the right to drink. Equally, the shameful and unruly public drunkenness of convicts, and other drinkers deemed deviant, symbolized their exclusion from political society, since they were understood as unwilling or unable to display the self-control required of citizens. Even as New South Wales became an electoral democracy on a broad male franchise, political agency was imagined as the exclusive privilege of those capable of proper restraint, symbolized in respectable drinking.

Performative Political Imaginaries

My argument draws on a long theoretical tradition to interpret ritualized drinking practices as political performances.[17] Based on the pioneering work of Erving Goffmann, I see all public drinking as a form of self-presentation for the audience of society.[18] Following Clifford Geertz and the many ethnographic historians influenced by him, I interpret cultural practices in theatrical terms, and see drinking rituals in particular as scripted performances that can be understood through "thick description" of what they meant for participants.[19] Drinking rituals in general and toasting in particular were "repeated, standardised and public" behaviour that was distinct from everyday life and took on symbolic meaning accordingly.[20] Toasting is politically performative – a speech act that asserts a particular social hierarchy – within a scripted tradition that is dynamically shaped by actor and audience. As Judith Butler argues, performative speech acts are "one of the powerful and insidious ways in which subjects are called into social being"; and rituals of assembly can serve as a performative democratic claim to speak for the people.[21] When the Turf Club mocked Governor Darling they were playing their scripted parts in a well-known ritual, but they were also subverting that ritual to offer a political critique and claim a political citizenship that did not exist in law. In this interaction between script and performance – drinking traditions and drinking practices – as well as actor and audience – drinker and society –

I find evidence for the historical development of a democratic political imaginary.

My understanding of politics is shaped by cultural history, and specifically by recent efforts to move the history of political thought beyond high politics and the history of ideas.[22] This project emerges from the long tradition of studying mentalities in cultural history, but I am especially influenced by Charles Taylor's more explicitly theorized notion of social imaginaries: "that common understanding that makes possible common practice and a widely shared sense of legitimacy."[23] While Taylor is (largely) concerned with modern disenchantment and immanence as the background to secularism, his concept of a historically contingent background of common understandings that underlie ideas can be usefully applied to the political thought of the nineteenth century.[24] Taylor also draws on Benedict Anderson's "imagined communities," but his imaginaries are not explicitly tied to nations and national identity and have a reflexive relationship with the practices that evoke and sustain them.[25]

Taylor's focus on imaginaries is echoed by recent trends in intellectual history, which has increasingly shifted from the history of ideas to what Elías José Palti calls a history of political languages. This new intellectual history is focused not on the surface ideological content of ideas but on "the argumentative apparatus that undergirds them," the "contexts of debate," or "the deep assumptions that constitute the language in which ... ideas are articulated."[26] I am more interested in performative practices than the political language of democracy, but I share this theoretical framing of the problem and its concern with underlying and unarticulated political thought. The toasting of Darling exemplifies a tradition and reveals the implicit political understandings that informed it, but it also demonstrates the ways in which this political background was challenged and performatively shaped by the public who collectively imagined it.

As I argue, this political imaginary was increasingly democratic. Democracy is a concept that notoriously evades easy definition; it is amorphous, contested, and plural. Benjamin Isakhan summarizes the core principles of democratic societies as "citizens ... invested with the full rights and responsibilities of citizenship; governed by a set of laws or norms that both protect their citizenship and hold to account those in power; and actively encouraged to contest, cooperate and participate in political life."[27] However, I am less concerned with democratic institutions or principles than with the shared sense that the public had a legitimate and authoritative political voice, a development that I argue preceded the granting of elections in colonial New South Wales. This understanding of democracy has its origins in the nineteenth century, especially in the work of Alexis de Tocqueville, who influentially read American democracy as a culture as much as a political system.[28]

I also draw on Jürgen Habermas's influential notion of an emerging bourgeois public sphere in early modern Europe in which the expansion of the press, and of the reading public and their discussion of politics, "connects society with the state and thus has a function in the political realm."[29] Subsequent scholarship has shown that the notion of a rational – and at least metaphorically sober – public was a discursive construction that limited political citizenship. As Joan Landes argues, the construction of feminine concerns as private and masculine ones as properly public was a "constitutive" feature of the bourgeois public sphere and meant that men were "better suited" to perform the "disinterestedness" and "rationality" required in public.[30] In contrast, Ian Newman argues for the emergence of what he terms a "convivial public sphere" in the second half of the eighteenth century, that "drew on fashionable sociability to produce a much more ludic and celebratory form of gathering organized around rituals of drinking, singing, and toasting," and centred on principles of "humour, sentiment and mutuality."[31] I argue that, in the British political imaginary, these idealized forms of fraternal sociability – sober debate and drunken conviviality – formed a kind of dialectic, helping to produce masculine political authority, which was especially important to public life in a male-dominated convict colony.[32]

My approach embraces what James Vernon has called "a new cultural history of the meanings of politics … the ways in which politics defined and imagined people."[33] Similarly, it echoes Patrick Joyce's focus on a "democratic imaginary," the subject of "demotic identities, often formed outside and prior to politics."[34] Importantly, this cultural history of democracy supports a healthy skepticism about the difference between democratic ideals and practice. As Vernon argues, English politics "became progressively less democratic" in the mid-nineteenth century, despite the rhetoric of reform, and the normalization of the term.[35] In a broader theoretical critique, Sheldon Wolin understands democracy as "a project concerned with the political potentialities of ordinary citizens," argues that "institutionalization marks the attenuation of democracy," a means of restraining the public will, and in consequence, sees true democracy as "fugitive" and momentary.[36] Building on Wolin, I characterize democracy in New South Wales and the wider British Empire as elusive, in the sense that the rare moments where the public had a meaningful voice often occurred in spite, not because, of formal political institutions. It is on this basis that I focus on the underlying political imaginary and not political events or even explicit political debate.

New South Wales held its first election (for the Sydney Council) in 1842, and by 1860, it was a self-governing colony, significantly more democratic than Britain in Isakhan's terms. Most scholarship on colonial democracy focuses on political ideas, notably Australian republicanism, electoral politics in the decades after 1840, and the campaign for responsible government (granted by Britain in 1856).[37] Terry Irving's work on mid-nineteenth-century Sydney is more relevant to mine because he is concerned with "the spread of the democratic sensibility" rather than the formal politics of the legislature, arguing that working men were mobilized to form "an alternate public" through "a model of acting democratically," primarily in public meetings.[38] I am especially influenced by Alan Atkinson's lyrical account of the mid-nineteenth-century Australian colonies, in which he argues that democracy was "a great shift in common imagination ... [that] had gradually taken root in Australian minds" for several decades before the first elections, and illustrates this in relation to both public meetings and the engagement of a growing literate public in the public sphere.[39] I argue similarly that public drinking practices can reveal an increasingly democratic political imaginary that preceded, underlay, and informed the better-known electoral politics. But, as I show, the drinking public was always a more or less exclusive fraternity, and the limitations on who was imagined as a legitimate public drinker, and the authority they acquired through public drinking rituals, symbolize the broader political exclusion on which "democratic" politics relied.

My argument is also influenced by debates around Russel Ward's concept of an "Australian Legend," a kind of "national mystique" and an "apotheosis" of character traits that were allegedly typical of convicts and rural workers. Ward famously defined his legendary Australian as a man who "swears hard and consistently, gambles heavily and often and drinks deeply on occasion ... He believes that Jack is not only as good as his master but ... probably a good deal better. [He] will stick to his mates through thick and thin, even if he thinks they may be in the wrong."[40] Ward was always ambiguous about the degree to which these traits were real or ideal, and the distinction matters for my argument: arguably, heavy fraternal drinking became less and less typical over the nineteenth century, even as it was increasingly idealized.[41] But I argue that such egalitarian mateship – crucially, limited to men – was a core democratic element of the political imaginary, frequently manifested in drinking practices.[42] I also suggest that such conviviality was always in tension with restraint in a crucial dialectic that helped to form masculine political authority.

Feminist critics have attacked Ward's work since its publication as representative of a tradition of national identity "written by males about males, yet claiming to tell us about *national* characteristics."[43] Influenced by this critique, I understand Ward's character traits as idealized features of a particularly influential kind of Australian masculinity. I draw here on Raewyn Connell's concept of "hegemonic masculinity," a theory of gender and power focused on normative gender roles that reinforce patriarchy, in part by subordinating, marginalizing, or securing the complicity of other kinds of gender performance.[44] Marilyn Lake argues that legendary masculinity really developed in the late nineteenth century as a rejection of respectable domesticity – the hegemonic masculinity of the time – and manifested as a "masculinist" call for male political freedom, especially from the feminized domestic sphere.[45] Importantly for my argument, Lake sees alcohol as a crucial symbolic and instrumental battlefield for this cultural contest. The pub could serve as "a haven away from ... home" for men, with drinking an increasingly "masculine prerogative," while the belief that alcohol caused domestic violence was "the springboard of [female] political mobilisation," especially through an increasingly feminist temperance movement.[46] Building on Lake's analysis, I argue that the roots of this culture war anticipate the organized feminist movement and can be found in the temperance struggle to domesticate male citizens, and the implicitly feminist critique of the cultural power and political authority men drew from fraternal public drinking.

More broadly, these arguments shape my understanding of the colonial political imaginary as fundamentally masculine and white. As Lake has also argued, "the self that claimed self-government in British colonies of settlement was gendered and racialized in conception," and recent scholarship has illustrated the growing efforts to limit the franchise to white men, even as property qualifications were abandoned.[47] Democracy developed in New South Wales during the global nineteenth-century settler revolution, and was profoundly shaped by what Lorenzo Veracini terms the "world turned inside out" – a transnational political imaginary of mimesis in which settlers sought to remake the Old World in the New while disavowing its violent conquest. As Veracini argues, a slow "imaginative shift" during the mid-nineteenth century transformed New South Wales into a settler-colonial society that imagined an ideal future as a white citizen democracy within a wider British Empire of white citizens and non-white subjects.[48] Loyal toasting only grew in importance as New South Wales democratized, because it continued to symbolize the source of men's imagined political authority: the empire that empowered them to settle and rule the colony.

Alcohol, Drinking, and Drunkenness

I use alcohol as a means to explain these political imaginaries because of its instrumental and symbolic importance. Alcohol is "an especially prized form of embodied material culture" with powerful symbolic meanings, frequently used to "mark social categories, boundaries, and identity" and in "the manipulation of power and the construction of authority."[49] Applying these insights historically, Susan Barrows and Robin Room argue that alcohol "[highlights] the structures and relations of a society and the processes of stasis and change."[50] It was and remains a vital and powerful substance in British cultures: an intoxicant, a source of sustenance, a taxable commodity, an industrial product, an accompaniment to recreation, and a perceived cause of social problems – both widely used and its use widely debated. Drinking is fundamental to many forms of social interaction: it symbolizes bonds of allegiance and solidarity and it marks the transition between work and play. Drunkenness functions as a release from social restraints, but as such it is also a powerful symbol of deviance. Alcohol is often strictly controlled, its sale and consumption licensed, while drinking and drunkenness are subject to moralizing scrutiny, policed, and medicalized.

In my understanding of alcohol I seek to marry two distinct traditions: a broadly anthropological interest in drinking culture, and a broadly governmental concern about the perceived problems associated with drinking and the best means of controlling them. The governmental perspective was decisively shaped by the temperance movement during the nineteenth century, and anthropology has largely reacted against the "moralizing and individualism" implicit in this "dominant alcohol-as-pathology literature."[51] As Mary Douglas observes, anthropologists "do not necessarily treat [drinking] as a problem," and this provides an important check on the dominant perspective of alcohol studies.[52] My reading of drinking culture reflects Douglas's observation that drinking is "essentially a social act, performed in a recognised social context." Rather than assuming standard effects of alcohol consumption, this cultural model of drinking focuses on "patterns of belief and behaviour" associated with alcohol consumption in different, often subcultural, contexts.[53] Abandoning the assumption that alcohol is inherently problematic, I read discourses about drunkenness as a cultural history that reveals the political imaginary.

One crucial anthropological insight for my work is Craig MacAndrew and Robert Edgerton's notion of drunken comportment – how people behave under the influence – as a form of conventional wisdom, socially and historically constructed and culturally specific, rather than simply the physiological effects of a drug.[54] They demonstrate the enormous variety of such "shared understandings of the nature of drunkenness," but also show that within particular societies drunken comportment is orderly and predictable, breaching some societal norms but governed by its own rules, and that drunkenness often functions as a limited "time out" or excuse from normal responsibility, notably in Britain and its former colonies.[55] While alcohol has real effects that are presumably historically constant, I understand behaviour under the influence as learned and performative, subcultural (even individual), shaping and shaped by the understanding of alcohol in the social imaginary. I adapt MacAndrew and Edgerton's concept to my study of colonial New South Wales but distinguish three styles of drinking (or abstinent) comportment with distinct political meanings, which I term drunken, restrained, and sober.

Historical scholarship on alcohol is also shaped by this divide between culture and control, largely because it is reflected in the available source material. While some historians have sought to explore drinking cultures, older historical research tended to focus on the changing incidence and construction of alcohol problems facilitated by the archival resources of government and of individuals and organizations concerned about drunkenness.[56] The strength of this archive, constructed by opponents of alcohol, draws into sharp relief the dearth of sources from below, since accounts of popular and working-class drinking are largely written by elite reformers. In an Australian context, discussion of drinking culture is dominated by antiquarian and populist treatments of Australians' supposed predilection for beer and more scholarly studies of the pubs in which it was served.[57] But Australian histories of alcohol have largely concentrated on efforts to control alcohol problems, especially the crisis of the early settlement, with its so-called Rum Rebellion, and the heyday of the temperance movement and medicalization after 1850.[58]

Historians have traced the history of the nineteenth-century "drink problem" and the ways this was reflected in increasingly complex regulation, especially of licensed premises.[59] Like much of this work, one key focus of my argument is the role of temperance – as both an organized social movement and an ideology of sobriety – in transforming attitudes to alcohol and more broadly to politics. Brian Harrison's classic study, *Drink and the Victorians*, argues that English temperance was best understood in terms of ideals of respectability and social mobility that cut across class lines, and that its prohibitionist campaigns were as much symbolic as instrumental. Michael Roe makes a similar argument for New South Wales, positioning temperance as central to the ideology of "moral enlightenment" – a liberal, romantic, Protestant "faith" that "urged that everyone could, indeed must, become good, wise, prosperous, and responsible" – that dominated mid-nineteenth-century Australia.[60]

Many scholars, especially in an Australian context, have drawn attention to the connections between temperance and feminism, and more recent work focuses on the way that temperance societies and the temperance cause were a significant space within what Megan Smitley calls "the feminine public sphere."[61] I look at an earlier period when women were largely excluded from any official role in the organized movement but argue, similarly, that the ideology of temperance helped to politicize women and legitimate their voices within political debates. Another strand of temperance historiography examines temperance as a lobby and more broadly its influence on public attitudes to moral regulation.[62] This connects with a larger project to historicize the medicalization of alcohol problems, based especially on Harry Levine's influential argument for a new medical paradigm of addiction that developed around 1800, and was closely aligned with the emergence of the modern liberal state and a "social order [that] depended upon self-control."[63] Building on this work, I read temperance as another expression of the democratic political imaginary, one concerned with social mobility and active civic participation, notably in the temperance movement's public campaigns for alcohol regulation.

Some recent histories of alcohol have focused on the political meaning and significance of drinking culture. British historians have linked new forms of drinking – including the evolving ritual of public toasting – to a distinct British tradition of fraternal sociability that developed over the long eighteenth century. As Brian Cowan argues, new practices of sociability, often involving alcohol, linked the consumer revolution, the emerging public sphere, and the culture of politeness in politically significant ways, helping to foster an era of relative political stability in England.[64] More specifically, there is a growing scholarship on the political significance of wine culture and toasting rituals.[65] Much of this work draws on Pierre Bourdieu's sociology of taste as a reflection and source of social differences, and specifically his argument that social elites use claims of the superiority, rarity, and authenticity of their consumption as a means to distinguish themselves and legitimate their cultural authority.[66] Charles Ludington builds on this approach to argue that changing tastes for wine over the long eighteenth century illustrate the contest for power between different social groups and have a reflexive relationship with the changing nature of British society.[67] In an Australian context, Julie McIntyre's history of wine as a "civilizing" drink in colonial New South Wales informs my reading of public toasting, which was, almost invariably, conducted with wine.[68]

I am also influenced by recent scholarship that historicizes the meaning of intoxication, and specifically modern constructions of drunkenness. As Phil Withington argues, "one of the key aspirations and sources of legitimacy for civil and colonial authority since the fifteenth century … [was] the conceit of controlled consumption. In theory at least, to be able to retain demonstrable levels of self-discipline and stamina in the midst of both immanent and purposeful intoxication distinguishes (usually male) elites from the incontinent and indiscriminate masses."[69] Building on this comportment thesis, I argue that forms of controlled consumption – what I refer to as restrained drinking – were a crucial source of political authority and served as a metaphorical test of democratic citizenship. Turning from drink to drinking places, scholars have drawn attention to public houses and their social and political importance in nineteenth-century Britain and its colonies, locating the pub as a crucial and contested public space in the transition to a modern economy and modern forms of leisure, and recognizing the political potency of forms of sociability centred there.[70] Similarly, I argue that public houses increasingly served as a stage for the performance of fraternal egalitarianism, symbolizing the spirit of colonial democracy.[71]

However, there is no work on New South Wales, and very little on Britain more broadly, which explicitly uses alcohol as a means to discuss political thought, let alone the political imaginary. Scholars of the drink problem have analyzed parliamentary debates and lobbying but rarely the wider political meanings of drinking.[72] This also tends to be true of work on the politics of alcohol outside of Britain, including scholarship on prohibition, in the United States and globally.[73] A rare exception is James Nicholls's analysis of the way English debates about alcohol "expose underlying cultural and political tensions" throughout the early modern and modern periods.[74] He argues that, "because drinking is such a ubiquitous social activity, the way it is framed in public discourse ... acts as a barometer of the cultural anxieties and political attitudes which are at work in any particular period."[75] I apply a similar approach in my more focused study of colonial New South Wales, using debates about alcohol as a means to understand politics. But I focus less on the overt politics of the drink question and more on the ways that drinking practices and rituals reflect underlying British political thought.

Sources and Method

This project depends upon a particular approach to politics and the evidence that can reveal it. As I argue, democracy was elusive in both Britain and its colony, and existed as much outside of as within formal political institutions. In consequence I turn away from the conventional sources of political history, and locate the political in everyday public practices, especially performative rituals, and specifically those involving alcohol. Due to the importance of toasting in Britain, as New South Wales became a self-governing democracy, public drinking served as a symbol of settler-colonial citizenship. We can therefore understand important aspects of the British political imaginary through the study of colonial drinking practices.

However, this approach is limited by the available sources. While there is abundant evidence for the economic, social, and cultural importance of alcohol, it tends to normalize elite and respectable drinking, while demonizing public drinking, and especially drunkenness, among the lower orders. This is especially true of people who were already underprivileged, marginal, or deviant, notably, though in different ways, for convicts, women, and Aboriginal people. While the public dinners of gentlemen are valorized and affirmed in the press, we most often encounter non-elite drinking in the moralizing narratives of its critics, and, like Mary Burt, in court reporting and records. These sources are valuable and can be read against the grain, but their limitations must be borne in mind.[76] We have very few accounts of drinking from the perspective of ordinary drinkers, especially from early in the nineteenth century, and almost none from women or Indigenous people, a problem that is compounded for intersectional identities. However, the symbolism of drunkenness in elite discourse is itself revealing, a script that denied the drunkard the status of a political subject.

More broadly, my argument depends upon the profusion of accounts of elite and respectable drinking and sobriety, forms of sociability that filled colonial newspapers and formed a key component of the nascent public sphere. Normal drinking – by which I mean drinking that accorded with societal norms, including specific expectations linked to gender, race, and class – has often been taken for granted by historians, treated as the background to events, if it is considered at all. Indeed, even historians of alcohol have tended to focus more on problem drinking because of the profusion of evidence. But as I show, even as the temperance movement flourished, and alcohol was intensely regulated, drinking remained an essential part of public life that left a prolific and largely neglected archive. I focus especially on this evidence of normal public drinking, analyzing drinking practices and, crucially, who was accorded the privilege of participating in them. By reading drinking as an expression of underlying thought I draw attention to the way alcohol and politics are publicly and collectively imagined.

Contents and Argument

I begin, in chapter 1, by exploring the instrumental and symbolic importance of alcohol in the late eighteenth-century British world. Alcohol was a necessary evil in British society, and in the planning of its new penal colony. It was valuable, useful, and meaningful, but subject to extensive regulation and critique. A stimulant and reward in the traditional moral economy of labour, alcohol lubricated commerce and sociability, and served as a sacrament in rituals that reinforced the social order, but drunkenness was also a symbol of sin, crime, and idleness.

Chapter 2 briefly surveys colonial politics to 1860. I identify three distinct eras: an early period of ferment ending in the Rum Rebellion of 1808; a longer period of greater stability with a factional politics centred on the authority of the governors; and the two decades of electoral politics and radical mobilization after 1842. New South Wales was transformed from a penal colony under autocratic rule to a democracy with universal male suffrage. But genuine democracy remained elusive, especially for women and Aboriginal people.

In chapter 3, I begin to show how drinking can reveal the imaginary that underlay this history, focusing on plebian drinking as a performance of drunken freedom. I establish the broad context in the availability and average consumption of alcohol, the places where drink was bought and consumed, and the patterns of drinking that resulted. I analyze the relationship between alcohol, work, and leisure, especially the use of alcohol in the convict moral economy of patronage and deference, the binge-drinking patterns of rural workers, and the round-drinking rituals that emerged among workers in urban areas.

Chapters 4 and 5 look at public dinners and the toasting ritual at their centre. In chapter 4, I explore the longer history of toasting in Britain, and the form that toasting took on public occasions. I trace the development of the public dinner in the long nineteenth century, the increasingly formal ritual of toasts, accompanying speeches and their reporting, and its connection with politics, especially as a highly scripted performance of loyalty that was capable of radical subversion. Chapter 5 focuses on this tradition in New South Wales as an expression of the democratic political imaginary. I analyze the importance of orderly and restrained drinking, the politics of inclusive fraternity and exclusive hierarchy, and the way that reporting of dinners and toasts scripted public opinion and was contested on that basis.

In chapters 6 and 7, I turn to temperance, arguing that both the organized movement and the broader ideas it promoted were fundamentally democratic. In chapter 6, I trace the history of the movement both internationally and especially in New South Wales. It transformed from a top-down project of elite philanthropy to a bottom-up movement marked by increasing radicalism, shifting from a politics of persuasion to one of regulatory compulsion that relied on effective lobbying to influence political outcomes. Chapter 7 focuses on the broader idea of temperance as a reflection of the democratic political imaginary. Performative sobriety served as a form of identity politics, an assertion of bourgeois respectability and responsible citizenship, while temperance helped to politicize its supporters, especially women. Temperance also helped to reimagine alcohol as a structural cause of social problems, and demanded stricter regulation accordingly, an argument that contributed to a revolution in government and a new conception of the state's responsibility for its citizens.

In chapter 8, I analyze the gendered history of drinking practices, which I read as symbolic performances that help constitute both gender roles and political authority. Male drinking was a test of manliness and an assertion of agency, and men's toasting performatively scripted the gendered public sphere. Female convict drunkenness was a notorious stain on the colony, symbolizing shameful sexual immorality and political disorder, and this made the performance of public sobriety and decorum essential for respectable women, notably through temperance.

In similar ways, the construction of Indigenous people's drinking illustrates their political disenfranchisement. In chapter 9, I survey what I term the "trope of the drunken savage" – the British perception that Aboriginal people could not perform restraint – exploring how drunkenness was understood as both a symbol and a cause of the perceived decline of Aboriginal people into anomic despair and supposed extinction. The assumption that Aboriginal people were not capable of political responsibility is symbolized in the ban on supplying them with alcohol and the patronizing lenience of courts toward their drunkenness.

The book's short conclusion draws my argument together by looking at the "National Banquet" held to mark the granting of responsible government in 1856. This celebration of colonial democracy, in and with alcohol, only shows how elusive it remained.

1

A Necessary Evil

ALCOHOL IN EIGHTEENTH-CENTURY BRITAIN

In October 1792, the first governor of New South Wales, Arthur Phillip, wrote to his British superiors about the role of alcohol in the new colony. Thanking them for supplying additional liquor in order to maintain the official ration, granted to all officers in the colony, he commented, "the permitting of Spirits amongst the civil and military may be necessary but it will certainly be a great evil."[1] Phillip's observation captures the fundamental tension around alcohol in British culture. Though drinking accompanied almost every aspect of social life, drunkenness was a traditional sin and was increasingly understood in secular terms as a cause of social problems. This chapter illustrates the paradox of alcohol in eighteenth-century Britain by looking in detail at its importance in the planning and voyage of the First Fleet, contrasting this with the critical discourse around drunkenness.

Preparations for the establishment of the penal colony formally began when the home secretary, Lord Sydney, drew up the first detailed plans in August 1786. Government rations were necessary for the voyage itself and for the new settlement until it became self-sufficient, and careful and detailed work went into supplying the pioneering colonists with all their wants.[2] Perhaps the most debated aspect of this provisioning was the supply of alcohol. In present-day terms, the naval ration of half a pint of rum per day equates to more than ten Australian standard drinks.[3] All sailors received this while on board their ships, as did members of the Marine Corps, who were to form the colonial garrison. However, once they were on land, marines were granted an allowance to purchase food but had to supply their own liquor.[4] This traditional approach to rationing was complicated by the remoteness and novelty of New South Wales, since no alcohol could be purchased there. In December 1786, Phillip wrote to Sydney fearing "discontent in the garrison" if the marines were denied the drinks "to which they have ever been accustomed," and the following year they submitted a memorial of complaint to their commanding officer, Major Robert Ross. They were "sorely aggrieved" to find that they would have no access to "an indispensable requirement for the preservation of [their] lives, which change of climate and the extreme fatigue ... may probably endanger."[5]

Anxious to avoid discord in the fleet and the new colony, Sydney responded. He noted that at first an alcohol ration "had not been thought advisable," but given the circumstances, he agreed that Phillip should purchase spirits and wine for the colony "to be issued ... at such times and in such proportions as you may judge requisite," although he warned that "no further quantity" would be provided to the settlement.[6] In consequence, Phillip was ordered to purchase wine and spirits for the settlement when the fleet stopped at Rio, at which time he duly purchased 115 pipes – about 50,000 litres – of rum, enough for the rations of all non-convicts for at least two years.[7]

The official elite of the prospective colony – largely naval officers – were more privileged. Standard naval practice granted them a ration of wine and entitled them to bring a personal stock of drink to supply their messes, which were essential sites of convivial sociability. Those who could afford to liberally exercised this right. Phillip, for example, brought 2 pipes and 104 cases (about 1,800 litres) of port, 2 puncheons (about 600 litres) of rum, and 12 barrels (about 1,400 litres) of porter. This amounted to more than twenty-one additional standard drinks for every day of the next two years, a surplus that would allow him to reinforce his authority through acts of patronage, rewarding deserving colonists with alcohol.[8] Besides this, Phillip was also ordered to purchase wine at Teneriffe for those "entitled" to a wine ration. Writing privately to a friend, one such officer, Lieutenant Ralph Clark, complained of "a very great hardship on use [*sic*] all to have nothing but water to drink for four Years."[9] Ironically, Clark himself was practically a teetotaller. He saw this as a hardship because his alcohol ration – which he did eventually receive – was a customary right that operated in practice as a form of pay.

Finally and most radically, the convicts were to be denied any access to alcohol.[10] Preventing prisoners from drinking might seem obvious, but in fact this was a novel, almost unprecedented proposal, shaped by recent criminological thought. A growing emphasis on the reform of criminals as the leading aim of punishment, combined with long-standing arguments that drunkenness was a cause of moral decline, leading inexorably to crime, led to calls for enforced sobriety. For example, John Howard influentially attacked English prisons as "seats and seminaries ... of idleness and every vice," pointing particularly to the practice of selling alcohol to prisoners – a key source of income for private jailers – as corrupting of the institution and the prisoners within it.[11] In response to such reformist criticism, the Hard Labour Act of 1777, which permitted prisoners sentenced to transportation to be housed in hulks on the Thames and set to work, became the first legislation to forbid prisoners access to alcohol.[12] Sydney adopted this new approach in his plans for New South Wales. Convicts were to receive a standard naval ration each day, apart from rum.

These plans and the controversy around them illustrate the crucial but contested place of alcohol in eighteenth-century Britain. Access to alcohol on the voyage and in the prospective colony helped to delineate status within a hierarchical and status-conscious society. Members of the convict labour force were theoretically sober, the marines and officials were plentifully provisioned by the state, and those who could afford to supplemented this with personal supplies that they drank, gifted, and traded. Compulsory convict sobriety reflected the planners' desire for the colony to function as a moral reformatory for a criminal class.[13] Public drunkenness was a symbol of sin and immorality, and drinking was seen as a cause of poverty, disease, idleness, and crime, so keeping alcohol from the convicts was essential to the proper functioning of this penal experiment. But the generous rationing of the marines and their officers demonstrates the centrality of alcohol to everyday life. Alcoholic drinks were ubiquitous and consumed widely and regularly; their production, trade, and consumption were valuable and highly regulated; and drinking and drunkenness were culturally powerful, intensely debated, and invested with political meaning. Alcohol was both an instrumentally and symbolically important substance in eighteenth-century Britain.

British Drinking Culture and the First Fleet

Alcoholic drinks were the standard accompaniment to meals and most social activities. Not only were they cheap and readily available, but they were also frequently the safest beverage in an industrializing society where water supplies were often unsanitary and tea and coffee were still largely luxuries.[14] However, it is difficult to draw meaningful conclusions about the quantity of alcohol individuals consumed. Official data is available only from the turn of the nineteenth century, when there was approximately eight litres of pure alcohol available per person each year – or thirteen standard drinks per week – a level slightly greater than Britain or Australia today, despite the much less developed economy.[15] Though this is a useful basis for comparison, there must have been enormous variations in individual consumption, as is the case in all drinking cultures, and we can only understand these variations speculatively and in general terms. Women typically drank less than men – female drunkenness was certainly subject to much greater stigma – and the rich certainly drank more than the poor, both because they could afford to, and because they usually drank at home and were hence less subject to the regulation of public drinking.

Drinking tastes also varied. Almost half of the alcohol consumed in Britain was in the form of beer or other easily fermented drinks, most of which were weak by modern standards, and formed the staple beverage of the common people. This traditional pattern, where the poor drank beer or cider, and the rich imported wines, was gradually transformed by mass access to spirits as a result of industrial distillation. Beer remained the main means of quenching thirst, but spirits were increasingly used as an intoxicant and their consumption increased exponentially in the century after 1650. This change was due partly to the improved technology of distilling but also to changing tastes in a commercial society in which people increasingly defined themselves through their consumption.[16]

High levels of drinking were partly due to the financial and economic importance of the alcohol industry. Despite the persistent concerns of social reformers, there were few successful efforts to regulate drinking in the eighteenth century, largely because of the increasing importance of excise on alcoholic drinks as a source of government revenue. In the period 1788–92, nearly 40 per cent of British taxation fell upon alcohol and its ingredients.[17] More broadly, alcohol was a valuable commodity produced by large and influential industries. Both brewers and distillers had a significant lobby in Parliament and were seen as essential sources of demand for domestic agriculture.[18] The British Empire, both the first, centred on the American colonies, and the second acquired during the Napoleonic Wars, was also bound together by trade in alcohol, especially spirits, which often served as a convenient ballast with a predictable demand. The Atlantic economy relied heavily on the clockwise circuit of ships from Britain collecting slaves in Africa, carrying them to the plantations of the West Indies, and returning to Europe with sugar, rum, and molasses, which fuelled domestic and continental drinking and distillation. The new colony likewise became part of an emerging Pacific and Indian Ocean economy, which also relied heavily on the rum trade, and rum was a key commodity for the first colonial merchants.[19]

Drinking on board the First Fleet echoes this broad pattern, not least in the reliance upon spirits, which allowed the navy to save precious cargo space. The naval ration equated to about five times the average national consumption, a fact that presumably supported the navy's well-earned reputation for drunkenness, but also provided sailors with a tradeable resource.[20] The level of rationing also reflected the practice of making potentially tainted water supplies potable by mixing them with spirits, and the widespread underlying view that alcohol was healthy, stimulating, and medicinal, necessary for hard physical work or coping with extremes of climate or exertion.[21] This view informed the marines' claim that their ration was an "indispensable requirement for the preservation of our lives," but it was also widely held among the medical and official elite.[22] John White, the chief surgeon on the fleet, actively promoted "the salutary effects" of wine as a cure for disease among the convicts, and Phillip specifically linked this to their otherwise enforced sobriety, arguing that "wine, at the discretion of the surgeon, is very necessary for the sick, as the convicts are not allowed anything more than water."[23] While the medical critique of alcohol was becoming more common in this period, it did not influence the plans for the colony.[24] Indeed Phillip was ordered to purchase thirty pipes (about fourteen thousand litres) of wine "for the hospital" (in addition to the rations for the officers) while the fleet resupplied at Rio.[25]

The idea of alcohol as a stimulant was shaped by the traditional pattern of drinking in association with manual labour. In rural society weak alcoholic drinks – "small beer" or cider – were often consumed regularly throughout the day; indeed they were a customary right and a form of payment in many parts of the country.[26] However, this was changing as Britain urbanized and industrialized. In pre-industrial towns, work rhythms tended to be episodic and involve hard work during a short week and hard drinking on the weekend, frequently extending into "St Monday," an unofficial holiday taken by artisans when they completed a task.[27] This pattern, along with the ritualized use of alcohol by tradesmen with their systems of fines and footings (hierarchical obligations that often involved inferiors buying drinks), was intimately connected with the nature of eighteenth-century industry with its small scale, organization into guilds, and emphasis on piecework. As John Dunlop, a temperance advocate and critic of such "artificial and compulsory drinking usages," observed in the 1830s, drinking in Britain was invariably a social activity governed by a "system of rule and regulation," though such drinking norms varied with context, notably between different trades.[28]

These habits clashed dramatically with the demand for a disciplined workforce in the new industries of the Industrial Revolution, and as Britain industrialized drinking was increasingly confined to leisure time in the evenings and the weekend.[29] But industrialization also supported a new drinking culture. The monotony and physical demands of industrial labour encouraged a resort to the public house in leisure time; and it created fruitful conditions for the growth of sobriety as a tool and symbol of self-improvement.[30] The need for "precise and continuous labour" over "spasmodic exertion of … crude physical energy" changed alcohol from an accompaniment to work to a means of relaxation and escape afterwards, and cemented alcohol's role as a marker of the cultural divide between drunkenness and sobriety, a process ongoing when the First Fleet sailed.[31]

The sailors and marines certainly demonstrated the traditional pattern of regular drinking accompanying labour and drunken celebrations of leisure time, but also the growing demand for sobriety and discipline. John Easty, a marine on board the *Scarborough*, regularly recorded variations in the liquor ration in his journal, reflecting its importance to naval life and work more broadly.[32] Drunkenness was also common, especially when the ships reached port and duties became less onerous. Jacob Nagle, a sailor on the *Sirius*, later recalled a naval career in which drinking and drunkenness were both normal and desirable, a means of proving oneself as a man. At every port on the voyage to New South Wales he reported participating in a drinking binge, notably at Rio de Janeiro, where he became so drunk he fell asleep in the market and lost all his possessions.[33]

Drunkenness in service was a serious concern for the officers who regularly complained about the excesses of their men and punished offenders. Easty listed several occasions when marines were punished for drinking, including an incident where he was "Confin[e]d and put in Irons for being Drunk on Duty."[34] White hinted at the reason for such severity when he suggested that delays to the departure of the *Sirius* in May 1787 were "more from intoxication than from any nautical causes."[35] Similarly, while anchored at the Cape, Clark reported that the second mate on the *Friendship*, Patrick Vallance, fell overboard and drowned, trying "to ease himself," almost certainly under the influence.[36] Even the men acknowledged the problems drunkenness could cause. On the *Scarborough*, Easty reported that "the Marines [drew] up an … agre[e]ment amongst themsel[ve]s to punish any body as was in Liqu[o]r," and subsequently stopped the rum ration of William Jones for a week as an informal sanction.[37] So while drinking was a central part of sailors' lives, and arrival in port was celebrated with customary binges, there was also a widely shared expectation that men would be capable of performing their work and an acknowledgment that excessive drinking could impede this.

The desire for alcohol was not confined to those who were entitled to it. The novel efforts to deprive the convicts of liquor were resented and resisted as much as penal discipline allowed. Watkin Tench, a senior officer in the Marine Corps, observed that the convicts awaiting the departure of the fleet were constantly requesting tobacco from their friends and relatives, suggesting that their desire for this luxury was stimulated by their inability to get alcohol.[38] More importantly, the sailors' rum was regularly stolen by, or illicitly traded to, convicts, leading to drunkenness. In one instance, Arthur Bowes Smyth, an assistant surgeon, reported the theft of rum by Thomas Kelly on board the *Lady Penrhyn*, "having broach'd a puncheon of Rum between decks & drank & given to the Women a Considerable quantity."[39] Adding to the problem, the fact that wine was used as a medicine for sick convicts allegedly encouraged malingering.

Such behaviour was unsurprising given the central role that drinking played in British social life and indeed in the lives of many of the convicts prior to their arrest. Public houses, the main source of liquor for most people, were more than mere drinking places, they were centres of communal life, the chief location for public recreation and public meetings, especially for the poor. They were also important spaces for mixed-gender socializing, often providing much needed privacy, while drunkenness afforded a social licence for flirting and sexual conduct that was otherwise deviant. Pubs were often the only place where poor people could enjoy basic comforts like light, warmth, and decent food, but in addition they sponsored local sports and festivals, provided rooms, held funds, and kept records for voluntary societies and clubs, and supported a host of subsidiary occupations like itinerant traders, auctioneers, and prostitutes. Coaching inns, in particular, functioned as the nodes of a burgeoning transportation network that was vital to the Industrial Revolution, and in consequence, public houses were centres of news distribution, where patrons could read or hear others read the proliferating press, and leave and collect mail.[40]

The radical tailor and social reformer Francis Place reported on the essential role of pubs for workers in London during his youth at the turn of the nineteenth century. He claimed that it was customary for men who had the means to spend their evenings in the pub, because they were often "the only place in which [they] can find congenial companions ... associates ... [and] recreation." Combatting the discourse that linked drunkenness to sin and crime, he also stressed that working men generally sought only to "muddle" themselves in a "pleasant delirium," rather than drinking to excess.[41] Convict trials also illustrate the social importance of drinking and public houses for the lower orders. For example, Elizabeth Dudgeon and Susannah Garth were each sentenced to seven years' transportation for robbing William Waterhouse, a drunken sailor, in August 1783. Waterhouse met them outside the Two Brewers on Banbury Street, where they asked him to buy them drinks and he treated them to several pots of ale.[42] Now visibly drunk, a friend tried to help him home, but the women persuaded him to resume drinking until he was "so much in liquor" he joined Dudgeon in bed, but awoke to find both women and his money gone. Their story reflects the traditional association of public houses with vice and crime, but also the central role of drinking and drinking places in social life.

More broadly, drinking in the late eighteenth century was associated with every kind of entertainment and social ceremony, from theatre to funerals. A social lubricant among every rank in society, alcohol was relied upon as an aid to courtship and general camaraderie and was critical as a symbol of exchange, both in business, where deals were frequently sealed with a drink, and in other transactions, like the solemnization of marriage. Alcohol was thus essential within the ritual celebrations of individual lives through anniversaries, wakes, and weddings, and of society as a whole in religious celebrations, localized annual fairs and fetes, and national and secular holidays. Drunkenness was tolerated and even encouraged by the traditional elite in such contexts, with alcohol often solicited as part of customary doles of food and drink. This tradition was socially and politically significant, releasing tensions built up within a strictly hierarchical society and channelling public emotion into collective carnivalesque celebration. In such contexts, alcohol was a catalyst for outbursts of public emotion, but also a symbol of the ties of patronage and deference that held society together.[43]

Drinking was also democratic in some fundamental ways. Alcohol encouraged men and women of different ranks to socialize and freely express their opinions, but it was partly for this reason that temperance critics like Dunlop worried about drinking rituals. In an earlier version of these arguments, Thomas Trotter, a doctor who published one of the first medical critiques of drunkenness, in 1804, noted that "the convivial disposition" of British people, and the political freedoms of British society, encouraged drunken socializing and "all its evils."[44] Illustrating this political resonance, gifts of alcohol – known as treating – by candidates were a standard feature of elections in this period, and indeed until the late nineteenth century, despite being technically illegal.[45] Frank O'Gorman has shown that electoral treating needs to be understood within a moral economy, in which gifts of food and drink were among a series of "accepted and normatively approved displays of electoral generosity that were designed to create or to maintain electoral goodwill between patron and voter."[46] As such, elections were a measure of local public opinion even beyond those with the franchise, and treating rituals – which in some contexts included forms of subsidised public dinner – were directed at the entire community, not just voters.[47] Indeed, in my sense we might suggest that they demonstrate a nascent democratic political imaginary, with the community understanding that it had a right – if not a duty – to express its political opinions at election time, irrespective of the franchise.

Drinking was also politicized by industrialisation. E.P. Thompson has identified the significance of alcohol as a marker of the shift in work rhythms, associated with the transition from a moral economy to a political economy of capitalists and wage-earning workers.[48] Marianne Adler emphasizes the apocryphal saying "With beer one thanks but with money one pays" to emphasize the difference between the two political imaginaries, embodied in this changing relationship between drinking and work. In an archetypal moral economy, the provision of alcohol bound servants to masters with ties of "reciprocity and communality," while drunken festivals "served to regenerate ritually the politically constituted social order."[49] But such practices threatened the political economy of capitalism, within which work and leisure were distinct domains, navigated by rational and self-reliant individuals who bought their own drinks.

The importance of alcohol in binding together all ranks of society is clearly illustrated in the journal of Ralph Clark, who recorded the drinking practices on board the *Friendship* in considerable detail, even though he very rarely drank. He regularly complained about the drunkenness of his fellow officers, although it was his abstinence that was deviant in the context of the traditions of the navy and of English gentlemen in general. For example, he lodged a formal complaint – without result – after he was drunkenly insulted by Second Lieutenant William Faddy, and he also reported that James Maxwell, the oldest marine officer on the fleet, was "drinking himself to death as fast as he well can."[50] Clark's Evangelical faith, evident in his frequent appeals to God for the health of his family and the success of the fleet, in part explains his performative sobriety and judgmental view of drunkenness. But his detailed account of the officers' drinking shows how central alcohol was to the social life of British gentlemen, and the importance of alcohol as a catalyst for the release of social tensions.[51]

Clark's account also illustrates the importance of alcohol within the ship's economy. His complaint about the prospective loss of his liquor ration might appear incongruous, if not hypocritical, given his sobriety, but though he did not drink, Clark regularly collected his ration and used it to pay for services, reward friends, and encourage camaraderie. He records that he gave a quart of rum to the boatswain and carpenter, another quart for a glass of grog to pay his tailor and hairdresser, and traded another glass for metal to make some hinges. He also regularly gave additional rum, on top of the ration, to the men working under him when their work was especially onerous.[52] Perhaps most significantly, he gave rum to both his friends and subordinates to help them celebrate festivals and anniversaries. On 23 August he celebrated his son's birthday, recording, "dr[a]nk my Ralphies [his son] and my Betseys [his wife] – god out of his great goodness Bless them their health is a bo[w]l of Punch. So good night as I shall not be able to write more as it will be late before we break to night as I will make my Mess mates drunk if I can as I don't drink any thing but Lemonnade." Similarly, on New Year's Day 1788, he gave his men rum to celebrate the new year and drink to his wife and son's health.[53] These gifts of liquor from a temperate moralist illustrate the significance of alcohol as a social lubricant.

Clark's tirades against convict drunkenness are perhaps most revealing of all, demonstrating the hierarchical and gendered nature of drinking and of British society more broadly. In July, Clark recorded an incident in which Elizabeth Barber, a convict transported for her part in a violent robbery in a public house, attacked the character of the surgeon, Thomas Arndell, accusing him of trying to sleep with her. When interviewed by Captain Meredith she was instead found to be a liar, "very much in Liquor," and was ordered to be placed in irons as punishment. Unintimidated, she told the captain to "come and kiss her C … for he was nothing but a Lousy Rascal," and hoped that "she Should See use all th[rown] over board before we got to Botany Bay." Meredith responded by having her hands tied behind her back and her mouth gagged, and Clark concluded his account complaining that he would rather manage "a hundred more men than to have a Single Woman."[54] Given the prodigious drinking Clark repeatedly complained about, and the fact that the officers had just finished dinner, it is hard to believe that Barber had drunk more than her judges. But as a convict she was not supposed to drink at all, as a woman her drunkenness was not just illicit but scandalous, and the accusation – if not the assumption – of drunkenness in a social inferior was a common means of asserting authority. If Barber was intoxicated, she must have received the liquor from one of the men entitled to alcohol: a marine, or even, perhaps, Arndell himself. But for Clark, her insolent conduct was best explained by wilful drunkenness, which deprived her of any meaningful agency. In the eyes of the male authorities, she was not even a rebel, but merely a drunken whore.

Clark clearly had a deeply conflicted attitude to alcohol – much like British society as a whole – but even an abstainer like him recognized its practical and symbolic value. Alcohol purchased goods and services, and drinking the health of loved ones, or social superiors, was a vital ritual, which Clark facilitated even as he renounced the drink itself. Alcohol was not only ubiquitous, it was also deeply meaningful. And just as important as its role in social ritual was its symbolism as a marker of deviance in the discourse of reform.

The Gin Crisis and the Symbolism of Public Drunkenness

Drinking and drunkenness were certainly linked to social problems, and public houses were often the scene of crime. But these real problems were also exaggerated, with the public drinking of the lower orders commonly read as disorderly unless authorized by patronage, and their perceived drunkenness made a crucial symbol in a broader narrative of sin, crime, and idleness. Reformers of all kinds – religious and secular – constantly used the symbolic figure of the idle drunkard and the moral dangers of the public house to embody their arguments about social problems. Such reformist discourse increasingly argued that alcohol caused these problems, and on this basis demanded stricter control of public drinking. In a typical example, the Scottish magistrate and advocate for professional policing Patrick Colquhoun claimed that "perhaps the greatest source of delinquency and crimes is to be ascribed to ill-regulated Public-Houses, conducted by men of loose conduct and depraved morals ... There is scarce any moral evil by which Society is afflicted – the mind debauched – the virtuous parent and master distressed, and the ruin of families and individuals affected, which is not generated in Public-houses."[55]

This understanding of alcohol as a symbol or cause of social problems in need of reform had its roots in two closely related traditions. In post-Reformation England, the tradition of moral reform was generally associated with Puritans, Dissenters, and Evangelicals who saw sins like drunkenness, idleness, and Sabbath breaking as both economic and moral problems, threatening to good order, hurting the efficient use of resources, and offending God.[56] At the same time, social elites and government officials were concerned with increased disorder associated with urbanization, industrialization, and population growth in a modernizing society. Throughout the eighteenth century, experts and interest groups called for the reformation and improvement of manners, institutions, and governments, and frequently invoked drunkenness in their arguments.[57] By 1788, while drunkenness was still recognized as a sin, reformers were more likely to stress that it was unhealthy, wasteful, and encouraged immorality and crime; indeed, these were Clark's main objections. It was becoming a cause as much as a symbol.

The moral panic over gin drinking during the second quarter of the eighteenth century aptly illustrates the changing meaning of drunkenness for reformers. This crisis had its origin in the extraordinary and rapid increase in gin production and consumption around the turn of the eighteenth century. The growth of both supply and demand led to an explosion of practically unregulated gin shops and gin vendors across London, and by the 1720s they were a serious concern for the city's authorities and reformers. Gin vendors were seen as encouraging idleness and disorder and gin itself became associated with a wide range of social problems, including increased crime and rising mortality, leading to calls for government action. As a consequence, seven acts attempting to regulate drinking were passed in the three decades after 1720 in an "unparalleled attempt" to make gin too expensive for the poor.[58]

The most famous act, passed in 1736, claimed that "the drinking of Spiritous Liquors ... is become very common, especially among

1.1 (*above and facing page*) William Hogarth, *Beer Street* and *Gin Lane* (1751).

GIN LANE.

Gin cursed Fiend, with Fury fraught,
Makes human Race a Prey;
It enters by a deadly Draught,
And steals our Life away.

Virtue and Truth, driv'n to Despair,
It's Rage compells to fly,
But cherishes, with hellish Care,
Theft, Murder, Perjury.

Damn'd Cup! that on the Vitals preys,
That liquid Fire contains
Which Madness to the Heart conveys,
And rolls it thro' the Veins.

Price 1s

the People of lower and inferior Rank, the constant and excessive Use whereof tends greatly to the Destruction of their Healths, rendering them unfit for useful Labour and Business, debauching their Morals, and inciting them to perpetrate all Manner of Vices; and the ill Consequences of the excessive Use of such Liquors are not confined to the present Generation, but extend to future Ages, and tend to the Devastation and Ruin of this Kingdom."[59] This emphasis on political economy, public health, and crime typified the emerging secular understanding of alcohol as a cause of social problems and shows the importance of drunkenness in reformist discourse. In a striking example, the Rev. Thomas Wilson attempted to calculate the financial loss to the state from drinking, taking these arguments to their ultimate secular conclusion: the problem of alcohol was less about morality than about health and less about the individual than about the nation as a whole.[60]

The most widely distributed and well-known representation of the crisis was William Hogarth's paired street scenes, *Beer Street* and *Gin Lane* (1751; see figure 1.1), which perfectly captured the dual meanings of alcohol in eighteenth-century Britain. In the former image, the inhabitants are well-fed, prosperous traders and workmen whose drinking is restrained and salutary, conducted in and around respectable public houses, after work, as an aid to relaxation, courtship, and community. In the latter, they are thin-faced slum-dwellers stealing, fighting, and frequenting a pawnbroker; their drinking is solitary, frenzied, idle, and irrational, conducted in the street. The central figure of a drunken mother letting her child fall to its death – probably referencing a notorious trial in 1734 in which a drunken gin addict, Judith Defour, was found guilty of murdering her daughter – illustrates the gendered concern about so-called Mother Gin. Gin was stereotypically a woman's drink, and female drinking and drunkenness were shameful because they subverted feminine expectations of good motherhood. Indeed, Hogarth's bad mother embodies a key element of Wilson's arguments about national health: a nation of drunken women would not raise healthy male children to serve in the military or work industriously, threatening national security and the economy.[61] The peace, prosperity, and good health of *Beer Street* are defined by what was increasingly seen as a traditional, manly, and patriotic drink; while the crime, disorder, and despair of *Gin Lane* are explained by the dangerous, novel, and foreign spirit, consumed by unfeminine women.

The significance of drunkenness for reformers was also clearly visible during public debates about crime in the 1780s and contributed to the plans for a new convict colony. Indeed, Sydney's radical plan to prevent the convicts from drinking was probably shaped by his membership in the newly founded Proclamation Society, which lobbied for and subsequently promoted a royal proclamation against vices, including drunkenness.[62] Britain had strategic and commercial interests in the South Pacific, but the colonization of New South Wales was in large part an expedient to resolve the growing problem of criminals sentenced to transportation and stowed in growing numbers in disease-ridden and escape-prone hulks due to the loss of their former destination, the American colonies. Sydney's plans for the penal colony were also influenced by the long tradition of reform that saw transportation as not merely convenient for society but a form of philanthropy, offering the destitute, debtors, refugees, and criminals an opportunity to redeem themselves in a new and productive life.[63]

Phillip's final instructions before departure ordered him to "enforce a due observance of religion and good order," but an earlier draft elaborated on this in greater detail, requiring him to "cause the Laws against Blasphemy, Profaneness, adultery, Fornication, Pol[y]gamy, Incest, Profanation of the Lord's Day, swearing and Drunkenness to be rigorously executed and ... take due care for the punishment of the aforementioned Vices."[64] Similarly, the first colonial minister, Richard Johnson, brought with him on the First Fleet one hundred copies of a popular Evangelical tract by Sir James Stonhouse, which cited biblical verses and relevant laws to warn that "Drunkenness is a Vice which destroys your Health, wastes your Time and Money ... robs you likewise of your good Name, brings a Reproach on that holy Religion you profess ... is not consistent with a due use of your Reason ... [and] will certainly exclude you for ever from the Kingdom of Heaven."[65] When the colony of New South

Wales was founded, drunkenness was well-established as a cause of social problems and a symbol of immorality, idleness, and crime.

Drinking the Health of the New Colony

The First Fleet arrived in Sydney Cove on 26 January 1788 after they found Botany Bay unsuited for a settlement. As the then naval officer Phillip Gidley King recorded in his journal, the British flag was planted, "possession was taken for His Majesty whose health, with the Queens, Prince of Wales & Success to the Colony was drank," a celebratory volley of gunshot was fired, and the landing party gave three cheers. The toasts to the King, Queen, Prince of Wales, and their new colony were led by Phillip, joined by all the "principal Officers of the Settlement, and many of the private Soldiers," with "all that display of form which on such occasions is esteemed propitious."[66]

The ritual was repeated on 7 February when Phillip formally took command of the new colony. After the deputy judge advocate, David Collins, had read the commissions of the leading officers, Phillip thanked the assembled marines and then addressed the convicts. He warned them that British law would be strictly enforced but stressed that he believed many of them were "good Men ... who, unfortunately, from falling into bad Company, from the Influence of bad Women, and in the rash Moment of Intoxication, had been led to violate the Laws of their Country." He then invited the officers to a formal dinner at which "many loyal and public toasts were drank."[67]

Phillip's warning may have been inspired by the unofficial celebration, which took place the night before when the landing of the convict women – almost all the women in the colony – led to what has sometimes been characterized as a drunken orgy. Arthur Smyth, an assistant surgeon, reported that the sailors, to celebrate the successful completion of their mission, requested, and were granted, an extra ration of grog, and soon achieved a general state of drunkenness that "beggars every description, some swearing, others quarrelling, some singing," and all "quite incapable" of performing their duties, while a "Scene of Debauchery & Riot" took place. Marian

Aveling has rightly cast doubt on this account and its construction as an orgy by a series of male historians, but despite her revisionism, the story continues to be repeated, even in recent historical work.[68] In fact, the one part of Smyth's account that stands up to scrutiny is the drunkenness of the sailors aboard the *Lady Penrhyn*, where Smyth spent the night. Smyth expressed horror and surprise at what was a commonplace of the eighteenth-century world, for the drunkenness of the navy was proverbial and the granting of an extra ration to reward sailors on making landfall was standard practice.[69] So rather than a narrative of extraordinary licence we are actually confronted with a typical instance of military discipline, with the drunken celebration a customary reward, and the alcohol supplied by the naval officers, thereby reinforcing their authority. If anything, Smyth's horror illustrates the clash between military and civilian – and especially Evangelical – sensibilities, which would prove a persistent problem in the colony.

Ironically, Smyth himself recognized the importance of celebrating with alcohol. He was not present at the governor's dinner on 7 February and bitterly complained that "the general Officers only were invited, & not the least attention whatever was paid to any other person who came out from England."[70] As he recognized, exclusion from such celebrations and the ritual toasts that accompanied them was a social snub that indicated a lack of political power. Throughout the voyage, he had regularly dined with the officers on the *Lady Penrhyn*, recording on Christmas Eve 1787 that they "all drank a chearful [*sic*] Glass to the health of our Friends in England (as indeed we do every Saturday night)."[71] Smyth's apparent hypocrisy, perhaps more than anything, captures the importance of alcohol to the British colonists. Alcohol was used widely and regularly; it was valuable and valued; it was a sacrament in the rituals that ordered this orderly society; and it stained those deemed to abuse it as sinners, idlers, and criminals. Efforts to reconcile these incompatible uses and meanings were a persistent feature of the new colony, and, in consequence, alcohol was a highly politicized substance.

2

Politics in Colonial New South Wales, 1788–1860

My discussion of the British political imaginary as revealed in public drinking practices is focused on the colony of New South Wales and, accordingly, depends upon an interpretation of the history of colonial politics. I categorize the period 1788–1860 into three distinct eras. First, an early period of political upheaval in which the governors struggled to assert their authority over a unique convict society, culminating in the crisis of the Rum Rebellion. Second, a longer and more stable period of gubernatorial government in which the authority of governors was largely secured, but colonial politics became increasingly factional and centred on the struggle to secure democratic reforms. Finally, the era of electoral politics, which began in 1842 and culminated in the granting of responsible government with a universal male franchise, and New South Wales becoming a settler-colonial democracy. This division largely corresponds with the administrative terms of different governors, both because these are a useful means of organizing the period, widely followed in the historiography, and because this convention reflects a truth. At least until the first elections, and for all that their authority was persistently challenged, colonial politics always centred on the governor.

This broad history of New South Wales's transition from authoritarian penal colony to settler-colonial democracy provides crucial context for my argument about the British political imaginary. In this chapter, I survey my three eras of colonial politics before briefly concluding with some observations about the symbolic importance of alcohol in the way this story is told.

Authoritarian Government, 1788–1810

The first two decades of New South Wales took place against the backdrop of the age of revolutions, with fears of sedition and rebellion in Britain and near constant and global war against France.[1] In Britain, radical ideas briefly flourished in the wake of the French Revolution but were soon brutally repressed by the anxious British state. These ideas inspired political movements against colonial rule throughout the empire, most relevantly in Ireland, where a failed revolution in 1798 ended in bloody reprisals. Partly due to these events, the penal settlement of New South Wales was an afterthought in British politics, and it was not until after 1808 that the British government paid considered attention to its newest colony. Colonial politics was decisively shaped by these conditions. Radical ideas were circulating throughout the British world, and the significant minority of Irish convicts, including political exiles after 1798, posed the threat of a convict uprising.[2] This threat was real but exaggerated. There was a failed convict rebellion in 1804, put down by a decisive military response; but this only fed a paranoia about Irish conspiracy that reinforced the authoritarian instincts of the colony's leaders.[3]

Such instincts were empowered by the legal and political foundations of colonial government. At least in theory, New South Wales was an authoritarian regime that ran on the orders of the governor, who had the power to regulate almost every aspect of society. Technically subservient to British Parliament – and in practice to the officials of the Home Office and (from 1801) the War and Colonial Offices – the governors had considerable independence and were empowered to rule through a peculiar hybrid of military and civil authority.[4] But such authority and power were heavily constrained by the possibility of appeal to Britain, by the presence of an independent military, by the use of the courts to resist official commands, and perhaps especially by the governors' inability to enforce their own orders. As a new society with a workforce largely comprised of convicts, New South Wales lacked both the institutions and the personnel on which British social controls traditionally relied. There was no organized church and only a single minister for most of this period, no parishes or parish councils, and no respectable public to serve as amateur officials on whom British local government depended. This led to a series of expedients – most obviously the use of convict constables and the dependence on corporal punishment – that allowed the governors to maintain a basic social order, but the colonists often resisted official commands. In particular, the governors were unable to implement the kind of strict surveillance of convicts that was seen as necessary for the colony to serve as a reformatory.[5]

Colonial politics was decisively shaped by remoteness from the metropolitan centre. Communication between Sydney and London in this period took an average of six months in each direction, which forced the governor on the ground to either issue orders that might be overturned or delay decisions pending official advice.[6] This problem contributed to resentment of the governors' powers, and it led to unrealistic orders. British officials often struggled to understand the practical challenges their governors faced and demanded outcomes that were inconsistent with the realities of governing a penal colony. Distance also helped shape a political culture of appealing to Britain for recourse. Leading figures in the colony were connected to networks of political patronage, which they leveraged to influence the oversight of London officials, lobbying for favour and against local authorities. The politics of what would become known as "old corruption" played out in New South Wales on a time delay, and this resort to distant patrons consistently undermined the governors' local authority.[7] Finally, distance exacerbated the unique challenges of colonial political economy. While the voyage of the First Fleet and the survival and growth of the colony was in many ways a remarkable feat of British logistics, the early governors all struggled with the practical challenges of creating a self-sustaining economy, notably in controlling rum, which had an especial importance in the early colony due to supply constraints and its value in motivating convict labour.[8]

The unique demographics and circumstances of the colony also shaped its politics. Less than a third of the population were female, mostly convicts, and this imbalance both empowered women within the sexual economy and accentuated the masculine tone of politics in a patriarchal society.[9] The colonial workforce was almost entirely comprised of a convict underclass of unfree labour, theoretically subject to official discipline, and imagined in terms of what Hamish Maxwell-Stewart and Michael Quinlan term "convictism": "the means by which the past moral failings of transported workers were used to justify labour exploitation." In practice, convicts had considerable agency, resisted authority, and demanded remuneration for their work, often in the form of alcohol.[10] Last but not least, early New South Wales was situated on the colonial frontier, and the expansion of the British settlement was achieved through expropriation of Aboriginal land and violent repression of Aboriginal resistance. At the same time, as Grace Karskens has shown, the frontier was always porous and Aboriginal people were a constant presence within the early colony; relations were often peaceful and friendly, but Aboriginal people were always and increasingly conceived as outside of the British political community.[11]

These inherent challenges were compounded by political divisions. By appointing a series of naval officers as governors while, from 1795, employing an army unit – the New South Wales Corps – under its own commander to secure the colony, the British authorities set the terms of the division between civil and military that would climax in the Rum Rebellion. The corps were subject to their own chain of command and their own forms of justice and used these powers to challenge the authority of the governor. In the interim between the departure of Governor Phillip in 1792 and the arrival of Governor Hunter in 1795, Major Grose served as acting governor and ran the colony under military law, while granting land, convict servants, and permission to trade for profit to his officers.[12] While Hunter restored the authority of the civil magistrates, this period of military rule entrenched the current and former military officers as the core of a commercial and agricultural elite who dominated early colonial society and challenged the official vision of New South Wales as a convict reformatory. As the jury in the colony's only court, the military shaped emerging legal norms, and as landowners and masters of convicts, they were central to emerging colonial agriculture. Just as importantly, their access to commissariat bills – the main form of money flowing into the colony – allowed them, initially, to dominate trade, including in rum, which was an especially profitable commodity for those who could buy it wholesale. The commercial interests of these first colonial capitalists clashed with the imperative for strict control of convicts, and much of early colonial politics concerned official patronage and the economic opportunities that land grants, convict servants, and imported goods could provide.[13] Moreover, this military-dominated elite saw themselves as representatives of the traditions of British gentlemen, loyal to a hierarchical system of power, and proudly entitled to liberty under the rule of law.[14] Not only were such views intrinsically hostile to the extraordinary authority of the governors, but they also found expression in an honour culture, based in performative *amour-propre*, in which perceived slights were bitterly resented, becoming the subject of duels and the foundation of lasting feuds.[15] As a result, every governor clashed with the military officers as individuals and as the leading members of a faction that was the de facto opposition in early colonial politics.

I understand this tempestuous politics in terms of a conflict between the political imaginary of the colonists and the practical reality of governing a remote penal colony. The colonial elite viewed themselves and aspired to be seen as gentlemen, but largely saw their tenure in the colony as an opportunity for profit and advancement rather than a service. They expected and increasingly insisted on political rights, sought to establish a colonial hierarchy modelled on the ideal of rural England, and competed for access to the spoils of office and trade. Even the convicts imagined themselves as political subjects in ways that challenged official authority: their use of the courts shows their sense of political liberties within a kind of moral economy of punishment and reward.[16] They asserted their own rights to compensation for their labour, to leisure and free time, to fair treatment by their masters, and to the promise of freedom when their sentences were completed. These practices reflected a shared though contested understanding of what it meant to be a British man, of political rights grounded in law, of the proper limits of government, of the privileges accorded to status, and of the mutual responsibilities of members of a society. But this imaginary was fundamentally in tension with the strict government of convicts in the interests of moral reform. For example, the right of property owners to distil their crops was incompatible with efforts to prevent convict drunkenness.[17]

This tension between the governors' constitutional and practical authority and the political imaginary of the colonists played out in a series of power struggles, which characterized the politics of the period, including a significant and ongoing contest over trade in rum. Each of the early governors were ordered to prevent convict drunkenness and control the importation and exchange of spirits, each found these orders impossible to effect, and each was criticized by the British government for their failure. Phillip was unable to prevent convicts from drinking and sought, unsuccessfully, to introduce free trade under a duty; Hunter was recalled partly in consequence of reports of officials profiting from rum trading; and Governor King was undermined by complaints about corrupt allocation of permits to import spirits.[18] This pattern culminated on 26 January 1808, when the corps, in a bloodless coup traditionally, though perhaps inaccurately, known as the Rum Rebellion, removed Bligh from his post.

While recent scholarship on the rebellion has tended to downplay the instrumental importance of rum, Bligh's struggles to control the spirit trade embody the larger crisis of colonial authority and illustrate the clash between the centralized power of the governors and the political imaginary of the colonists.[19] Bligh and the rebels imagined the colony and the role of alcohol within it very differently.

For Bligh, spirit trading corrupted his convict reformatory; for the rebels, trading was a right that lubricated the nascent political economy, encouraging trade, conviviality, and progress. These divisions over the purpose of the colony, the authority of the governors, and the rights of different classes of colonists would continue to dominate colonial politics.

Gubernatorial Government, 1810–42

The era from the arrival of Governor Macquarie in 1810 to the first colonial elections in 1842 was dominated by strong governors whose authority was progressively challenged by colonial liberals and democrats. By placing the armed forces under the direct authority of the governor and regularly rotating units out of the colony, the military never again served as a rival source of power, and opposition to governors now centred on factions of civil society. But conflicting visions of the colony remained a source of political strife, especially between "exclusives," the landowning elite who favoured a strict social and political divide between masters and convicts, and "emancipists," former convicts and their allies, who campaigned for full political rights for all colonists. This emancipist campaign was supported by most of the so-called native-born (or "native") colonists and by the growing numbers of poorer free immigrants without access to land.[20] In the absence of democratic institutions, these struggles played out in the courts, the increasingly free press, and the wider public sphere, including in politicized toasting at public dinners.

Women remained less than a third of the population but increasing immigration and expiration of sentences resulted in growing numbers of non-convict women in the colony. Combined with official policies encouraging marriage, this helped create a more normal society, but it also exacerbated the gendered politics of respectability. Respectable women were especially concerned with preserving their reputations from the taint of convictism, including through performative sobriety, and married women were key managers of the politics of society, which centred on Government House.[21] In contrast, the Aboriginal inhabitants, sometimes known as "native blacks," were increasingly understood as either threatening savages on the frontier, or inevitable victims of colonization, clinging to the fringes of civilized society, and in either case they were explicitly excluded from any discussion of political rights.[22]

Lachlan Macquarie arrived in the aftermath of the rebellion with a mandate to stabilize the colony and restore order while improving morals and promoting economic growth. While Macquarie was not vulnerable to a military coup, political authority remained concentrated in the executive, and this continued to cause political tension. Opponents among the exclusives used rival sources of authority, especially the church and the law, to challenge Macquarie in a campaign that centred on the contentious issue of emancipist rights. They effectively mobilized patronage networks in England to attack the governor in Parliament, resulting in a highly politicized commission of inquiry into the colony that inspired Macquarie's eventual resignation. Public opinion played an increasingly overt role in colonial politics in this period. Petitions to Parliament were a key tool used by Macquarie's opponents, while William Wentworth was the first to articulate the emerging demand for free institutions – including a free press, jury trial, and representative government – that would become central to the emancipist cause.[23] Under Macquarie the growth of the colony also accelerated frontier conflict as Aboriginal land was granted to settlers. The pattern of a steadily expanding frontier and consequent destruction of traditional lifestyles helped to create the trope of Aboriginal people as ruined by colonization, symbolized in the imagined figure of the drunken savage.[24] This trope in turn reinforced humanitarian calls for "protection" of Aboriginal people, which by the late 1830s would increasingly shape imperial policy.[25]

Macquarie's successor, Thomas Brisbane, arrived in 1821 as Commissioner Bigge was composing his reports, and his term of office was decisively shaped by their recommendations. Under the New South Wales Act of 1823, a Legislative Council was established to advise the governor and help pass colonial laws, thereby ending the era of autocratic orders. Since the council was solely advisory and appointed by the Crown, this was by no means a democratic reform, but it did fundamentally change the legal system of the colony, gave the chief justice a crucial constitutional role in certifying that proposed legislation was not "repugnant to the laws of England," and separated Van Diemen's Land from New South Wales as a distinct colony.[26] Bigge's reports called for stricter control of convicts, which in turn led to new regulations, and a system of secondary punishment for convict offenders, which drew increasing numbers of convicts into public works as opposed to assignment under private masters.[27] These policies provoked opposition from both major political factions. Exclusives resented their decreased access to convict labour and the centralization of legal authority in an expanding convict state. Emancipists opposed the repressive convict police regime that demonstrated their lack of civil liberties. The convicts themselves also asserted their political rights, increasingly protesting against what they saw as breaches of the moral economy, including their right to free time and rewards for their labour.[28] Female convicts also asserted their rights against the gendered and sexualized judgment of their conduct, forcing the political status of women in a penal colony into the public sphere.[29]

From 1826, under Governor Ralph Darling, the relative stability of colonial politics was disturbed as the increasingly strident political factions asserted themselves. Two independent newspapers, the liberal *Australian* and the more radical and pro-emancipist *Monitor*, helped establish a more open and rancorous public sphere, not least by publishing reports of public dinners. The actions of the government were often subject to criticism, and the emerging free press helped encourage a broader democratic campaign for political rights. Darling sought to restrain the pace of political reform but his efforts to control the press and silence his critics backfired. Charging editors with seditious libel only created a cause for the opposition to campaign against, while the increasingly independent chief justice of the Supreme Court, Francis Forbes, blocked his repressive regulations. Darling's attempt to rationalize the system of land grants and convict assignment along the lines prescribed by Bigge were also controversial because they hurt the interests of colonial capitalists who wanted ready access to stolen land and unfree labour. Their interests were increasingly, though indirectly, represented by the members of the Legislative Council, expanded in 1828 by the Australian Courts Act, which also granted civilian juries for civil cases in the Supreme Court. The council now had greater independence, with a majority required for legislation to pass, and members granted the right to submit bills and publicly dissent from decisions. Juries provided another forum for resistance to gubernatorial authority, as they often exonerated prominent radicals prosecuted by the government.[30] More importantly, Darling's efforts to retain authoritarian powers and resist the expansion of civil liberties only inspired his political opponents to redouble their demands. In particular, Wentworth assumed a position of leadership in an increasingly well-organized democratic movement, not least through the informal politics of public dinners, like the insulting toasting of Darling in 1827.

The arrival of Richard Bourke in 1831 proved a circuit breaker for the spiteful politics of the Darling era, but as a Whig, his efforts at reform were resisted by the exclusives who dominated the council and owned the majority of land. Bourke expanded jury trial to criminal cases and reduced the summary jurisdiction of magistrates over convicts, but large landowners opposed both reforms.[31] Similarly controversial was the Church Act of 1836, which formally disestablished the Church of England and granted equal state funding to all denominations based on the size of their congregations. This important reform, championed by Bourke based on his experience in Ireland, made New South Wales a secular state that officially avoided discriminating against any Christian faith; but partly in consequence it also led to increased sectarian resentment, especially toward Catholics.[32] However, despite considerable public support, Bourke's calls for further reform of the council and the introduction of elections were resisted by the British authorities. A Select Committee on Transportation, chaired by Sir William Molesworth, sat in 1837–38, but heard often hostile evidence that only confirmed the view in Britain that a convict colony could not be trusted with democracy. Molesworth recommended that transportation to New South Wales cease (the last convicts were landed in 1842) and the colony was informed that elections would only be granted thereafter.[33] This decision linked the cause of colonial democracy to the emerging anti-transportation movement in ways that would become especially significant in the late 1840s.

The rapid expansion of the non-convict population also transformed colonial politics. An early migration boom from the late 1820s until the depression of the 1840s supplemented growing numbers of emancipists and locally born "natives," fundamentally changing the nature of the colonial public. While increasing rates of transportation in the 1830s meant that convicts under sentence were still 40 per cent of the population in 1840, a decade later, they were less than 1 per cent. These changes were significant even in the 1830s because the growing numbers of "free" people – whether emancipists, native-born, or immigrant – fundamentally changed the nature of society, expanding the public sphere, and encouraging open public debate among a wider range of political interests. Increasing numbers of immigrant women and respectably married families also exacerbated the stigma associated with convictism.[34]

Rapid population growth contributed to rapid expansion of the colonial frontier under systems of licensing that encouraged so-called squatting – running large herds on what were deemed "waste lands" beyond the existing boundaries of settlement – by pastoralists, which further accelerated frontier conflict with Aboriginal owners.[35] Under the new governor, George Gipps, who arrived in New South Wales in 1838, such frontier conflict accelerated and became a public issue, notably in debates around the Myall Creek massacre – the murder of at least twenty-eight Wirrayaraay people by a posse of mostly convict shepherds in a supposed reprisal for attacks on stock.[36] The trial and execution of the murderers provoked a storm of controversy that ensured no such prosecution would succeed again, and cemented the public understanding of "savage" Aboriginal peoples – those still living traditional lifestyles on their country – as a threat to colonial prosperity. It is no coincidence that democratization in the 1840s and '50s was accompanied by increased frontier conflict. As the colonial public expanded and democratic institutions were introduced, land was intensely politicized, understood as both a resource to be exploited by capital and a right of citizens. Both projects required ignoring Aboriginal ownership and violently repressing resistance, and both contributed to the ongoing disenfranchisement of Aboriginal peoples, whose voices had to be ignored to preserve the legitimacy of settler-colonial democracy.[37]

Gipps's governorship (1838–46) was a transitional period for the colony since it saw the first colonial elections, those for the Sydney Municipal Council in 1842 and the expanded and reimagined Legislative Council in 1843. With transportation ending, Gipps sought to reform the management of colonial land and, in line with the ideas of Edmund Gibbon Wakefield, to link land policy to immigration by charging squatters increased rents to subsidize assisted migrants. While the economic depression of the 1840s rendered the plan a failure, Gipps's approach and Wakefield's ideas would influence future systems of assisted migration and sale of what was deemed "Crown" land. More important in the short term, his policies inspired concerted opposition from an alliance of the former landowning exclusives and the new pastoralist squatters, who would come to dominate the Legislative Council during the 1840s.[38]

Overall, the period from 1810 to 1842 saw broadly stable politics centred on the authority of the governors, but with a growing public increasingly confident in demanding political rights. Throughout this period the governor remained the central figure. He drove the legislative agenda and was integral to colonial society, the closest thing to nobility in a society obsessed with status, gentility, and breeding.[39] Notwithstanding the growth of the public sphere, governors came to use their power in increasingly sophisticated ways: laws were tightened and more strictly enforced through a centralized administrative and judicial system. However, at the core of my argument is my claim that, during this period, the public – and the authorities themselves – increasingly understood politics in democratic terms. Independent of expanding civil liberties and democratic institutions, the public understood themselves as entitled to a say in their government and their voice became more influential.

This public sense of political rights and a political voice would only grow as the colony was granted democratic institutions, but in turn, the question of whose voice counted was increasingly politicized.[40]

Democratic Government, 1842–60

New South Wales was transformed in the 1840s and '50s. Transportation had ended, emigrants rushed to the goldfields, and the post-convict, white, male public was granted representative democracy on an increasingly liberal franchise. As a migrant society, shaped by radical and Chartist ideas and creating new institutions rather than reforming traditions, New South Wales granted the vote to all adult men in 1858. This was much earlier than the United Kingdom (1918), although the speed of this change was aided by the liberal turn in British politics and imperial policy, and the resulting support for responsible self-government in the settler colonies. The frontier continued to expand at the expense of Aboriginal people, and the Indigenous survivors of frontier conflict were understood in patronizing terms as incapable of citizenship and requiring the "protection" of government.[41] The temperance movement peaked in popularity in the early 1840s, but the broader ideology of moral enlightenment helped make sobriety, domesticity, and respectability dominant values. Despite this, women were cast into domestic roles as adjuncts to male citizens and had to fight to have a public voice.[42]

The discovery of gold in 1851, and the mass migration that followed, further transformed the economy (exports tripled and imports increased fivefold in the following decade), the population (which almost doubled in that period), and hence the political public. Mass migration accelerated the settler transition, such that New South Wales was increasingly a settler-colonial society, imagining itself as a reflection of Britain, only fairer, freer, and more democratic. It also accelerated the emergence of modern class-consciousness among both workers and the liberal middle classes, whose representatives were uneasy allies in their political struggle against the conservative influence of the squatters.[43] Even as convictism ended, there were intense concerns over social mobility in this rapidly changing society. The gold rushes inspired official and respectable anxiety about the growing power of workers, the labour shortages provoked by their rush to the goldfields, their increasing independence and lack of deference, and the implications of these dynamics for the emerging democracy. These anxieties inspired a recurring moral panic around public drunkenness, culminating in a select committee to investigate "intemperance" in 1854.[44] Meanwhile workers were increasingly active in organizing to secure their rights. Miners protested against the introduction and increase of mining fees using democratic arguments, pointing out that they were taxed without proper representation. Urban workers responded to inflation by unionizing and lobbying for improved conditions, while a broader campaign sought to open up the land, largely leased to pastoralist squatters, for selection by working-class families.[45]

The first elections in New South Wales were held in 1842 for the Sydney Municipal Council. As Terry Irving has argued, that year was a critical one for colonial democracy, with numerous public meetings and a significant radical campaign for greater representation.[46] The Constitution Act, which passed in Britain that year, was, however, a conservative document. While it increased the size of the Legislative Council to thirty-six members, two-thirds of whom were now elected, the property qualification for electors was high enough to disqualify most men and ensured that the council was dominated by squatters. But as Irving has shown, popular politics in Sydney, influenced by Chartism, was much more radical than the constitution or the council. This democratic moment was made possible by a flourishing popular press, and by organized electoral lobbies and less formal groupings of recent emigrants, emancipists, and "native" Australian-born working men, who would mobilize around their interests, organize public meetings, and petition the more liberal members of council, including the governor. In addition, colonial politics was shaped by both the threat and the reality of urban political violence with organized mobs, largely comprised of unenfranchised working men, rioting at most elections in the 1840s, in support of their patron-candidate, and often fuelled by free drinks.[47]

In alignment with events in Europe and Britain, the years between 1848 and 1856 were especially fraught. The Presbyterian minister and republican John Dunmore Lang was one of a series of early councillors elected to Sydney seats based on radical public campaigns in support of their candidacy. The arrival of the *Hashemy* in 1849, the first convict ship since 1840, provoked a mass campaign against transportation, which successfully prevented the landing of further convicts. The anti-transportation campaign was significant because most squatters, and hence the Legislative Council, were committed to reintroducing convicts or other forms of unfree labour into the colony, but were resisted by an alliance of workers, who saw this as a threat to wages, and the respectable middle classes, concerned about the convict stain.[48]

Democratic politics in the 1850s centred on the expansion of the franchise and responsible government – removing British control by making the colonial executive responsible *to* the legislature and the public who elected it, and responsible *for* the taxes that the public paid.[49] In 1850, Britain agreed to this in principle, granting New South Wales the right to develop its own constitution for a new bicameral legislature, separating Victoria as an independent colony, and halving the property qualification, thereby significantly expanding the electorate. But there was more public protest over a new Electoral Act in 1851, which deliberately sought to undermine the more democratic franchise by discriminating against Sydney in the division of electorates, a gerrymander designed to ensure more power for squatters. In addition, strikes in the early 1850s among the more organized trades led to improved labour rights, including the granting of the eight-hour workday to some artisans.[50]

Wentworth, whose Whig principles now made him a conservative in the context of 1850s Sydney, sought to limit the power of the public by arguing for a hereditary upper house, modelled on the House of Lords, a proposal roundly mocked as a "bunyip aristocracy."[51] In contrast, some radicals, like Lang, were also republicans who argued for full independence from Britain as the means to free the colony from the corrupt hierarchy of traditional British society and ensure meaningful democracy. But in general, democratic politics was strictly loyalist and settler-colonial, employing the rhetoric of popular constitutionalism and celebrating the supposedly immemorial rights of Britons, grounded in access to lands seized from their Indigenous owners and granted to white settler-citizens.[52]

The new constitution, emerging as it did from a complex negotiation, was a compromise, providing an upper house nominated by the governor on advice of the executive. This meant the executive could "swamp" a hostile Legislative Council by nominating additional members, and it gave the elected Legislative Assembly the de facto power to amend these rules on a simple majority vote. More importantly for democracy, in 1858 the assembly passed a new electoral act that granted manhood suffrage and required use of the "Australian Ballot" – voting in secret on official printed forms – which helped transform voting from the rowdy street politics of the 1840s into a "well-mannered civic ritual."[53]

More broadly, during the 1850s there was a vibrant politics of public meetings, which organized support for candidates sympathetic to Chartist aims. From 1848 to 1855, Irving estimates there were at least one hundred "public meetings … in which radicals and liberals were engaged in building a democratic movement," and argues that these meetings were just as important a political forum as the Legislative Council.[54] As he notes, such meetings relied on a much wider culture of fraternal sociability through clubs, societies, unions, associations, and other public institutions, which taught men how to engage politically in the public sphere. Many of these bodies met in public houses, held public dinners, and lubricated their political opinions with alcohol. Equally, the temperance movement was the symbolic centre of a rival cultural politics of respectability and performative sobriety, which also attracted a mass following.

Overall, the period of electoral politics saw the formal political system increasingly match the democratic political imaginary of the public. But the public meetings and street protests of the late 1840s and early 1850s were arguably a rare moment of democracy in which a mass public demanded a say. Orderly elections, more professional politicians, and organized factions, and later parties, tamed this democratic energy. By 1860, public opinion was widely accepted as the source of political legitimacy, but this public was systematically and normatively confined to adult white men, and even their voices were largely limited to the exercise of the vote.

Drunken and Sober Histories and the Democratic Political Imaginary

The political history of colonial New South Wales has traditionally been interpreted as a Whiggish story of inexorable British progress: from convict colony to liberal democracy. The colony's first historians projected a glorious future in overcoming the stain of convict origins, and embracing what were seen as the British political virtues, even as they radically disagreed about what these virtues were, or what they meant.[55] Wentworth, the first self-conscious colonial historian, was a pioneer of this tradition, arguing that "the superior freedom of [Britain's] laws, which have engendered her a freer, more virtuous, and more warlike race of people," had led to "a dominion, unparalleled in the history of the world." Writing in 1819, Wentworth read recent colonial history, and especially the Rum Rebellion, as a battle between British freedom and the unconstrained authority of the governors, claiming that New South Wales was "the only one of [Britain's] possessions exclusively inhabited by Englishmen, in which there is not at least the shadow of a free government."[56]

Such early histories, told by self-professed patriots, were a self-conscious exercise in imagining a national community, and from at least the 1820s they were often performed to an audience of drunken gentlemen at public dinners like that held by the Turf Club. In 1826, at a dinner to celebrate what was now known as "Foundation Day" – 26 January, the date when Phillip first toasted the new colony – Wentworth presided over toasts to "Trial by Jury," "A House of Assembly," "The Freedom of the Press," and to three former governors – Phillip, Darling, and Brisbane – all boisterously cheered, in contrast with the current governor, Darling.[57] In doing so, he and his fellow diners were constructing a public history through alcohol, the spirit of which is captured in a poem, written for the occasion by Michael Massey Robinson, an emancipist clerk who wrote a series of celebratory and commemorative odes in the 1810s and '20s:

Then true to the sport,
My boys, let us sup [on] port,
And relish the boon we inherit,
Ever proud to proclaim
We are Britons by name,
Let us prove ourselves Britons in spirit …
"Advance" then "Australia," …
thy watch-word be "Freedom for ever!"[58]

In contrast, another version of this political history is a story of the colony overcoming its drunken origins, of progress *from*, not progress *to*.[59] Echoing the form of the classic temperance narrative – a literary genre, popularized in the mid-nineteenth century, in which a drink-induced crisis leads to remorse and self-improvement – such temperance histories understood progress very differently.[60] The most influential exponent was Lang, whose *Historical and Statistical Account*, published in a series of distinct editions in the 1830s, made rum a symbol for the corrupt trading spirit and immorality of the colonists. For example, he claimed that under Governor King the colony "consisted chiefly of those who sold rum, and of those who drank it," and that Bligh's efforts to change this caused the rebellion of 1808.[61] He also cited Wentworth's celebratory fete for the departure of Governor Darling as an example of the drunken style of colonial politics, claiming "a taste for rum implies a taste for ribaldry, for gross personal vituperation, and for an indiscriminate abuse of all the measures of government."[62]

More broadly, Lang argued that the colonists were characterized by their "blustering and rather offensive affectation of liberty and independence," and he personified this in the image of an emancipist mother who celebrated her freedom by drinking, and taught her children "a boisterous assertion of rights which nobody ever thinks of calling in question."[63] The drunken comportment of the working classes – at least those who had not turned to temperance – were, for Lang, a symbol of their lack of deference and order. He took the first temperance pledges in Sydney from a shipload of immigrants he organized in 1831, and his opposition to transportation and advocacy for Protestant immigration was framed in terms of the need for a sober public for the democracy he championed. Indeed, he claimed in 1837 that "the whole body politic of the colony has at length become completely saturated with intoxicating liquors, and the entire mass of its humours completely corrupted."[64]

I am not alone in finding in drink a potent metaphor for colonial democracy.

3

Drunken Freedom and Fraternity

THE POLITICAL MEANING OF POPULAR DRINKING

Alcohol remained a necessary evil in New South Wales between 1788 and 1860, but drinking was politicized in distinctive ways that reflected the unique conditions of a penal colony, isolated from Europe, and swiftly becoming more democratic than the metropole. Popular drinking was performed and read as drunken – loose, free, reckless – and as the colony democratized this freedom, and the egalitarian rituals with which it was celebrated, came to evoke the democratic political imaginary. To put the political meaning of toasting in context, in this chapter I briefly summarize drinking in general before turning to focus on the drinking of convicts and workers.

I begin by explaining the availability of alcohol in relation to changing systems of production and trade and describe colonial drinking culture by looking at drinking places and patterns. Building on this foundation, I argue that distinct styles of drinking had important political meanings. I concentrate on the drunken comportment of convicts and workers, arguing that it evinced their freedom from authority, both for the drinkers themselves, and for elite audiences who often read such drunkenness as dangerous and threatening to the political order. The transition from a moral economy of patronage to a political economy of purchase imbued key rituals like binge (or "spree") drinking and drinking in rounds (or "treating") with democratic symbolism, embodying an egalitarianism that was limited to the fraternity of male drinkers.

Alcohol in Colonial New South Wales: Supply, Demand, and Consumption

Alcohol was in high demand in colonial New South Wales, but supply was limited by distance, rurality, and status, shaping patterns of consumption. The data on alcohol in the colony is useful but flawed, relying on official measures of drinks on which tax was paid; hence calculating how much people drank is, necessarily, a speculative exercise. I give some crude estimates for how many standard drinks were available per person in the colony – and for convenience, I sometimes term these figures average "consumption" – but they are mainly useful for comparative purposes since individual consumption must have varied enormously from the mean (and over time), as it does today. In particular, I think that the available data for the first two decades of the colony significantly understates actual supply due to smuggling and illicit distillation, and my estimates reflect this assumption.

During this earliest era, alcohol had a special importance in colonial society and the nascent colonial economy over and above its already essential role in Britain, largely due to scarcity, not abundance. Since local production was limited – distillation was banned, while brewing and wine making only developed slowly – the vast majority of legal alcohol consumed in the early colony was imported, and the bulk of that was spirits, but there was also a flourishing illicit trade in illegally distilled or smuggled rum.[1] Even allowing for this dark figure, there was almost certainly less alcohol available than in contemporary Britain: perhaps eight weekly standard drinks per colonist compared with thirteen in Britain, and mostly spirits, not beer.[2] However, unlike in Britain, there were huge variations in the availability of alcohol in New South Wales over time, as a result of the colony's remoteness, cynical monopolizing of supplies, and regulatory constraints. Due in part to a lack of hard currency, but also to the peculiar nature of the convict workforce, spirits became an important form of barter and a crucial means of payment for labour, over and above British precedents.[3] The combination of reduced and irregular supply and inflated demand created enormous opportunities to profit from the trade in alcohol, often exacerbated by government controls that failed to prevent convict drunkenness but did entrench the monopoly of the privileged elite, who were granted permits to purchase wholesale liquor from visiting merchants.[4]

From 1810, alcohol regulations were gradually brought into line with those in Britain, supply and demand stabilized, and consumption increased, but fluctuated significantly. After a brief experiment with a licensed monopoly on spirit trading to fund the construction of the Sydney hospital, Governor Macquarie introduced free trade under a tariff, and other than changes to the rate of taxation, there were no significant constraints on supply.[5] As prices stabilized, available alcohol, and hence alcohol consumption, increased and people of all classes drank more and more regularly. The 1830s were almost certainly the peak of alcohol consumption in Australian history, with the average colonist consuming as many as sixteen standard drinks per week, considerably more than in Britain in the same period, though this extreme level may in part be a consequence of the disproportionately male population. However, these levels declined rapidly and strikingly in the 1840s, when the combination of stricter licensing regulation, a colonial recession, increasing numbers of women, and the influence of the temperance movement more than halved consumption to below a standard drink per person per day. In contrast, the economic boom of the gold rushes saw consumption increase significantly in the 1850s – to near British levels, perhaps ten standard drinks per week – before it declined again in the 1860s, stabilizing at about one standard drink per day (approximately half the level in Britain) for the rest of the century.[6]

Complicating this pattern, there was also a gradual shift from spirits to fermented liquors, especially among the working classes. While beer did not become the main source of alcohol until mass production and refrigeration in the late nineteenth century, both beer and wine consumption steadily increased, and beer and wine may have constituted a quarter of available alcohol by 1860.[7] Wine was the drink of the social elite both domestically and on public occasions like the Turf Club dinner. As Julie McIntyre argues, wine was a key cultural signifier that marked out gentlemanly status and was even promoted as a solution to colonial drunkenness, because it supposedly caused the restrained comportment associated with its consumption.[8] On this basis, increasing consumption of wine can be understood as a kind of performative social mobility by a growing colonial middle class. However, the main, indeed iconic drink in colonial New South Wales remained rum, which often served as a generic name for distilled spirits of all kinds. In the 1840s, Charles Rowcroft, author of an early novel that fictionalized his experiences as an emigrant, reported a conversation with a publican who was shocked when he asked for beer or water and told him, "You'll find no beer up the country. Rum's the stuff; that's our drink in this colony."[9] In particular, while wine carried elitist connotations and was often served and consumed in elaborate (and expensive) rituals, both spirits and beer were more egalitarian, typically shared from a communal vessel or bought in rounds. Unlike "Mother Gin" in eighteenth-century England, rum in Australia was stereotypically a man's drink, presumably due to the absence of many alternatives – and indeed of women, and especially female drinkers, to stereotype.

Overall, alcohol became steadily more available in New South Wales and as it did so, drinking culture more closely aligned with British norms. From the 1820s, alcohol was consistently available to urban drinkers, prices stabilized, and a consumer culture that linked particular drinks, venues, and drinking practices to status and identity took hold. However, consumption levels were highly influenced by economic conditions and, more relevant to my argument, by the transformation of colonial society as it democratized. Among the growing respectable classes, restraint, if not sobriety, became an important means of performing cultural identity, especially for women; and increasingly even gender ratios may help explain declining consumption per person after 1840. This overall pattern also conceals enormous variation, not least between urban and rural areas. Outside of towns, access to alcohol remained more limited and sporadic, a fact that likely contributed to the binge-drinking pattern of rural workers.

Drinking Places and Patterns

Beyond the blunt measure of available alcohol, regulations and norms governing where and when it was acquired, and when and how it was drunk, shaped patterns of drinking. In the early decades of the colony there were few licensed premises, and in most cases little difference between licensed and unlicensed houses. Most drinking places were not buildings designed for or dedicated to drinking, but private houses whose owners sold liquor with or without a licence.[10] Officers and the colonial elite had personal stockpiles of liquor, purchased wholesale and drunk in private; in contrast, convicts were usually forced to drink in more public settings, either in these licensed and unlicensed houses or, frequently, outdoors. In these early years the official elite drank wines and spirits constantly and heavily, but convicts depended on illicit trade or forms of quasi-legal patronage to access alcohol, mostly watered-down rum, known as grog, and often drank in intense binges when it was available.

Under Macquarie and his successors, free trade was accompanied by a much stricter system of licensing, including distinct classes of licence, and efforts to shut down sly grog shops.[11] As licensing was more closely monitored, dedicated drinking places became more common, and licence holders invested more in their businesses and targeted particular customers. This led to more clearly stratified categories of public house, ranging from large and expensive hotels aimed at travelling rural gentry, upmarket inns for professionals, to taverns and sly grog shops for convicts and urban workers. Peter Cunningham, a surgeon and early settler who published a popular account of the colony in 1827, described the range of venues, claiming Hill's tavern – the scene of the Turf Club dinner – was one of a smattering of hotels that could "vie with those of any English town of the same size." It was, however, outnumbered by "a great variety of taverns of an inferior description, and tippling houses to no mean amount."[12]

Alexander Harris, an emigrant labourer and trader in the 1820s, who published accounts of his working life in the colony in the 1840s, described a visit to a sly grog shop, the "Sheer Hulk" on Gloucester Street, which was owned by a ticket-of-leave holder and had once been licensed but now formally operated as a lodging house. It flouted the licensing law through the payment of "sweeteners" to local constables, afforded by the substantial profit of the trade, which Harris estimated at thirty shillings a night.[13] Harris claimed that in the 1820s there were twice as many unlicensed as licensed houses in Sydney, and that almost every house in the Rocks – the notorious district on the western shore of Sydney Cove where the Hulk was located – operated in this way, acting as drinking den, fence, and flophouse for the criminal underclass of convicts, prostitutes, and sailors who populated the growing port.[14] Supporting his claim, Sydney publicans in the late 1820s raised private funds to reward constables for prosecuting their unlicensed competitors.[15]

The failure to control the sly grog trade encouraged greater liberalization of licensing as a consensus emerged that "more drunkenness ... takes place in those places where spirits are illegally sold."[16] From 1826, pubs were permitted to serve convicts, and during the 1830s the number of legal houses increased significantly, while professional policing improved enforcement of the law. Supervised convict drinking was normalized in this period with the legalization of what had always been standard practice of providing convict workers with drink, as rations, rewards, and payments. The Licensing Act of 1830 permitted up to a third of wages to be paid in alcohol, though this was limited in 1838 to one gill (approximately three standard drinks) per day and the paying of wages in pubs – encouraging them to be spent on alcohol – was banned.[17] But it remained deviant and often illegal for convicts to drink without permission, outside curfew, and especially in public to intoxication. Illicit sale of alcohol certainly continued but rarely in dedicated venues or in towns, heightening the differences between urban and rural drinking. Furthermore, much of the illicit trade in rural areas was tolerated, if not actively controlled, by local landowners who wanted to discourage their labourers – and their pay – from leaving the estate.[18] Rural drinking also retained a traditional rhythm shaped by patterns of work and difficulties of access. Like convicts before them, post-convict rural workers tended to have long periods of sober labour, punctuated by short drunken binges.

In urban areas, public drinking now largely took place in licensed venues, though these took many different forms and catered to very different kinds of clientele. Importantly, as J.M. Freeland argues, changes to licensing laws "killed" cheap, unruly, and sometimes unlicensed taverns like the Sheer Hulk, and led to raised standards in the appearance and outfitting of houses, which increasingly featured a distinct public bar, separate from storage areas for liquor, and from the parlour, which offered food and drink for overnight guests.[19] Harris also describes a visit to such a public bar in the "Market House" in Sydney, a "large tap-room" crowded with "a strange assemblage" of convicts, emancipists, and native-born colonists mingling with immigrants from across Britain, and even foreigners. There were only a few women, accompanying their husbands and uniformly "sober and quiet." In contrast, the men were loud and drunken, all smoking and "drinking rum in drams, or very slightly qualified with water."[20] Urban drinking like this increasingly took on a more modern pattern, taking place outside of work hours and especially on the weekend, a fact reflected in the spike of arrests for drunkenness on Sundays and Mondays. An editorial in the short-lived working-man's paper the *Sydney Journal* explained this pattern in terms that echoed those of Francis Place: "the previous steadiness and sobriety of the lower orders, is the result of [saving] to enable them to spend at least one day in happiness … [while] over-stepping of the bounds of moderation … [is due to] relaxation from the daily toils of an otherwise monotonous round of manual labour."[21]

By the democratic era, drinking places and customs were distinct markers of identity. Thomas McCombie was a Scottish immigrant who arrived in the colony in 1841 and tried to establish himself as a squatter before settling in Melbourne as a journalist and politician. In 1845, he published *Arabin; or, The Adventures of a Colonist*, a colonial tale of adventure loosely based on his own experiences, and centred on Geoffrey Arabin, an English doctor, trained in Edinburgh, who came to Australia to make his fortune. McCombie advocated temperance – meaning moderation, not abstinence – and his novel is intimately concerned with drinking and its consequences.[22]

At one end of the social spectrum, Arabin drank punch in the house of a squatter, Captain Thomson, who stressed his sympathy for the temperance movement, but "swallowed glass after glass without being the worse," persuading a reluctant Arabin to drink with him in order to honour his hospitality. He is called out to see a "settler" (in McCombie's usage, a middle-class immigrant farmer), Mr Willis, who "was labouring under fits of insanity, occasioned by too frequent indulgence in intoxicating liquors," using his story as a warning about the risk of normal drinking becoming habitual.[23] He also visited a respectable country hotel, divided between a "tap-room" that was "crowded every hour of the day with carters, bullock-drivers, and tradesmen," a parlour for settlers, and a house where travellers slept. In the bar the men take turns "standing treat" (buying rounds), a practice that leads McCombie to editorialize about "the wild riots which daily occur in the taps of these houses … [and] are a disgrace to the Colony." His snobbish description of the crowd of workers in the bar is especially significant: "they have no satisfaction beyond drinking rum, and, when their money is exhausted, in asking the landlord out of bravado 'if they owe him anything?' What pen could describe their self-importance when the landlord would smile upon them benignantly and declare they had paid him like gentlemen? … What consequence! … *they are drunk, and owe nothing.*"[24]

McCombie's account illustrates both the diversity of colonial drinking culture and the way popular drinking was stigmatized by respectable observers. While Arabin was a reluctant drinker, he felt compelled to participate in the rites of hospitality; in contrast the captain embodies the heavy-drinking culture of colonial gentry, and Willis, the dangers of such drinking. Working-class drinkers were victims of exploitative publicans and popular drinking culture was riotous, disorderly, and threatening. At the same time, McCombie's descriptions of drinking workers are open to a different reading. Their drinking habits were threatening to respectable observers like McCombie, precisely because they evoked a kind of drunken freedom and a lack of respect for the traditional ordering of British society.

Styles of Drinking and the Politics of Drunken Comportment

Where, when, and how people drank in public was thus a key marker of identity in the status-obsessed colony. People drank – or were perceived to drink – in distinct styles with their own cultural meanings and political significance. Such drinking styles are also part of the political imaginary, cultural templates that script performances and the reactions of the social audience. This connection between drink and identity was both an agentive performance and a discursive construction: both the act of drinking and its reception mattered. Drinkers actively performed their identity through their comportment, but public drinking was also the subject of fraught anxieties and social judgments that reflected power dynamics. For some drinkers in some contexts, drunkenness provided the kind of "time out" from norms that MacAndrew and Edgerton describe.[25] But drinking was also governed by its own strict though unwritten rules, which served as a test of the drinker's responsibility. With this in mind, I distinguish three styles of drinking (or abstinent) comportment that had especial political significance in colonial New South Wales. I term these drunken, restrained, and sober comportment.

Drunken drinking was characteristic of popular celebrations and emphasized excess – drinking everything available – in a carnivalesque release from conventional norms, and it was, accordingly, often politically subversive.[26] Drinkers acted drunk, in MacAndrew and Edgerton's terms: they behaved as if they had a cultural time out from conventional manners, not least taboos against interaction between genders, sexual conduct, and violence, but also, importantly, from deference to the social hierarchy. To be excusable in public, popular drunkenness had to be authorized. It was traditionally associated with festivals, at which times there was some social licence for unrestrained behaviour, but there were always drinking places, licensed and unlicensed, that cultivated this kind of celebratory drunkenness and release from norms among their clientele. In particular, convict drinking often took this form, regardless of occasion. In part this was a consequence of efforts to limit convicts' access to alcohol, which encouraged excess when it was available. But elite observers were also inclined to read convicts as drunken, irrespective of how they actually drank. Similarly, Aboriginal drinkers were usually perceived as drunken savages incapable of holding their liquor, while drunken women were seen as shamefully unfeminine, and understood as sexually available.

The drinking performed by gentlemen at public dinners was, at least superficially, more restrained. Restrained drinking complied with accepted norms of public conduct and demonstrated self-control. It was polite and orderly, restricted to those deemed sufficiently responsible, and governed by complex codes of manners, the successful observance of which sanctified the behaviour of the participants. Performing drunken restraint – abiding by the unwritten rules of drinking – demonstrated responsibility, while being judged to have failed in such a performance was evidence that the drinker was insufficiently responsible. Clearly, when gentlemen drank twelve toasts at a wine-soaked dinner they were likely to be affected by the alcohol consumed. But regardless of the degree of intoxication, restrained drinking was understood by those who performed and witnessed it as something very different from convict drunkenness, as the reported "harmony and conviviality" of the Turf Club dinner illustrates.[27] While such public dinners are a key focus of this book, and the most obvious example of a drinking practice that was widely understood as restrained, many drinkers in other contexts sought to perform restraint with varied levels of success. Women drinking in mixed company typically performed a kind of restraint to demonstrate their respectability. The increasing wine consumption of middle-class men can also be understood in these terms, with their choice of drink serving as a coded means of distinguishing the drinker from the associations of popular drunkenness. The successful performance and reception of restraint reflected the political authority of those involved. To be allowed to drink in public –

to be read as suitably restrained – was a mark of status that, I argue, became symbolic of citizenship in the democratizing colony.

In contrast, a third distinctive style emphasized both literal and figurative sobriety, deliberately drawing the contrast with restraint, but especially with drunkenness. Sober comportment was not simply failing to drink; it was a style of performative abstinence through not drinking when others were, refusing drink when offered, and, often, through publicizing such sobriety so as to draw attention to it. Most obviously linked to the temperance movement, such sobriety symbolized religiosity, moral uprightness, and a scrupulous concern for public reputation. Like the other styles outlined above, sober comportment had highly gendered meanings. For most women, it was normative, the default in public or where there was any question about the respectability of the company. Some respectable women did drink in mixed company but only in private, or when chaperoned by men among company of suitable status and moral reputation. In contrast, for men, sober comportment was socially deviant, a breach of expected masculine conduct. Men who publicly refused to drink were often seen as effeminate and puritanical. Perceived to be holding themselves to a different standard, they were ostracized from fraternal company and created their own sober subculture accordingly.

I discuss gentlemanly toasting, the iconic form of restrained drinking, and temperance as performative sobriety, extensively in later chapters. Here, I briefly explore the political meaning of drunken comportment, in general as an aspect of popular drinking culture. In what follows, I sometimes use E.P. Thompson's term "plebian" (or "plebs") to characterize the social status of colonial workers (both convict and "free") because this avoids the complex questions posed by social class in a convict society.[28]

The evidence for convict popular culture must often be read against the grain of hostile sources, but convicts clearly drank heavily when they could. David Collins published the most widely read and influential account of the early colony and was obsessed with the disorder he associated with convict drunkenness, the consequences of which constantly came before him in his role as judge advocate. For example, on Sunday, 12 October 1794, an emancipist settler, Simon Burn, was murdered by a convict butcher named John Hill after he tried to intervene in a domestic dispute between Hill and his mistress. Collins commented that the crime was compounded by the fact that Burn died "with the sin upon his head of having profaned the Lord's Day by rioting and drunkenness." In similarly sanctimonious terms, he claimed that Burn's friends and relatives "celebrated the funeral rites in a manner and with orgies suitable to the disposition and habits of the deceased, his widow, and themselves."[29] But we should understand the drunken comportment that Collins snidely condemns as an important ritual – a wake – and one in which alcohol played a central role, as it would have done in Britain.

Indeed, much of the drunkenness lamented in the available sources can be read as perfectly in line with mainstream British popular culture, viewed through the eyes of a judgmental elite. Notably, David Mann, an educated convict (a convicted forger) who remained in the colony for almost a decade after his 1802 pardon, thought that the colonists drank in a similar manner to the British. While he strongly condemned the spirit trade and convict drunkenness, Mann argued that colonial morals "are by no means so debauched as the tongue of prejudice has too frequently asserted ... [and] instances of drunkenness, dishonesty, and their concomitant offences, are not more common than in the mother country."[30] Tellingly, though, both Collins and Mann saw convict drunkenness as symptomatic of idleness and subversion, with Mann even suggesting that the opportunity for easy wealth through rum trading undermined the social order by encouraging "a consciousness of independence, which was fatal to that strict subordination which ought to be maintained and enforced ... [leading to] the assumption of a degree of importance and independence which induces [the convict] to place himself above his master, and thus controverts the natural and necessary distinctions of society."[31] Such elite reports on convict drunkenness were highly politicized and tell us more about perceptions of public order than actual levels of alcohol consumption.

Harris's descriptions of drinking with convicts are more clearly based on personal observation and sympathy; indeed, he had problems with alcohol throughout his life. While he also wrote from a broadly temperance perspective, condemning drunkenness as "the great moral disease of the colony," he also understood the drinking of workers as a "habit" encouraged by the climate and the working and social conditions in New South Wales.[32] When working as a sawyer on the Illawarra he described a large group of convicts, including known bushrangers, gathered on a beach, drinking from ten-gallon kegs of rum that the timber boats had smuggled in for them, calling them an "unlicensed and reckless mob … prolonging day and night their carousal until all the liquor was gone."[33] Such unlicensed recklessness, wilfully ignoring the rules and authorities, drinking all available alcohol, and the egalitarian solidarity between participants, including those living outside the law, typified this kind of drunken plebian celebration. On another occasion, Harris was working as a trader, buying timber on the Hunter, when a large crowd of drunken convicts who had exhausted the rum their master had given them swarmed his wagon and demanded liquor with threats of violence. Again, Harris focused on the wild and reckless nature of the drinking that ensued, but he observed that it reflected a customary pattern, broadly tolerated in the colony, including by masters, noting that "such affairs are pretty well understood to be only jokes, and no ill will is allowed to be borne about them afterwards."[34] When licensed by elite patronage, drunken celebrations were no longer subversive but reinforced the political hierarchy.

The evidence of court cases that sometimes resulted when such drinking turned violent is also revealing. Though this was a common context for charges of assault and murder, we should be careful in assuming that violence was a common feature of plebian drinking. Rather, as today, it seems more likely that drinking parties were accompanied by a release from social restraints, a time out that made violence more likely but by no means ubiquitous. In an example from 1813, two linked trials centred on a murder among a drinking party of seven convicts and emancipists, five men and two women, who testified that they had gathered together "for the purpose of drinking spirits."[35] Karskens cites a similar example of a Christmas party that ended in violence to illustrate drinking among the convict- and emancipist-dominated communities of the Hawkesbury. She notes that festivals like Christmas often featured gatherings of people from different ranks and genders drinking together and describes alcohol in such contexts as "cathartic [and creating] a heightened sense of merriment and joy."[36] Such drinking parties were distinguished by their drunken freedom, and while it is rarely possible to quantify, this often clearly involved drinking to get as drunk as possible. In an 1834 trial, Henry Whiley gave evidence of drinking at Windsor hospital with "the whole of the servants of that establishment," who "commenced a drinking bout" during which the six of them consumed twelve gallons of beer in two hours (at least thirteen standard drinks each), before some of them went on to a brothel.[37] Convict drinking often occurred in unlicensed venues or outdoors, and the alcohol was often acquired, if not produced, illicitly, which helped promote a deviant subculture where drinking was fast and reckless.

As numbers of non-convict people – "native," emancipist, and immigrant – increased, workers often drank together, regardless of their status, and by the 1830s this was largely legal. Popular drinking culture took on distinct features in urban and rural areas, with drinking "sprees" especially common among rural workers. In urban areas, working men typically drank in public, not in private, increasingly in licensed houses, and their drinking culture emphasized their manly independence through a practice of round drinking in which men were expected to "treat" each other. Harris's accounts of drinking with convicts and other workers in the 1820s and '30s illustrate this emerging drinking culture and the way it, too, was perceived as drunken. His description of the "Sheer Hulk" focuses on the noise – a "perfect frenzy of drunken vociferation," which could be heard from a hundred yards away – the crowded, smoky, dingy conditions, and the risk of being "hocussed" (given drugged drink) and robbed or cheated at the gambling tables. But reading against the grain, we get hints of a kind of drunken egalitarianism, with the grog ordered half a pint at a time, "delivered in a tumbler ... dealt out into wine glasses and drunk neat."[38] His description of the public bar of the Market House further illustrates this kind of culture and the way it was becoming more respectable. Men were clustered in small groups, everyone smoking and drinking, and many drunk. Though Harris was not impressed by their conversation, claiming it chiefly consisted of boasting about their livestock, farms, or "the quantity of work they could perform," he emphasized their generous fraternity, the fact that they frequently offered to share their liquor, and stressed that "there was no offensive intrusiveness about their civility; every man seemed to consider himself just on a level with all the rest, and so quite content either to be sociable or not, as the circumstance of the moment indicated as most proper."[39]

The drinking practices found in the public bar were still often read as drunken – including, at times, by Harris – but they also performed a kind of egalitarianism that would become especially symbolic as the colony democratized and the franchise expanded. Interestingly, Harris emphasized that these drinkers constituted an emerging "class" of workers, those who, "whatever advantages they had had in the colony, still continued unexalted by improved opportunities"; in Marxist terms, a *Lumpenproletariat*.[40] However, as Ward argues, there is considerable evidence that such drunken fraternity increasingly extended across class boundaries, or at least was imagined to do so.[41] The egalitarianism of the convict and working classes, symbolized in their drinking culture, would become a distinctive feature of the legendary masculinity that characterized Australia's democratic political imaginary, and excluded women from it.

Hierarchy and Fraternity: Alcohol, Work, and Leisure

This plebian drinking culture and its drunken fraternity developed a distinctive colonial form as the colony democratized and the economy shifted toward paid labour in the 1840s. As in Britain, a key feature of this economic transformation was a sharper boundary between work and leisure, marked by alcohol, and the political meaning of popular drinking changed accordingly. This transition from a moral to a political economy was even more politicized in New South Wales, where convictism gave way to a settler-colonial sense of entitlement among workers. In the early decades, and in rural areas, the economy was especially reliant on convict labour and alcohol had an exaggerated importance as a means of motivating workers, with such patronage affirming the hierarchical nature of convict society. As transportation ended, this traditional association contributed to the practice of celebratory drunken binges, especially among rural labourers, evoking their freedom. Meanwhile urban workers drank more regularly, typically in public houses, after work, but their drinking culture emphasized reciprocal treating – buying rounds – as a gesture of fraternal fellowship. In both cases, the drinking of post-convict workers renounced hierarchy and emphasized a radical egalitarianism in which all were fundamentally equal in their capacity to treat, and in their drunken freedoms.

The traditional provision of alcohol by masters to servants was a customary feature of rural convict labour. The extensive investigation of the Castle Forbes revolt, an 1833 uprising by convicts on James Mudie's estate on the Hunter, illustrates how such patronage operated in New South Wales.[42] Mudie's convicts told the subsequent inquiry that they were regularly given alcoholic drinks, both to help with their work and as a reward during key celebrations.[43] Mudie later claimed that alcohol "was required on all occasions, when I allowed it, as a medicine" – as, for example, at harvest time, when "the weather is excessively hot" and he gave his men a glass of gin with breakfast and dinner. He also gave his men alcohol "once or twice during the year ... as an indulgence," a practice he claimed was "notoriously known in the colony," even serving as a "waiter" and pouring drinks for his servants during Harvest Home (the celebration of the end of the harvest) in a traditional ritual of role reversal.[44] Mudie's management of his estate is a classic illustration of paternalism. He granted his men alcohol as a reward for deferential service but sent them to the bench for a flogging if they were absent seeking to buy drinks for themselves. Arguably, his defence of these practices aligns with his opposition to democratic reform in New South Wales.[45]

Forms of patronage using alcohol were not confined to agricultural workplaces but were commonly found in other contexts with a clear and accepted hierarchy and an accompanying moral economy. Governors often provided drinks to convicts during public celebrations such as the flag-raising ceremony in 1788, and even to Aboriginal people, during annual feasts at which blankets were distributed. In each case, the drinking of a subaltern population was not understood as drunken because it was licensed by a ritual of patronage and deference that reinforced the social order. An interesting transitional example was the fete organized by William Wentworth to celebrate Governor Darling's departure from the colony. *The Monitor* told readers that "there will be lots of Cooper's [gin] and Wright's best [beer], to enable the visitors to pour out copious libations on the joyful occasion," while *The Australian* reported that "upwards of 4000 persons" enjoyed the food and drinks, before hoisting their patron on their shoulders and chairing him around the lawn. In this case, Wentworth was engaged in a more democratic form of patronage since his guests were not formally under his authority but were celebrating his leadership of the public campaign against Darling. Wentworth acknowledged this with a series of lamp-lit illuminations on his lawns, including a crown flanked by two stars and the slogans "God save the king" and "Down with the tyrant."[46]

Patronage evolved throughout the democratic era, and an especially fraught form was electoral treating. While colonial elections were far less corrupt than those in Britain in this period, election meetings were usually held in public houses, and there is good evidence that free "refreshments" were often provided for the audience.[47] Treating was explicitly banned in every electoral act but the offence was almost impossible to prove because the prosecutor had to show the treat was offered "with a view of influencing the vote." There were, nonetheless, regular accusations of alcohol-related inducements to voters.[48] A civil case in 1848, in which a publican sued for debts incurred in an election campaign, hints at the reality of electioneering and the role of hospitality. The suit was unsuccessful – since treating was illegal, debts could not be recovered, a principle that was subsequently codified – but the evidence showed that potential voters were given free drinks.[49] A larger controversy surrounded the candidacy of George Hill, a successful butcher and racing promoter who became mayor of Sydney in 1850 and held a series of fancy balls and picnics for his constituents.[50] During the election campaign in 1851, supporters of a rival candidate, the teetotaller George Allen, alleged that Hill's civic festivities were designed to "bribe the citizens to bestow upon him a certain sort of popularity," and the liberal daily *The Empire* dubbed him "the picnic king" and implied that his victory was corrupt.[51]

In general, patronage with alcohol was less common among urban workers and declined in rural areas with the end of convictism, as paid workers came to purchase their own drinks. However, many rural employers used their privileged access to alcohol as a means of exploiting their workers, continuing the tradition of the early rum traders. Joseph Mason, an assigned convict during the 1830s, reported that "settlers are allowed to retail spirits on their farm in exchange for labour," and often sold drinks on credit to draw their servants into debts that kept them labouring even after their sentences had expired.[52] Similarly, Mudie defended his patronage by arguing that it was better for his men, claiming that convicts easily acquired liquor from sly grog shops and that non-convict labourers also demanded alcohol in payment.[53] These practices continued into the 1840s. An anonymous writer in *The Temperance Advocate* claimed to have encouraged his shepherds to become teetotallers and that they increasingly requested tea with their work, but noted that he was "obliged" to offer spirits during shearing in "self-defence"; since other settlers did so, shearers expected it, he claimed, and given the level of wages, it was the only way to make labour affordable. Indeed, he suggested that the custom of working men blowing their cheques in a "spree" was "absolutely necessary in order to their being [*sic*] any servants in the country districts," since otherwise they would leave to get drunk in town.[54] Freedom to drink was seen to threaten the social order and the economy.

Such sprees among rural workers evolved from the traditional moral economy of convict labour. As Ward argued, itinerant bush workers in the later nineteenth century retained this pattern of "work and burst" – that is, working for a season before drinking their earnings in an epic spree.[55] He attributed binge drinking to the persistent gender imbalance in rural areas, the "universal" system of paying workers in a single cheque at the end of their contract, and to colonial land laws, which allegedly discouraged workers from saving. More broadly, he also linked the practice to his Australian legend. Building on Ward, I understand binge drinking as a democratic and egalitarian ritual among working men, an assertion of freedom and a rejection of the Protestant-capitalist ethic of responsible, temperate domesticity that was later idealized by the proponents of legendary masculinity – including, ironically, Ward himself.[56]

There is plenty of evidence of spree drinking in the mid-nineteenth century, but almost all of it is from the perspective of judgmental (and often temperate) observers. Arguing for the end of transportation, John Dunmore Lang told the Molesworth Committee that, once emancipated, even well-behaved convicts would often "revert all at once to habits of drunkenness and dissipation … employing [themselves] from time to time in honest labour only till [they have] acquired the means of repeating [their] brutalizing debauch … and drinking for weeks together till their last shilling was gone!"[57] His view fits with his broader temperance historiography, and he would later call for opening up the land to settlement as the only means by which working men could be kept sober.[58] But the pattern he observed clearly had some basis in reality since it became a cliché in accounts of rural life, and while it is almost always described by critics, their observations illustrate the egalitarian nature of the ritual.[59] An article by "The Old Shepherd" claimed that drinking sprees were "absolutely necessary" for most unmarried rural workers once they finished a contract. The author described how shepherds "knocked down their cheque," leaving it as credit with the landlord. After drinking "with a vigour acquired from his three months of forced abstinence," the shepherd "begins to 'shout' – which means that through generosity or ostentation he insists on every one [*sic*] in the house drinking at his expense; and many a quiet inoffensive man have I seen insulted or even beaten for refusing the proffered treat."[60] Allowing for some exaggeration, there was clearly a strongly felt expectation that those fortunate enough to afford a drunken spree should also pay for others, but equally that such generosity obligated appreciation, and reciprocity. While urban workers were less likely to be rewarded with alcohol and their drinking rhythms were typically weekly, they shared the sense of obligation linked to drinking, as Harris experienced in the Market House.

Many of the customary "drinking usages" Dunlop complained of in Britain also persisted in the Australian colonies, and similarly speak to a sense of fraternal obligation. Alcohol was an important accompaniment to commerce, opening purses, and in some instances becoming an expectation, necessary to a successful transaction. William Howitt, who visited and wrote about the colonies during the 1850s gold rushes, reported a man buying meat from a public house who told the publican, "I must have a nobbler out of this," and also described visiting a smithy to fix his dray, only to be told that they "would not undertake to do the job at all without a nobbler, and they would not finish it without another."[61] Harris also noted such customs, reporting that sawyers expected "the usual starting glass (a half pint of rum)" before commencing a logging trip and that his expenses included "those innumerable gills of rum, that a sawyer is called upon for in Sydney, when he is known to be pretty well off, by his less thrifty brethren."[62] Godfrey Mundy, another British observer of the colonies in the 1850s, described a fair in Wollongong at which "every bargain, every meeting, greeting and parting was solemnized by liberal libations," which loosened up manners so that men "shook hands, laughed; d[amne]d each other's old eyes and limbs … slapped on the back and 'treated' each other over and over again." Two drunken men who could not agree on the price of a horse only came to a bargain when the seller offered to "drink a sovereign of [his price] now" with the buyer.[63] These customs were traditional, but in contrast to patronage, they evoked the equality of buyer and seller, treater and drinker, in a democratic society.

The key drinking ritual of post-convict workers, urban and rural, was the round, and the closely linked practice of treating or shouting liquor.[64] Treating could resemble patronage; in some contexts the term was used to describe an unrequited gift of alcohol from a patron, notably in relation to elections, where voters were often "treated" by the candidate to bolster their support. However, I am concerned here with the practice of mutual treating, the expectation of hospitality between equals, which was fundamental to colonial drinking culture. Another 1850s visitor, Frank Fowler, describing the legendary drunkenness of the colonies, claimed that "nothing is done without the nobbler," and that "even respectable men" and merchants offered visitors a drink and were offended if it was refused: "In fact, not to drink is considered a crime ..., if you will not 'stand,' you may walk."[65] Illustrating this, in Harris's novel *The Emigrant Family*, the temperate protagonist, Martin Beck, visits a convict hut and declines a drink when offered one, thereby "producing offence and mistrust." The situation was only saved when Beck's friend, a fellow convict, told the drinkers that "he never does drink, lads ... but he has always got a good glass to give the likes of us at his own hut," which "restored the general community of sentiment."[66] Like Ralph Clark's, Beck's abstinence does not prevent him from gifting alcohol as a necessary ritual of solidarity among equals. A poem, "Cleared Out," published in *Bell's Life in Sydney* in 1849, captures the spirit of reciprocity inherent in treating, with the narrator telling his companion, "If to-night for your friend you the needful will raise, / And meet me to-morrow, I'll stand treat for you."[67] Court cases from the period also show that reciprocal treating was understood as an obligation. The expectation was often manipulated by criminals to discover potential marks; and threats and violence could result where the perceived obligation was not honoured.[68]

The implicitly democratic politics of treating are captured in a newspaper serial entitled "Tim Tippet's Ticket: A Colonial Tale," published in 1845 in *The Star*, a penny paper whose original subtitle, the "Working Man's Guardian," gives a good sense of its politics. While it broadly adopts the form of a temperance narrative, the story is more sympathetic to, and more insightful about, its convict hero and the dangers and pleasures of drink than most other sources. Tim is an Irish convict who sets out from Windsor to Parramatta, with his "all-important pass," allowing him to travel freely, to apply for a ticket of leave – a permit that would let him live independently of his master, and (importantly for the story) to marry.

On arriving in Parramatta, Tim "passed resolutely by several public houses, whose open doors, offered a tempting invitation to the thirsty wayfarer," but meeting a former shipmate, Harry Larkin, he is drawn into a drinking session at the Thistle, a dingy tavern full of unsavoury characters, all male apart from a single drunken woman. Once Larkin buys him a round, Tim feels obliged to "treat Harry in return," and is rapidly drawn into a larger round with a carpenter, who "offered to shout for glasses for three." Again, Tim feels obliged to "stand his glass" and, when he tries to leave, is bullied to "stand something all round." All the patrons of the tavern then gather around a single table, with the eldest serving as "temporary president" for the crowd, who begin a series of drunken toasts and songs. Predictably, the drinking ends in a drunken brawl during which Tim has his pass and money stolen and is arrested by venal constables, seeking their share of any fine.[69]

The serial ends mid-tale with a remorseful and hungover Tim seeking to recover his pass and secure his ticket, but still provides useful insights into working-class drinking culture and its political meaning. Tim's drinking companions are exclusively male, and the only woman present is shamefully drunken and degraded. Among the male drinkers, there is an intense sense of fraternal obligation: once treated, you must treat in return, though the story is clearly framed to show that the obligation is dangerous. Moreover, their drinking is clearly shaped by the practices of gentlemen, practices that were in the process of being democratized. The table of drinkers informally elects a president who directs a series of drunken toasts and songs, establishing convivial fraternity. Finally, the drinking ends in cathartic violence, something that marks the distinction between the restraint required of such gentlemen and the freer drunkenness of workers. Tim may be a fictional character, but his story brings us as close as the sources allow to the political imaginary of plebian drinking. The egalitarianism of the public bar would come to symbolize the imagined freedoms of democratic society, the elite fears of social disorder that accompanied it, and the gendered and racialized limits of public participation in a settler colony.

4

Toasting and Dining

THE POLITICS OF PUBLIC DRINKING IN THE BRITISH WORLD

As the Turf Club dinner showed, public toasting and dining were powerfully symbolic rituals and could be overtly political acts. This distinction between the overt and deliberate *use* of toasting, on the one hand, and its larger and implicit *meaning* on the other, is critical to my argument. In Britain in general, but specifically in colonial New South Wales in the period 1820–40, toasting and dining were important tools of political organizing. But I also interpret toasting as an expression of an underlying political imaginary using the performative reading of drinking practices outlined in the introduction.

The practice of drinking healths – drinking as a means of well-wishing – and more broadly of toasting – honouring an individual, cause, or sentiment through drinking – were rituals with a long history and a dense meaning.[1] Toasting was a highly charged performance of sociability, a choreographed tradition shaped by the drinkers and their social audience, and the contours of that performance changed over time. While toasting occurred in many contexts, and was often a largely private matter, it came to have a distinctive political resonance when deployed in public, especially at so-called public dinners, where large numbers of diners – and even larger numbers of subsequent readers – could witness the political statement involved.

I focus here on the practice of toasting and its ritual importance in British society, tracing its history and especially the forms it took at the turn of the nineteenth century. I then turn to the public dinner, arguing that in New South Wales, in the absence of more formal political institutions, such events took on especial importance as a means of asserting group identity among distinct sections of an ever-expanding social elite, including the military, British ethnic groups, and, increasingly, political factions. I look especially at the political use of loyal toasting, and the way such loyalty could be subverted and deployed by radicals and reformers to challenge the existing political order.

Toasting

Toasting is a long-standing tradition in Britain, but its modern political significance has its roots in the conflicts of the seventeenth century. As Rebecca Lemon notes, the drinking of healths was "the most popular and chronicled drinking ritual" in early modern England. In its basic form, healthing involved participants pledging each other's health reciprocally, either by draining a glass, or drinking in turn from a communal bowl, in a public display of their social bonds. But the practice became controversial in the late sixteenth century, attacked for compelling drinkers to excess, and depicted as a foreign (especially Dutch) innovation. Over the course of the seventeenth century, healthing was increasingly politicized, condemned and banned by Puritans, but celebrated by royalists as a now traditional display of loyalty.[2] Angela McShane argues that after the Restoration the elite practice of the "loyal health" became a kind of "profane sacrament," one that was "increasingly ubiquitous, both socially and geographically," as a compulsory test of loyalty to crown and church.[3] Healths were a kind of oath, a test of one's honesty before God, and in consequence drinking the health of king or church was used aggressively to weed out "traitors" who would refuse to drink against their conscientious beliefs, refusal that could be severely punished. Though the specific controversies of the seventeenth century were long forgotten in colonial New South Wales, the paradox of what Lemon terms "compulsory conviviality" – celebrating collective loyalty and the liberties it granted through obligatory and harmful excess – remained a key feature of toasting, as did its function as a means of unifying drinkers in their drunkenness and through exclusion of outsiders.

More directly relevant to the colony were the forms the tradition took among gentlemen at the turn of the nineteenth century, since these were imported to New South Wales. Following Lemon and McShane, Rémy Duthille argues toasting initially marked allegiance to a patron, but increasingly came to indicate allegiance to a political cause.[4] The practice formalized over the eighteenth century, taking distinct patterns in particular places, but sharing some standard features. In a clear though critical discussion, Henry, Lord Cockburn, recalled the toasting ritual among the Scottish elite of his youth in the 1790s, claiming during dinner "every glass ... required to be dedicated to the health of some one," with the proposer and honouree pledging each other's health and locking gazes while drinking. After the table was cleared, an even more formal ritual began in which "each person, following the [host], [had] to drink the health of every other person present, individually." Next, "before the ladies retired, there generally began what were called '*Rounds*' of toasts; when each gentleman named an absent lady, and each lady an absent gentleman, separately." In addition, there were toasts offered to sentiments: "short epigrammatic sentences, expressive of moral feelings and virtues," which varied "from the elegant and romantic, to the political, the municipal, the ecclesiastic, and the drunken."[5]

One unusual feature of Cockburn's account is that women participated equally. In most contexts it was increasingly disreputable for women to associate with drunken men, and in elite society they often withdrew from the table after the cloth was drawn, leaving the gentlemen to drink and toast alone. Nonetheless, Cockburn illustrates some common features of the ritual, notably the different forms of toasts. Toasts were made between those at the table, but more commonly, and distinctively, to honour the absent; and also, additionally, to a broader range of sentiments. The sentiments, and, similarly, the drinking songs that often accompanied toasting, allowed for more explicit political statements reflecting the context in which they were performed. Adapting Duthille's distinction, the toasting of sentiments could take two basic structures (sometimes combined), which I will term "to" and "may."[6] Toasts "to" honoured some person or thing, and toasts "may" allowed for a broader range of wishes, often humorous, and just as often explicitly political.

Lists of such sentiments were not only published in accounts of public dinners but were also gathered in popular collections that typically framed orderly toasting as a form of good manners and insisted on a narrow and conservative version of loyalty, sanitizing actual practice. The anonymous author of the *Toast Master*, published in 1789, claimed that "decency ... urges the necessity of drinking to our companions" but warned against drunken sentiments that set a "bad example," calling for "sentiments of duty, respect, and love." Similarly, Robert Pocock's *Everlasting Songster* of 1804 (figure 4.1) aimed to present songs, toasts, and sentiments "which will at once inspire mirth and cheerfulness, [while] avoiding those that have a tendency to inculcate either disloyalty to the government, or to wound the chaste and modest ear."[7]

The rarer exceptions to this conservatism give us a clearer sense of the true breadth of political sentiments. The *Royal Toast Master* of 1791 offered sentiments drawn from all sides of politics, but justified this in terms of the need to tailor one's toasts to the company, stressing that the "great variety" of toasts would allow the reader "to answer the ruling opinion of the time" regardless of who they were drinking with.[8] A later guide, seemingly published amid the censorship battles of the 1820s, included an even more diverse range of political sentiments, including the loyalist pledge to "Church and King" (which Dissenters were unable to drink) and the radical wish that "revolutions never cease while tyranny exists."[9] Toasting was increasingly adaptable to different political contexts, solidifying distinct forms of allegiance. As Ian Newman argues, toasting was "well suited to political topics during the period of democratic revolution, because the toast is fundamentally a form in which the

4.1 Unknown artist, frontispiece in Robert Pocock, *Pocock's Everlasting Songster* ... (1804).

potentially alienated individual gets to imagine him- or herself as part of a much larger, more powerful body of political opinion."[10] In New South Wales as in Britain, toasting practices became more liberal and overtly politicized in the 1820s and '30s, reflecting the expansion of freedom of speech and the press.

By the nineteenth century, toasting was a broad practice without an agreed form but with some standard features. Toasting was most common at a dinner, after the cloth was drawn; it was organized in specific ways that always involved the entire company at the table, often under the leadership of the host or, more formally, an appointed chairman; it almost invariably required publicly stating the object of the toast; and it always required at least two people –

a proposer and a respondent – to drink. Such features became especially formalized – and political – in the context of a public dinner, a setting from which women were almost always excluded.

Public Dinners

Public dinners were an especially significant site of toasting. They can be distinguished from dining more broadly by their celebratory and performative character: they are concerned with and for something larger than the company and the meal. Based on comparative ethnography, Michael Dietler identifies some distinctive political dimensions of feasting, which he defines as "a form of public ritual activity centred around the communal consumption of food and drink" but distinguished from ordinary meals by being self-conscious public performances. Feasts have an "integrative function" helping to bond the "consumption community," which may be inclusive or exclusive, and they symbolize idealized social relations based on "reciprocal obligations between host and guest."[11] Lluís Garcia and Enriqueta Pons draw a related distinction between a feast, which they define simply as an elaborate meal, and a banquet: a special meal, often ceremonial or honorary. Such banquets are "held in *celebration* of something," involve a "sumptuous" meal relative to the social standing of the guests, are attended by large numbers of people, and are governed by "more ceremonial rules" than usual.[12] In many societies – and notably early modern and modern Britain – alcohol served as a sacrament of feasting rituals, its intoxicating properties imbuing them with symbolic power. In early modern Britain, a tradition of toasting, often accompanied by songs and speeches, became a distinctive part of banquets and was politicized accordingly.

In the long nineteenth century, the so-called public dinner was the most prominent form of banquet. In its classic form it involved an advertised event, either by invitation or ticketed, with the proceedings reported thereafter. It is thus precisely the publication of the dinner, and not the openness of the proceedings to participants or witnesses, that rendered it "public." At the same time, the act of publication symbolically designated the attendees as representatives of the wider (reading) audience, allowing them to serve as a synecdoche for the public as a whole. As Newman suggests, the publication of toasts transformed them from a display of individual wit to a "form of collective political identity," which was presumed to authoritatively speak for the drinkers.[13] Published toasts were often linked to explicitly political causes, like election campaigns, to ethnic and political identity, celebrating an anniversary, hero, or event, but also took more civic forms in connection to the increasing numbers of public societies and charities in eighteenth-century London and other urban centres.[14]

Reporting of public dinners seems to have expanded rapidly from the 1760s onward, especially in political contexts associated with the campaigns of John Wilkes.[15] However, accounts of dinners printed in the press are not straightforward sources. As Duthille argues, in general they should be understood as "idealised, rather than realistic, rhetorical and political constructions." He notes that the press typically only reported the list of toasts, not what was actually said by the toaster, and he argues that in such cases the list became "shorthand for the ideological principles defended by a particular set of people."[16] Similarly, Newman argues that printed toasts "played a pivotal role in the development of public opinion" but were often made with this in mind and are perhaps best understood as "expressions of the idealised fantasy of collective agreement," designed to help *create* a consensus as much as display one.[17]

Charles Dickens was a prominent attendee at public dinners in London and a suitably acerbic observer of them. Writing in 1835, he described, in his inimitable style, an imagined though typical charity dinner, stressing the "astonishing [self-]importance of the committee," who had a special entrance to the hall, dined at a special table on a raised platform, and entered in procession and to applause. After the meal itself, the cloth was drawn from the table and the toastmaster called for silence for the singing of *Non nobis* – a traditional hymn – and then demanded, "Gentlemen, charge your glasses, if you please!" The "loyal and patriotic" speeches commenced with the chairman, and were confused and clichéd, only broken by cheers at stock phrases – "constitutional sovereign of these realms" – and for the toast itself, which was "drunk with a great deal of cheering and knocking." The evening concluded with the obligatory toast to "The Lady Patronesses now present!," with the diners turning to the "ladies" gallery and celebrating the fashionable women who attended as observers.[18] Dickens's account, while apocryphal, captures core elements of the ritual that we have already seen in the Turf Club dinner. These occasions were often obsessively formal and the office-holders took considerable pride in their honourable status; the toasts were the ceremonial highlight of the evening, but were simultaneously formulaic and predictable; and, the entire ceremony was an exclusively male affair, though sometimes, as in this case, witnessed by a non-participant female audience.

Most of Dickens's observations are equally applicable to New South Wales, though public dinners only really began in the colony in the 1820s. The earliest potential example is the "Commemoration Dinner" of 1813, which celebrated Macquarie's birthday and the anniversary of the foundation of the colony, but it was organized by the governor. Indeed, in this period, all public meetings, including dinners, required official approval under a stricter local version of the Seditious Meetings Act, which also regulated meetings in public houses.[19] In 1817, with the explicit permission of Macquarie, another anniversary dinner was held at the house of Isaac Nichols, a prominent emancipist.[20] However, these were outliers, and it was not until the mid-1820s – and, not coincidentally, the advent of a free press – that multiple public dinners were advertised each year.

Advertising the event in advance was an essential element of public dinners, and the press therefore played a crucial role. By the mid-1820s, such advertisements typically listed the chairman and stewards, explained where and how tickets could be purchased, and told diners when dinner would be served. Dinners themselves were reported in varying levels of detail, but the most comprehensive form began with a description of the room and its decoration, noted any notable (high-status) guests, and named the chairman and officers who presided. Some longer reports also described the food and wines, sometimes with generic praise that emphasized abundance and variety, but sometimes more critically, in contrast to the supposedly superior quality of "public" hospitality and taste found in London. Reflecting this critique, *The Gazette* reported in 1827 that during one public dinner "some wags" substituted Madeira cut with water for champagne; the result was widely praised as a "drink for the Gods [and] was paid for at 16s per bottle, while the sly manufacturers of it laughed heartily in their sleeve at the success of their hoax."[21] Especially in the early years of the tradition, colonial reporters seem anxious either to prove that Sydney hotels and their public diners could live up to English standards, or to criticize them for failing to do so.

But the bulk of such reports focused on the toasts, recording them in order and, increasingly, reporting in detail any accompanying speeches or music. As in England, public dinners in New South Wales were held for significant local societies like the Turf Club, the Masons, and the Agricultural Society, but also for the three major immigrant ethnicities – English, Irish, and Scottish – who each celebrated the day of their patron saint, and for the native-born colonists who celebrated 26 January as "Foundation Day" or "the Anniversary."[22] Attendance at such dinners marked the members as part of a kind of identarian aristocracy, since their elite celebration, sanctioned by the authority of the press, typically mirrored larger and more boisterous popular celebrations, especially among the Irish.[23]

Regardless of the occasion, dinners required considerable organization and promotion. A chairman, stewards, and other officials had to be chosen – sometimes by election at a planning meeting – a venue selected, funds raised, and the speakers and official toasts determined, since these were planned and sometimes published in advance, as part of the advertising that encouraged the purchase of tickets. The complexity of these arrangements is illustrated by a controversy over the poorly attended anniversary dinner of 1829, which attracted just twelve diners, held, like the Turf Club dinner, at William Cummings's Sydney Hotel. Cummings blamed the low turnout on E.S. Hall, suggesting Hall had promised that forty gentlemen would attend, but had set the price of tickets too high.[24] The legacy of the Turf Club affair certainly hurt attendance, since many colonists feared attending a dinner associated with Darling's enemies, but Hall also failed to advertise the event outside his own paper or form an organizing committee, key steps in the production of an effective dinner.

Another important feature of dinners was the drinks, almost invariably wine, and often criticized as inferior quality. The act of drinking itself was typically accompanied by boisterous cheers, or "given three times three" (three cheers) in the parlance of the time. This became an expectation, like applause at a concert, such that the level of enthusiasm was notable and could be reported, dissected, and indeed politicized. Manly drinking also typically involved draining a full glass – a "bumper" – for each toast. In 1838, John Dunlop claimed that the practice of drinking bumpers was a norm that was becoming unfashionable in the best society, though "large masses" still insisted on "'bumpers, true bumpers, real bumpers,' of liquid fire; and 'no heel taps'" – the latter an admonition against leaving any residue of drink in the glass.[25] As Charles Ludington argues, the worst excesses of the Regency era in England were moderating after 1820, but colonial drinking may well have retained its boisterous character for longer, since New South Wales was an intensely masculine society, and the 1820s were the period when the most alcohol per head of population was available.[26] In 1828, *The Monitor* reported in a tone of mock scandal that a dinner hosted by John Macarthur Sr on the occasion of the departure of his son James to England involved twenty-one bumper toasts, which equated to a bottle and a half of wine per person. This gives a useful approximation of both the volume of wine that diners consumed (at least twelve standard drinks) and the size of glasses (about half a standard drink).[27] Since this estimate ignores any incidental drinking either over dinner or after the formal toasts had ended, it is not unreasonable to imagine some attendees would drink twice this much in an evening. Illustrating the notorious drunkenness of public dinners, a humorous report described how to "sow up a company" by "planting half a dozen seasoned old topers, whose heads are liquor-proof," around the table to repeatedly "challenge [the company] with bumpers of port and sherry," and, "the instant the table is cleared, [to go] at them again with bumper-rounds of Claret."[28]

Political Dinners

Some public dinners were planned and performed as an explicit political statement or form of political organizing. Supporters of Wilkes were probably the first to fully utilize public dinners as a means of political agitation, and in the 1790s they became a key forum of radical politics, taking advantage of the fact that they escaped the provisions of Seditious Meetings Acts. Due to these radical associations, Whigs and Tories were initially opposed to explicitly political dinners, but by the 1820s politicians from all parties were utilizing a broadly similar form to promote their electoral campaigns. Peter Brett describes political dinners as "a significant element in the symbolic repertoire of the main political parties ... used as an organizational device ... to establish and consolidate party commitment and allegiance."[29]

As Frank O'Gorman notes, elections were inherently theatrical and ritualized occasions, and despite the limited franchise, these rituals were often aimed at "*the entire community*, not merely ... the electors." As he shows, elections were understood as such by contemporaries, who not only attended campaign rituals but also read reports of them in the press, and he reads the "stage-managed" performance of toasts at political dinners in these terms as "enormously powerful solidarity rituals" for a political community of supporters.[30] Similarly, Marc Baer argues that political dinners were a crucial element of the early nineteenth-century public sphere, since widespread reporting made them "an important alternative channel of political discourse" and "barometers of public opinion," an indoor hustings, "both significant and carnivalesque," that "lay at the intersection of the popular and political."[31] A related but distinct tradition of radical and Chartist dinners were less explicitly linked to elections but helped to organize non-party-political protest movements in part through commemorative toasting of what Matthew Roberts terms a "radical pantheon."[32]

Party-political dinners took a standard form, closely related to the public dinner discussed above. They were advertised and reported in the press, but were ticketed and often expensive, and hence public but not truly open; only the elite could typically afford the time and the cost of attendance. Guests were attracted by the political cause, the advertised speakers, but also the menu, decorations, and music. The toasts themselves were frequently planned and announced in advance, and the press were incentivized to send a reporter to record the speeches because they served as a very easy means of filling the paper. Brett suggests that this function as a kind of press release contributed to a decline in the political importance of dinners during the 1840s, since the reported content was increasingly predictable and only interesting to partisans. In addition, the rise of mass politics under Chartism made political dinners increasingly impractical, and open outdoor meetings and the mass platform gradually took their place in the political world, while the influence of temperance also helped to encourage a shift from drunken male dinners to more respectable, mixed-gender tea parties and soirees as the basis of political organizing.[33] In 1835, Dickens was already contrasting the "amusing" nature of public dinners in general with the "tedious" political dinner.[34]

In New South Wales, the peak era of the political dinner was slightly later than in England, but they were arguably even more important in a society without a formal democratic outlet for its opinions, which is precisely why Governor Darling was so concerned about the way he was toasted. The English form was adopted in the 1820s by democrats advocating for political rights, and then adapted to electoral politics from the 1840s on. In particular, public dining on 26 January became overtly politicized in the 1820s as a nativist celebration of nascent colonial patriotism, and associated with the campaign for emancipist rights, helping to consolidate a key political faction.[35] During this period, a considerable proportion of all press reporting in the colony was devoted to recording these events. O'Gorman's point about the breadth of the audience for political rituals also has important implications for pre-electoral politics in New South Wales. As in England, the colonial plebs were engaged in elite politics, even when they were not directly involved, as Wentworth's public festival to celebrate Darling's departure illustrates. Similarly, political dinners were not simply for the diners but also served as a wider statement of public sentiment, even beyond their literate audience in the press. The introduction of elections in the 1840s, the rapid expansion of the franchise, and the spread of Chartist and radical ideas among the newly enfranchised working class probably helped to extend the life of the political dinner in New South Wales. Terry Irving has argued that "the politics of the public meeting was just as important as the politics of the Legislative Council" in the 1850s; and I see public dinners, especially in the 1820s and '30s, in similar terms.[36] For three decades starting in the mid-1820s, dinners were a key form of political organizing in New South Wales.

Loyalty and the Politics of Toasting

Given these traditions, public toasting was widely used as a political statement, most obviously and importantly as a statement of loyalty. Drinking the health of the monarch was a crucial loyalist ritual, and more broadly, patriotic sentiments and the hierarchical order in which dignitaries were toasted also served to display loyalty to the nation and, often, the existing political system as well. As we have seen, in the seventeenth century, toasts were explicitly used to test conformity and identify traitors. While overt tests like these were rare in the nineteenth century, the proper execution of the ritual remained a performative demonstration of the loyalty of the participants. But radicals could also use professions of loyalty to frame their politics as constitutional and disarm accusations of treason.

As Matthew McCormack shows, "loyalty" was a "very loaded term" in eighteenth-century Britain and only became more politicized during the revolutionary era after the 1790s. He draws an important distinction, emerging around the time of the Glorious Revolution, between legal loyalty, especially emphasized by Whigs, and emotional loyalty, emphasized by Tories. While Whig notions of loyalty focused on the constitution, and justified disobeying an unlawful monarch, Tories defined loyalty "in terms of conscience and feeling."[37] Both aspects of loyalty are relevant to colonial New South Wales. While loyalty was obligatory and expressed in emotional ways, in the context of a penal colony, during a global war, colonial democrats used a more legalistic form of loyalty to frame their demands for reform in constitutionalist terms.

Radicals in the long nineteenth century used distinctive forms of toast as a symbolic language to challenge emotional loyalty. While radical toasting had some precedent in the politicized toasting of seventeenth-century royalists, and that of eighteenth-century Jacobites, it took a new and more popular form as part of the public dinners of the Wilkes campaign. This expanded further in the age of revolution, with what Duthille terms "transnational toasting" – "ritualised drinking in the honour of a person or group located in another country, or of a universal or transnational idea" spreading around the revolutionary Atlantic, in the wake of the French Revolution. The tradition developed over time, celebrating an evolving pantheon of British and international heroes, contemporary and historical, in "rituals of remembrance [that] helped to build a sense of historical continuity."[38] Toasting was a kind of performative solidarity, helping to forge a unified political movement around agreed symbols, heroes, and sentiments. Indeed, in the context of revolutionary America and Ireland, radical toasting and its reporting has been understood as a means of forging a new imagined community, as it was for colonists in New South Wales, celebrating the anniversary of the colony.[39]

James Epstein focuses on radical dinners in the 1820s, arguing that with the repression of public protest "commemorative dining took on expanded importance" since it remained technically lawful. Toasts became a "calculated [gesture] of defiance ... intended to provoke a reaction," perhaps especially the celebration of "the people" as "the source of legitimate power," or the refusal to toast the monarch and play the national anthem. Authorities feared toasts, regarding them as "an index of public opinion," and from the 1790s, loyal societies and the government actively sought to prosecute seditious toasters and intimidate publicans who hosted radical dinners.[40] Paul

Pickering argues that, by the Chartist era, radical dinners were indistinguishable from political dinners more broadly, stage-managed events that performed constitutionalist loyalty, including appropriately celebrating the Queen. Roberts offers a more nuanced account, demonstrating that Chartist toasts were tailored to their audience, and hence the performance of loyalty and respectability increased when dinners were public.[41]

There was thus a spectrum of radical toasting, as there was with radical politics more broadly, ranging from constitutionalist calls for reform to revolutionary demands for a new order. Thomas Muir was one of the so-called Scottish martyrs transported to New South Wales for allegedly revolutionary acts in the 1790s. As Duthille recounts, he subsequently escaped from the colony to France, where he was celebrated at a public dinner, accounts of which were also published in the British press. He thanked his hosts for drinking "to the Victims of English Despotism, and may the blood they have shed, speedily ripen in their Country the seeds of Liberty and Equality," and to the United Irishmen and Scottish Highlanders, promising in response to "break our chains on the heads of our Tyrants."[42] But it was in private and plebeian contexts, away from the formal setting of public dinners, that toasts were more likely to directly confront or defy traditional loyalty.

In the highly radicalized world of the seas, mutinies often featured rebel toasts that deliberately and directly opposed the tradition of loyalty.[43] During an alleged mutiny on a convict transport, the *Barwell*, in 1798, it was claimed that the ringleaders celebrated their conspiracy by calling for a bottle of brandy and sharing a toast of "Damnation to the King and Country."[44] The importance of alcohol to such plots is illustrated by another alleged, and probably imaginary, mutiny, this one aboard the *Chapman* in 1817. Among the evidence that inspired Captain Drake's fears were claims that the convicts were tempted to rebel by the promise of a "grand dinner" with "brandy ... Port and Madeira."[45] Radical drinking rituals were also linked to alleged conspiracies among Irish convicts. In 1800, Edward Dogherty was given two hundred lashes for "uttering seditious and inflammatory expressions ... and h[aving] drunk several disloyal and improper toasts tending to disturb public peace and stir up sedition."[46] Similarly, during the unsuccessful 1807 trial of Michael O'Dwyer, a significant proportion of the circumstantial evidence against him involved evidence of him drinking with other Irish "croppies," singing "disaffected" songs, and attacking other convicts for singing "loyal" or "orange" songs.[47] Clearly, rebellious toasts had a powerful place in the political imaginary.

However, radicals could also use loyal toasting for their own ends. During their transportation to New South Wales, two more Scottish martyrs, William Skirving and Thomas Palmer, were arrested and had their property impounded after they were accused of plotting a mutiny by treating their guards with liquor, and toasting "Damnation to the King, his Family and all Crowned Heads!"[48] After the trumped-up charges were dropped, the accused published a complaint about their treatment, stressing the hardship of being "deprived of both wine and spirits" – a personal supply that they had shipped out with them as a valuable resource. More importantly, they claimed that Skirving had merely given one of the men two glasses of port "on the condition that he drank his Majesty's health," and the man had subsequently become drunk. Leaving aside the justice of their punishment, Skirving and Palmer understood the power of loyal toasting and sought to use it to build connections with their guards (or to justify themselves afterwards), despite the fact that they were ostensibly exiled for challenging official power.[49]

More generally, democrats in New South Wales were almost invariably loyal and constitutionalist. I have not identified an instance of a public dinner at which the first toast was not to the monarch, and drunk with gusto, and reported toasts drew from a much more limited and loyal repertoire than was the case in contemporary Britain. There are occasional instances of toasting the people as "the source of legitimate power," but these were always included among a much broader list of loyal, liberal, and patriotic toasts, which always began with the monarch.[50]

Drinking the King's health was a necessary accompaniment to every public occasion in the early colony, as it had been at Phillip's ceremony of possession in 1788. The ritual was growing in importance in a Britain that was in the process of imagining itself as a nation, during a major war, and this was amplified in the colony.[51] Self-conscious assertions of British identity were a means of coping with the strangeness of the new environment and a way to draw a contrast with the supposed disloyalty of criminals and especially political exiles. We can see this particularly clearly in relation to the celebration of the monarch's birthday, the iconic festival of loyalty to the monarchy, and the traditional social hierarchies it evoked. Tracing the celebration and the toasting that usually accompanied it in different contexts can help to illustrate the significance of loyalty as a grounding for political thought.

While Phillip was governor, he marked the occasion of the King's birthday – 4 June – with an elaborate ceremony performed at one o'clock and again at sunset: a twenty-one-gun salute, the raising of the colours accompanied by volleys of musket fire, and the playing of "God Save the King."[52] He also held a formal dinner for the officers accompanied by extensive patriotic toasting, issued pardons, and ordered a public holiday and celebration for the convicts. The surgeon George Worgan reported in detail on the first such celebration in 1788, describing an elaborate dinner accompanied by wines and porter that "went merrily round in Bumpers," followed by toasts to the King, the Queen and royal family, the Prince of Wales, Prince William Henry, the newly established County of Cumberland, and the governor and the settlement. The governor responded to this last honour by drinking the health of all the officers and "wishing Harmony & Unanimity throughout the Settlement." The official party then visited the convict bonfires, where the governor was given three cheers and a party of convicts joined in singing "God Save the King." Most importantly, Phillip issued a pint of grog to the sailors and convicts at his own expense so that "every person in the colony was enabled to drink his Majesty's health." [53]

Thus, under Phillip, the King's birthday became a symbol of official authority, marked with a series of pardons and toasted with a universal rum ration. The act of drinking was used to emphasize the social hierarchy and unify the colony around it, with the governor as the King's representative, demonstrating his authority through patronage of a deferential convict plebs. The symbolic importance of alcohol to this ritual is demonstrated by the fact that such public communal celebrations were the only time when convicts were officially permitted to drink in public (although, of course, they frequently drank privately and without such official sanction).

However, Phillip's efforts to make the King's birthday an integrative ritual were immediately rejected by the New South Wales Corps. In 1791, a time of severe famine in the colony during which rations were substantially reduced, the corps protested the ritual because they felt "slighted by having an equal quantity [of rum] with the Convict."[54] In this unique society, access to alcohol symbolically delineated the crucial divide between convict and "free," substituting for the traditionally established hierarchies of British society. Tellingly, Phillip's integrative ritual seems to have ceased with his departure from the colony. Richard Atkins, soon to become judge advocate, contrasted the celebration in 1793, noting, "To the Convicts [Phillip] gave half a pint of Rum, There was a bonfire in the Evening, and the people express'd the Loyalty in the best manner they were able. Nothing of this kind has happened this time [1793], if the Lieutenant-Governor [Grose] gives a dinner it is only to a few individuals down at Sydney. In short that marked attention which [Phillip] shewed to every one whose rank entitled him to it, is totally laid aside, and a selfish partial principle substituted in the room of it."[55] Access to alcohol, and especially participation in the toasting ritual, was a powerful means of marking the limits of the political community. Phillip's beneficent patronage embodied his efforts to reform the convicts, but for the officers of the New South Wales Corps, their exclusive privileges were an essential symbol of their status, and the capacity to participate in loyal toasts distinguished ranks within a self-consciously hierarchical society.

The celebration of the King's birthday in 1819 shows how the provision of alcohol for toasting could reinforce the political hierarchy. At midday, Macquarie opened a public levee in Hyde Park, "numerously attended by the Officers, Civil and Military, and Gentlemen of the Colony," the 48th Regiment and the Battery at Dawe's Point fired a salute, and one of Michael Robinson's celebratory odes was read.

At one he went to the barracks, where the male convicts were given "Plum Pudding and an allowance of Punch" on top of their standard ration, and had the "gratification of drinking in a rummer of good punch to the sanctified remembrance of our beloved Sovereign." Macquarie delivered what he described as "a short plain speech" and then, with his staff and both judges, "drank to [the convicts'] Health & Prosperity." His departure from the convict feast was celebrated with "three cheers from the grateful people, who all appeared to be happy." At five, the governor gave a formal dinner for "the Civil & Military Officers and the other Gentlemen" at which "several loyal and constitutional Toasts were drank," and they afterwards joined "a select Assemblage of Ladies" in the drawing room.[56] We can observe a number of distinct features here that reflect the politics of the period. The governor's symbolic authority was essential to public celebrations, but these were highly stratified by status. Convicts were granted celebratory alcohol as a form of patronage, and non-convicts could attend a public ceremony, but only a restricted social elite could dine at the governor's table; indeed, the question of who would enjoy the privilege of dining and toasting with the governor was a cause of political controversy. Finally, despite such efforts by the governor and Mrs Macquarie to promote a more conventional mixed society in the colony, the toasting ritual was confined to men.

During the 1820s, public celebration was released from official control, with loyal toasting increasingly offering a larger and more democratic elite a means of demanding political reform. A dinner of "His Majesty's friends," held in Hobart in 1825, at a time when Van Diemen's Land was campaigning for formal independence from New South Wales, illustrates the increasingly overt politics of the occasion. Anthony Fenn Kemp, a leading rum rebel in 1808, but now a prominent Van Diemonian businessman, as well as a critic of Lieutenant-Governor Arthur, was elected president and took the chair. In his speech, which preceded the first bumper toast to the King, he stressed that as "British Subjects" they possessed "rights and privileges unknown to all others in the world; and that our King lives in our hearts by the constitutional liberties which under his beneficent sway we all enjoy." Other explicitly political toasts included those to "Sir James Mackintosh [a prominent Whig lawyer], and Trial by Jury," "The Liberty of the Press," and "The Independent Spirits of Van Diemen's Land."[57] While Arthur was not publicly insulted, as Darling would be, the event was organized by his political opponents and without his patronage, representing a similar form of opposition politics. Moreover, dining was becoming increasingly factional. For the King's birthday in Sydney in 1827, Darling ordered the traditional public celebration with military salute at noon and held a "grand Ball and supper." But at least two other rival dinners were held, one by Captain Rous aboard HMS *Rainbow* and attended by leading exclusives, including the colonial secretary, Alexander McLeay, and the governor's private secretary, Colonel Henry Dumaresq; and a second at the Sydney Hotel chaired by Dr Douglass and attended by many enemies of the governor and prominent emancipists.[58]

By the late 1830s, on the eve of democracy, while the monarch's birthday remained a day of celebration, these celebrations were broader. In 1838, Governor Gipps organized a regatta to complement the public festival and held a much larger and less exclusive ball for a broader social elite, inviting six hundred guests to an illuminated Government House.[59] In 1843, these official events were complemented by at least two subscription balls aimed at the respectable middle and working classes (indeed one was teetotal), illustrating the expanded public in the democratic era.[60] Even at the governor's ball, drinking was also less significant and there were far fewer toasts, though drinking to the health of the monarch remained an essential gesture of loyalty. Indeed, with a female monarch, the toasts took on a different character, reflecting the intensely masculine nature of the ritual, and the gender politics of colonial society. Loyal toasting remained significant throughout this period but was used in different ways, becoming an essential means for democrats to legitimate their movement. Their use of the ritual is highly revealing of the colonial political imaginary, as I discuss in chapter 5.

5

Public Dinners and the Political Imaginary in New South Wales

In 1825, the politics of public toasting came to the fore in New South Wales when the colonists sought to bid farewell to the departing governor, Thomas Brisbane. Initially, in early October, an exclusive and self-selected committee of stewards invited a "chosen party" of colonists they deemed "the gentlemen of the colony," none of whom had been transported to New South Wales, to dine with the governor. However, following complaints from prominent emancipists, a separate group centred on William Wentworth called a public meeting at which Wentworth challenged the "exclusionist" principles of what he deemed a "secret junta." The meeting voted their approval of a public address from "the Colonists" that included a request that Brisbane "embrace all opportunities" to persuade the British government to grant the colony "those two fundamental principles of the British Constitution, *Trial by Jury*, and *Taxation by Representation*."[1] At a subsequent meeting, they also voted to organize a rival dinner and elected a group of stewards, including "a wealthy Commoner" – D'Arcy Wentworth, William's father – as president. Brisbane initially sought to avoid taking sides in colonial politics and agreed in principle to attend both dinners while suggesting a compromise whereby the emancipist stewards would be invited to the dinner of the exclusives. But this compromise was peremptorily rejected by the original committee, who cancelled their event in a public advertisement that stressed that they refused to dine with "certain individuals ... whose presence had not been anticipated by the Subscribers."[2]

Seizing the moment, both colonial newspapers celebrated the sole ensuing dinner as a milestone of political progress and a symbolic forum of democratic politics. The editor of *The Gazette*, Robert Howe, himself the son of a convict, now claimed that the governor had chosen "very judiciously" to attend "that Dinner, representing by its Guests the Commonwealth at large." Similarly, Robert Wardell in *The Australian* noted that "when a public dinner is talked of every one naturally feels a desire to join in it, or not to join in it," and claimed that from this date it would be impossible to tell "any class" of colonists "that they are not fit to be jurors, that they are not fit to appear at a public dinner, that they are not fit to be invested with political existence." Both papers reported with pride on the success of the evening, with *The Australian* arguing that it showed it was possible "to bring together all classes in the Colony in social union," and that "the Colony was in a 'fit state' to undertake a good dinner."[3]

On Friday, 28 October, over a hundred gentlemen, including "most of those who fill the highest civil offices," stood in honour as the governor entered to "God Save the King." In a speech of thanks, Brisbane interpreted the occasion as a vindication by "the people of the Colony" from the slight of his official recall, and one that demonstrated "how much he prized public opinion." Significantly, he also endorsed the political rights that colonial democrats were requesting, fulsomely approving a toast to "the necessity of extending to this Colony the 'free Institutions of England'" and promising to support the colonial campaign on his return there. But William Wentworth, who took the chair due to his father's ill health, went further. He attacked the "expiring faction ... [who] opposed the free principles of the age," claimed that New South Wales had always been designed as a reformatory where convicts could redeem themselves and regain their political rights, and insisted that Brisbane's support proved that the colony was now "in a state fit to enjoy" English liberties. Robert Howe, the editor of *The Gazette*, spoke effusively to "the liberty of the press," while E.S. Hall, soon to publish the third colonial newspaper, *The Monitor*, called for "A House of Assembly, as the most powerful engine of augmenting our prosperity." The political spirit of the event was captured in another of Michael Robinson's celebratory odes, which praised "the trophies of freedom … dispers'd through the civilis'd world; / Wherever Britannia's flag was unfurl'd" and called for "Emancipists!" to "swell the proud goblet – full charge, now or never! / Whilst the toast is Our BRISBANE, and Freedom for ever!"[4]

This farewell dinner helped to establish the framework for future political debate and the controversies of the Darling era. Shortly after his arrival, the new governor reported to Lord Bathurst that by hosting the dinner the emancipists had "proved their strength and influence," and thus from the outset, Darling knew that public dinners and toasting were a measure of political feeling.[5] Wentworth, Darling, the wider democratic movement, the supportive press, and subsequent historians all understood that dinners were a means to mount a political argument. Carol Liston suggested that the farewell dinner was "deliberately engineered" to promote political reform, while Manning Clark understood the dinners of this era as form of political theatre.[6] John Dunmore Lang, the first historian of the farewell dinner, saw a larger political meaning in what he presented as a crucial turning point in colonial politics. He argued that Brisbane had attended to "attain popularity," a motivation and decision he condemned. Drinking with the emancipists was "tantamount to an authoritative lowering of the standard of morals throughout the territory" since, in 1825, "the great majority" had gained their wealth "by the sale of rum and the practice of enormous extortion." He claimed that Brisbane had assumed "a right to dictate to reputable men as to who should be invited to their company or society" and saw this as an extension of Macquarie's emancipist policies.[7] For Lang, in keeping with his temperance narrative of colonial history, Brisbane's attendance had empowered the emancipists with a dangerous sense of entitlement, which threatened colonial progress and morals. More broadly, he implied that such dinners were not merely a form of political organizing but also a symbolic performance of a politicized public that enacted their sense of British democracy.

However, in New South Wales in 1825, this imagined public were limited in two distinct ways. First, many of the social elite, including most military officers and a significant proportion of the original guests, declined to attend. To justify his absence, John Macarthur Jr, son of the rum rebel, even sent a list of the diners, with comments on each individual's character, status, and morals, to the attorney general in London.[8] Loyal toasting implied – and was understood to imply – a level of equality among the drinkers that was intolerable to the exclusives, concerned as they were about the convict stain. Second, and more important, no convict under sentence, Indigenous person, or woman attended the dinner or were understood as part of the colonial public. The democracy the colonists imagined, and drank to, had a restricted citizenship of respectable white men.

This reading of Brisbane's farewell dinner reflects the distinction between the political use and political meaning of public toasting, and in what follows, I move beyond the overt politics. From this occasion on, public dinners had symbolic status as a synecdoche of colonial democracy, with attendance delineating who constituted the public, and the newly freed press were increasingly assertive in demanding more open dinners as a principle of a free society. The toasts themselves were performative drinking practices that both reflected and shaped the imaginary. They give a sense of the underlying political ideas precisely because they helped – and were intended to help – script drinkers' political thinking. Reading dinners in these terms, I analyze public toasting in the decade after 1825 for its political meaning. The unwritten rules the ritual relied on illustrate the ways that colonists sought to order their society, and how they thought such order should be agreed on and enforced. By bonding groups of men together, toasting reinforced the politics of exclusivity and helped to forge distinct political identities, especially in a society transitioning from convictism to settler colonialism. Finally, the reporting of dinners and toasting helped give imaginative shape to a political community and script public opinion.

5.1 Thomas Rowlandson, *The Brilliants* (1801).

Keeping Order: Drinking Rules

One key feature of public toasting was its orderly nature, which echoed the crucial importance of order in British political thought. Toasting was a form of restrained drinking, governed by rules that mattered greatly to participants. Analyzing Thomas Rowlandson's satire of a male drinking club, "The Brilliants" (figure 5.1), Ludington notes the rules of the society printed on the wall: "1st. That each Member shall fill a half Pint Bumper to the first Toast. 2nd. That after Twenty-four Bumper toasts are gone round, every [man] may fill as he pleases. 3rd. That any Member refusing to comply with the above Regulations to be fine[d] a bumper of Salt and Water." He suggests that while these specific rules were satirical and humorous, they were "not entirely fanciful," reflective as they were of a culture in which rule-bound drinking was expected, especially in the context of clubs and societies.[9]

This reflected a broader pattern of orderly drinking in Britain. As the temperance author John Dunlop observed, "the system of rule and regulation, as to times and occasions of drinking, pervades all branches of society in Great Britain – at meals, markets, fairs, baptisms, and funerals; and almost every trade and profession has its own code of strict and well-observed laws on this subject." As an example, he quoted from a guide for commercial travellers that described the expectations on such men when staying in the commercial rooms at an inn and dining at a shared table. The men were to elect a president who would guide them through toasts to "The Ladies," "the health of the reigning sovereign," and potentially a sentiment from each person at the table, and only "when the bill is called for [can] any person rise and leave the table without any apology."[10]

Pocock's advice to singing (and drinking) parties demonstrates how intricate such norms could be. He noted that when men gathered "for the purpose of spending a jovial evening over a bowl of Punch, or a bottle of Wine," they should elect a chairman who, "by his authority and example, [will] be a check to those who may attempt to break through the barrier of decency and decorum." The chair should ensure that toasts were never "given either out of time, or out of place," always commencing with the monarch, then their spouse and heirs, before he called on the company in turn for a toast or sentiment, alternating with a song. Pocock advised toasters to "give [i.e., propose] some eminent person, not so much for his title or estate, as for his virtues," and appended a list of dignitaries in the church, the law, the army and navy, and various "Principal Officers of Public Societies," along with his suggested sentiments and songs. Finally, he also called for the chair to regulate the amount of drink, ensuring that no more was ordered than agreed in advance, and to settle the bill well before the end of the evening, since "no society of this kind will last long, where temperance and regularity are not suffered to preside."[11]

While these examples all pertain to less formal, private contexts, proper order was even more important when dinners and toasting were public. In general, the rules for such dinners were not written down; rather, they were performative – taught by example and evolving through practice – but some of this orderliness is visible in the extensive preparations that took place in advance. As the Brisbane dinner demonstrates, public dinners were organized in increasingly democratic ways, with officers elected, and the chosen toasts seen to reflect the collective views of the diners, who would endorse them in their drinking. Precisely for this reason, any variation from the agreed toasts was potentially controversial, a breach of the public consensus with political significance.

At a dinner for St Patrick's Day in 1830, John Macarthur Sr, the rum rebel and a leading figure of exclusive politics, was invited to speak to "the agricultural interests of the colony," but once on his feet he began a long invective against the colonial press, citing an editorial that had offended him. As the editor in question, Robert Mansfield, newly appointed to *The Gazette*, was in attendance, this was a particularly provocative gesture, but it also breached the agreement about the proceedings. Mansfield later reported that "the company was taken aback with astonishment, and numerous voices were instantly lifted up to protest against so unprovoked an aggression upon the good feeling of the party," and there seems to be no reason to doubt the accuracy of his claims, since they were echoed in other papers. Roger Therry, the vice-president of the dinner, and commissioner of the Court of Requests, "warmly protested against this extraordinary infraction of order," noting that he had agreed not to include a toast to "the liberty of the Press" precisely to avoid party politics. Mansfield insisted on a "right of self-defence" and rose to justify his coverage of Macarthur in general terms, though at the request of the chair (the Sheriff Thomas Macquoid), he refrained from entering into specifics. But the public at the dinner clearly took Mansfield's side in this controversy, booing Macarthur's speech and applauding Therry's response, and subsequently, Macarthur promised he would never sit at a public dinner table again. In the aftermath, Mansfield lamented the loss of convivial feeling in the colony due to political dissension and claimed that "men have been almost afraid to meet their fellow-citizens around the table or the hearth."[12]

The episode illustrates the way that such dinners were governed by both specific and general rules of conduct. There was a general norm of dining, frequently referenced in guides to etiquette, that toasts should avoid political controversy, which in practice meant echoing the political sentiments of the assembled company. In New South Wales in 1830, this was interpreted strictly because the small population of gentlemen – however defined – who constituted the public made political opposition among them inevitable.

Reflecting on a similar dispute in 1832, Hall claimed in *The Monitor* that there were two kinds of toasts, "official and non-official." The former were "proposed by the Stewards ... prepared with care, their quality being maintained strictly according to etiquette, and to the object or objects for which the dinner is given." After the official toasts were drunk and the president had departed, "the company that remain commonly get together at one end of the table, and begin to enjoy themselves as a private party ... to think, talk, and act as gentlemen who feel loosened from the bonds of certain strict rules, save those which always govern the deportment of gentlemen."[13] Hall thus identified two distinct drinking codes, one public and one private. Public toasts were a performance of public opinion; in private, drinkers spoke only for themselves.

Inclusion and Exclusion: Fraternity and Hierarchy

The toasting ritual was both intensely hierarchical and implicitly egalitarian. As Ludington argues, toasting was an integral part of a larger culture of "honourable drinking" that licensed drunkenness so long as it resulted from "drinking with other men while scrupulously following rules."[14] Drinking bonded gentlemen into a convivial fraternity of broadly equal participants so long as it was performed with suitable restraint. Such communal drinking also evoked the rite of Holy Communion in post-Reformation England, which was similarly open to the whole confessional community but excluded Dissenters and Catholics in what McShane terms a "test of both religious and political loyalties."[15] The alcohol itself was crucial to the toasting experience, both because its intoxicating effects encouraged feelings of comradeship, and because the shared exposure of intoxication was a symbolic leveller.[16] Indeed, failing to participate in the ritual and drink with other men was potentially dishonourable and liable to be viewed as effeminate. Moreover, in the context of a political dinner, such fraternal egalitarianism was tied to a political cause. Dinners became an essential form of political organizing, in part because they publicly demonstrated the strength and unity of political constituencies.

The assumption underlying such organizing was implicitly democratic: men who drank together publicly were understood to be equal participants in the political community. Indeed, the growth of the public dinner over the course of the nineteenth century, its transformation into a ritual practised by all classes of men, and for increasingly larger numbers of diners, paralleled the increasingly democratic nature of society, and the broadening of the category of gentleman.[17] But, this convivial fraternity was not universal. Only participants in the ritual were bonded together, often in deliberate distinction from other groups or from society as a whole. The size of the drinking public, and questions of who was and was not invited to participate in it, also carried powerful political meaning. Perhaps most obviously, the exclusion of women framed them as objects rather than subjects of politics.

Toasting was often used as a means of creating a more limited solidarity through practices of exclusivity, solidifying the in-group against outsiders. Such exclusivity was a distinctive feature of colonial manners, in part because the very masculine and military nature of society intensified concerns about honour and shame, but also because of the strict and intensely observed social hierarchy.[18] This hierarchy descended from the governor as the representative of the monarch (and often, also, the highest-ranked military officer), a position with both formal and informal political significance. But there was a complex politics of descending status that was both well understood and reflected in official lists of officers, which were public documents.[19] As Penny Russell argues, "Government House society" was "a microcosm of colonial culture" in a colony obsessed with social rank. She critiques as overly simplistic David Cannadine's claim that governors were "at the apex of the colonial social hierarchy," and instead argues for a more complex and contested status.[20] My analysis of toasting supports her conclusion, showing the way that rival elites used hospitality to assert social – and by extension political – authority, through who they ate and drank with, and how they acknowledged the governor.

In the context of a penal colony, much of this turned on what became known as the convict stain.[21] As with Brisbane's farewell dinner, members of the social elite would decline to socialize – and specifically to dine and drink – with emancipists so as to emphasize their own superior social status and morals. This reflected a broader practice of exclusivity that was especially acute between 1810 and 1840, the peak years of both transportation and political dinners. Even after transportation ceased, there was a ruthless politics of invitations and social snubs, increasingly grounded in social class and notions of respectability. Dining and drinking with the governor was a mark of social approval that mattered in colonial society throughout this period, and more broadly, whom one drank with carried significant political meaning. In private contexts, to be invited to dine marked the invitee as the object of patronage, and hence empowered the host as patron, while the hierarchy of toasts ordered the ranks. But the implicit equality of gentlemen who drank together made some colonists very particular about whom they drank and dined with.

Governor Macquarie publicly favoured and patronized a small number of wealthy and prominent emancipists whom he deemed respectable, using them as exemplars of his wider policy of encouraging convict reform through opportunity. This practice became a focus of criticism for the growing opposition to the governor and came to a head when Macquarie invited emancipists to dine.[22] Macquarie was clearly aware that his guest lists were contentious, since he thought it necessary to tell his British superiors, emphasizing (in

1810) that he had dined with "only four" emancipists.[23] By 1821, he listed seven emancipists "whom I have thought fit to invite to my table," and defended this in terms of a broader governing philosophy of "restoring men to that rank in society, to which, by birth and education, they belonged previously to their being transported."[24] At the same time, he also saw such dining as important, indeed a responsibility as the leader of the community. Requesting an additional "table allowance" to supplement his salary, he noted that he initially held a "public dinner" every week but could now only afford to do so every fortnight.[25] Similarly, a surviving plan for the seating arrangements of such a dinner (unfortunately impossible to definitively date), annotated in the governor's hand, demonstrates both the significance of these arrangements and the thought that went into their social politics. The only emancipist invited (Redfern) was carefully placed between the governor and the naval officer, Captain Piper, who was sympathetic to the emancipist cause.[26] Dinners like these were the forerunner of public dining in New South Wales, since they were often announced in *The Gazette*, although the toasts were rarely reported.

The main opposition to Macquarie's dining arrangements came from military officers, who, since they were only briefly deployed to the colony, were especially concerned about the potential taint of associating with former convicts. This concern peaked with the arrival of the officers of the 46th Regiment in 1814, who were drawn into the growing political conflict of the period and came increasingly to clash with the governor. Reporting on their quarrel, Macquarie noted that they were "received and Entertained by me with every possible Attention and Hospitality," including dining with those gentlemen emancipists Macquarie deemed reformed. However, the officers pointedly refused to reciprocate, because, prior to their arrival in the colony, they had "bound themselves never to Admit [anyone sentenced to transportation] into their Society."[27] Macquarie regarded this as "premature, Illiberal, and ... Almost Unjust," and argued that "a Courtesy was due to Me as their General, and Governor of this Territory, in regard to making my Table the Rule or Standard." He also complained of the "Mutinous Licentiousness" of "a political Faction" of officers who criticized his administration "At their Mess Table, and in Hearing of their Servants, as Well as at other Tables Where I am not present." The hostilities between Macquarie and this faction of officers culminated in the latter pointedly refusing invitations to Government House. In a further scandal, the regiment's commanding officer, Colonel Molle, felt obliged to censor a public letter written by some of the officers, suggesting that their mess table was "regarded as the Standard of Society in the Colony" – a remark Macquarie claimed in his official complaint was "Subversive of all good Order and Military Discipline.[28]

Brisbane's farewell was a catalyst for further politicizing attendance at public dinners. Indeed, Peter Cunningham reported that the organizers on that occasion scrupulously reviewed all the invited guests to ensure that none of the emancipists had committed an offence in the colony, so that "His Excellency might not be exposed to the unpleasant dilemma of rubbing his immaculate shoulders against a man who had been sullied by a *double* conviction."[29] More typically, there were complaints about exclusion. When the outgoing colonial secretary, Major Goulburn, prepared to depart the colony in early 1826, *The Gazette* expressed outrage at rumours that he was to be bid farewell at a "select dinner," insisting he should have "a magnificent and public-spirited Dinner from the Colonists collectively."[30] Despite his reluctance to socialize with the Turf Club, Darling clearly shared this view. Later that year, he reported to London that the attorney general, Saxe Bannister, had refused to attend a public dinner for the law officers because Wardell was a guest, suggesting that "any objection, which he might have to meet Doctor Wardle [*sic*] in private Society, should [not] prevent his dining in Company with him on a Public occasion."[31] It was increasingly understood that public occasions in general, and public dinners in particular, should be open to all gentlemen, that all "free" (non-convict), property-owning male colonists were gentlemen, and that this status was sanctified by participation in the ritual of toasting. However, in practice, dinners were often much more exclusionary than this ideal would suggest.

Another kind of social division, this one linked to class, became the subject of growing controversy. Complaints about the quality and expense of public dinners were long-standing, but by the 1830s, prices were becoming politicized. In 1832, the organizing committee for the anniversary dinner initially proposed a "liberal" dinner with wine, champagne, and music, but were quoted thirty shillings a head, a price that was rejected by some of the members as "exorbitant," causing the event to fold. Commenting on the affair, *The Monitor* contrasted a recent public dinner, "suitable for a young and poor colony," where tickets had cost only ten shillings, with a bottle of sherry per guest and the diners purchasing any further drinks themselves, and suggested, given recent droughts and bankruptcies, that greater "extravagance" amounted to "a sort of public immorality."[32] Ticket prices were understood – and doubtless served – as a proxy for social class and would become a means of limiting attendance and ensuring respectability in an increasingly open and democratic society. These were not the only objections. Temperance advocates employed a more extreme form of *The Monitor*'s argument, calling for tickets to include dinner only, and for guests to buy their own drinks, because some colonists had "a conscientious objection to pay for wine."[33]

By the 1840s, public dinners were increasingly exclusive and class-bound, but this was always framed in terms of respectability, which in practice often served as a euphemism for concerns about the convict stain. John Sweatman, then in his early twenties, sailed as a clerk on two surveying cruises around northern Australia in the mid-1840s, and during his time in Sydney he reported in some detail on the dinner parties he attended and the toasting customs practised there. He was a well-educated young man of respectability looking to make his career in the antipodes but possessing neither wealth nor standing. As such, he was concerned to preserve a basic social distinction between "the People" and gentlemen like himself, a position captured in his resort to the cliché that "any one [*sic*] who visited at Government House was a fit and proper person to associate with."[34]

In 1845, he and his fellow officers of the *Fly* collectively declined to accept an invitation to dine at the Australia Club because its rules excluded anyone below the rank of lieutenant in the navy, a slight Sweatman described as "unjust and insulting" since the club admitted all army officers as honorary members. Returning to Sydney in 1847, he noted "the distinctive distance between the free settlers & emancipists was most jealously kept up," and that accepting invitations from the latter, who were "very anxious" to know a naval officer as "a mode of increasing their own respectability," would lead to ostracism by the former.[35] In reference to the Government House principle, he stressed that the governors' wives were "known to be very particular whom they admitted," but that on arrival in port, officers would leave their cards at Government House, which would usually lead to an invitation into viceregal society. Even in the democratic era, dining and toasting retained their symbolic power.

Scripting Public Opinion: Reporting Dinners

Regardless of who attended, the most telling feature of public dinners and public toasting was their *public* nature. These events were always theatrical. Performed by and for the participants and a wider audience who read the reports in the press, they staged a vision of how colonial politics should work. Given their ritualized form and their widespread reporting, dinners were also especially performative occasions, heavily scripted but consequently easily subverted, with each iteration helping to shape the expectations of future dinners. In a colony lacking any official form of political representation, the theatrical performance of loyalty and disloyalty, often dissected in the press, became a key means of conducting colonial politics. The publicity of dinners and their prevalence in the press during the period when New South Wales was granted responsible and representative government allowed them to serve as an embodiment of the public sphere.

The significance of the ritual as a political script is made manifest on occasions when the script was contested, as with the St Patrick's Day dinner in 1830. Less than a year later, at the 1831 anniversary dinner, there was a similar controversy, this time focused on the reporting. Once again, the organizers made a deliberate effort to forbid the discussion of politics, thus promoting "harmony and good feeling" and preventing an inflammation of "party spirit," and to aid such unity, the dinner was used to inaugurate a new "Australian Society to promote the growth and consumption of Colonial produce and manufactures." But according to Edward O'Shaughnessy, writing in *The Gazette*, the toast to Darling was "received with loud cheers" but also "a very few ebullitions of vulgar interruption," which "the good sense of the more respectable part of the company, immediately repressed."[36] Pointed refusal to cheer toasts to Darling (and even the occasional heckling of them) had become increasingly common after the Turf Club controversy.

Even more shocking for O'Shaughnessy was the "uproar" provoked by Robert Nichols, a prominent emancipist who would soon become the first native-born Australian admitted to practise as a solicitor, and who would later serve as a prominent radical politician. Nichols spoke to "the health of the Natives of the Colony, and that of WILLIAM CHARLES WENTWORTH [*sic*], the patriot of Australia," but was "loudly and repeatedly called to order, on account of his wholly irrelevant allusions to the Colonial Government." Worse was to follow the departure of the chairman (Samuel Terry) and many of the guests. Nichols seized the opportunity of a further toast to speak to the "despotism exercised in this Colony," which again provoked loud objections and counter-objections, culminating in an unnamed individual throwing a punch, for which he was unceremoniously ejected.[37]

It should not surprise us that in a fraught political climate such drunken dinners could end in violence. What was unusual was that the disorderly incident was reported, breaching Hall's distinction between "official" and "unofficial" toasts, under which the most drunken part of the proceedings was not to be reported in any detail, but rather concealed beneath platitudes about "harmony" and "conviviality" that ensured the diners were seen to perform the proper restraint. In this instance, Hall, who also attended and spoke, conceded that Nichols may have "strayed a little into politics, and shewed a spec of Radicalism or Monitorism," but suggested that O'Shaughnessy had shown "bad taste" in drawing public attention to his conduct, and that the "little fracas" should not have been reported since it was not "compatible with the conduct of a gentleman to publish all that passes in a private company." Finally, and most pointedly, Hall claimed that the only punch had been thrown by O'Shaughnessy himself. Apparently, another guest had suggested, loudly, that since O'Shaughnessy was still under sentence as a convict (though he had long been on a ticket of leave), he should not have been invited to a respectable dinner, and that this was the cause of the drunken fight.[38]

Clearly what happened at dinner mattered beyond the occasion itself, and journalists (who were also participants) were concerned not only with writing the definitive account, but also with its proper interpretation. For O'Shaughnessy, Nichols's conduct was a disgraceful display of disloyalty and the dinner "the theatre of one of the noisiest mock-tragedies ever got up by political fanaticism." But for Hall, what it really showed was that "the dislike to the measures of the present Government is so deep and so rooted, that a few glasses of wine overturned all good resolutions." Nichols made similar suggestions in a subsequent public letter, claiming his speech was motivated by patriotism, that his views were widely supported, that the only opposition had come from "intruding spies, and favour-coaxing hirelings," and was "soon silenced by the overwhelming influence of patriotic and independent men."[39]

Everyone involved was also concerned about the rules governing dinners and their reporting. Nichols argued that he had not breached the rule against political discussion, since both commerce and agriculture "[depend] greatly on the nature of the political system by which ... [they are] governed." O'Shaughnessy disputed this, claiming that such public political debate encouraged "the baneful influence of party-spirit" and led to "the divided state of our little society." Mansfield, as the editor of *The Gazette*, defended both his reporter and the report, claiming that "the public dinner of a public Society" was "universally considered" a fit subject for the press and disputing that there was any meaningful distinction between official and unofficial toasts. Hall suggested that *The Gazette* was guilty of a double standard and eluded to a series of minor scandals involving swearing, gambling, small rows, and other drunken misconduct at public dinners among the governor's supporters, which he had chosen not to report previously.[40]

The reporting of public dinners mattered because the reports, as much as the dinners themselves, represented public opinion, especially in a colony without representative institutions. In another example from the period, Wardell was more explicit about the political significance of publication. In its initial report on a Freemasons dinner on New Year's Eve 1826, *The Australian* claimed that the toast to Darling was followed by "solemn silence" while Brisbane was drunk with "rapturous applause." Samuel Terry, who had chaired, felt compelled to write to *The Gazette* denying that any disrespect had been intended, and Howe, the editor at the time, characterized the original reporting as an "impudent and infamous slur."[41] Defending the accuracy of the report, Wardell suggested that the whole affair was contrived by *The Gazette*, which was displaying – indeed performing – a hyperbolic sensitivity about the governor's feelings.[42] But he also argued more broadly for the importance of reporting on public toasts and their reception as a significant form of political speech: "Public opinion is a valuable thing; and in whatever way it is shewn, its manifestations should always be recorded. It is the life and soul of an Englishman's liberty to avow his sentiments decorously of the acts of the government under which he lives; and it is the knowledge that that liberty will be used which restrains an administration often from doing wrong, and lording it at pleasure over the people."[43] Citing the hostile public reception of George IV during the Queen Caroline affair, he suggested that toasting was a crucial means of simultaneously displaying loyalty to British institutions while also expressing political opinions: "One of less loyalty than a Briton, if he did not like the King on the throne, would curse a kingly government altogether; but a Briton acts more rationally; he toasts the King or a Governor; because, in so doing, he toasts the form of government; he toasts the Constitution; and if he does not cheer when he drinks to the King or the Governor, it is not because he is disloyal, but because the King or the Governor is unpopular."[44]

According to Wardell, the colonial public were loyal to the governor as an institution but were increasingly disappointed in Darling himself and were demonstrating this in the way they toasted him, a display of "public feeling and public energy" that Wardell celebrated. In McCormack's terms they were legally but not emotionally loyal.[45] Indeed, Wardell called on the public to toast the governor "with feeling, proper feeling, with enthusiasm, or silence, and in a manner typical of the feelings, of A BRITISH PUBLIC!" For Wardell, toasting was overtly a form of political expression – and a necessary one, since the public had not just a right but a democratic duty to express their political views.

6

The Temperance Movement

PERSUASION AND COMPULSION

George Gipps, the ninth governor of New South Wales, arrived in the colony in 1838 as a product of the humanitarianism and moral enlightenment transforming the British world. A committed advocate of temperance, he became the first governor to chair a public meeting in New South Wales when he served as honorary president of the New South Wales Temperance Society, in June 1838. Addressing the respectable assembly of "gentlemen and a large proportion of ladies" who filled the hall of Sydney College, his speech embodied the spirit of moral reform through patronage and persuasion that underlay the early temperance movement. It was his "firm conviction" that the "greater portion of the crimes, the vices, and, consequently, the punishments that are inflicted in this Colony may be traced to the excessive use of ardent spirits," and he called for the audience to "use your utmost influence ... and bring the force of public opinion to bear" on the problem.[1]

In many ways, this early temperance meeting echoed the proto-democratic forms of public dinners. The governor served as chair and gave the opening speech to rousing cheers, other speakers obtrusively thanked him for his patronage, and the meeting was understood to represent a public statement of the temperance views of much of the political and social elite. Reporting on the occasion, the recently established *Australian Temperance Magazine* claimed it was "a Meeting worthy of an imperial dependency for its loyalty and good order, and would have done honour to a republic for its freedom and simplicity."[2] The governor both reaffirmed his own status by extending his patronage but also acknowledged that he was a public representative, that there were limits to his authority, and that public opinion was an essential element of colonial society and politics. Like toasting, the performative practices of temperance reveal something of the underlying political imaginary.

But within the temperance movement itself there were very different visions of the proper performance of temperance – between respectable restraint and more radical sobriety – and these divisions are also revealing. While the Temperance Society condemned spirit drinking, they and their patron continued to tolerate other forms of alcohol, notably wine, the drink of the elite. During a subsequent speech at the society's annual meeting in 1841, Gipps alluded to a growing divide within the movement, claiming the "chief maxim" of the Temperance Society was "put moderation in your enjoyments" and contrasting this with the newly formed Sydney Total Abstinence Society, which was "more rigid, more austere, and perhaps more perfect." He stressed his conviviality, arguing that "good cheer … produced good company," and cited as an example the public dinner he had recently attended to bid farewell to the attorney general, John Plunkett, which he claimed remained within "the bounds of moderation and propriety" and "sinned against no rule of [the Temperance] society."[3] However, this was a typical public dinner of the period, featuring fourteen official toasts, and it is unlikely the governor abstained from any of them. Indeed, Gipps had thanked the company for "the very flattering manner in which his own health had been drank, and begged to drink all their healths in return."[4] Addressing the Temperance Society in 1841, Gipps acknowledged condemnation of the practice of health-drinking within the wider temperance movement, but admitted that his first thought on hearing news of the Queen's first child (Victoria, born 21 November 1840) was to "propose the health of the young Princess in a bumper," an admission that was celebrated with "cheers" by the assembled membership.[5]

In contrast, more radical temperance advocates were increasingly condemning all drinking, calling for the government to ban alcohol, and specifically targeting health-drinking and toasting. At a meeting of the Total Abstinence Society a few months later, Rev. Mansfield, a Methodist minister and journalist who was then editor of *The Sydney Herald*, reflected critically on the governor's remarks, suggesting that it was "one of the worst fallacies to suppose that the comfort of the social table depends on the bottle."[6] His comments were expanded on in a lengthy discussion of toasting in the society's paper, *The Temperance Advocate*, presumably written by its secretary, John Saunders, a Baptist minister, temperance missionary, and editor.[7] Saunders noted that the British were "essentially a drinking people" but argued that "the same amount of good fellowship and of animated feeling, may be obtained without drinking either healths or toasts." He insisted that he intended no insult to the governor, "the chief friend of Temperance," and claimed that "His Excellency above all others" looked forward to the day when "his duty and affection to his sovereign will not be suspected by mentioning her name without raising the pledging cup."[8] Saunders's views neatly illustrate the changing political imaginary of the colony. The governor remained a central figure, and his patronage mattered. But his voice was merely an especially influential one within a wider public sphere in which the performance of sobriety, as much as restrained toasting, asserted political citizenship.

This controversy over the governor's temperance was a minor matter, soon forgotten in the intense politics of New South Wales in the 1840s. But it nonetheless illustrates the growing political and intellectual divisions within the early temperance movement between elite philanthropy, bourgeois respectability, and working-class radicalism, divisions that echoed those taking place on a broader scale in New South Wales as the colony democratized. Gipps was committed to the temperance of moderation, which relied on "moral suasion" – proselytizing lectures and pamphlets that admonished drunkards to change their ways – and individual commitment, symbolized in the abstinence pledge. The early temperance movement in the colony took this form, focusing on attracting the support of prominent leaders and encouraging working-class drinkers to follow their example and publicly commit to abstain from spirits. But increasingly some temperance activists adopted a far more radical critique of all alcohol, which, they argued, was the fundamental cause of social problems, demanding total abstinence among supporters, and actively lobbying for stricter regulation toward total prohibition. In addition, temperance became a mass movement with support drawn from a broader range of society, and as it did so, temperance societies became more democratic and bottom-up. For a mass membership, temperance was a means of social mobility, and a rejection of both popular excess and elite debauchery and corruption – in my terms, of both drunken and restrained drinking. Radical temperance rejected the idea that drinking could be orderly, saw conviviality as idle and dangerous, and insisted on the active performance of sobriety. The Gipps controversy illustrates both the internal politics of the temperance movement and the battle of ideas that underlay it.

Temperance thus serves as a counterpoint to the performative drinking of public toasting: both reflect and reveal a public who saw themselves as political agents and acted accordingly. Just as toasting was a ritual of loyalty that also affirmed a kind of proto-citizenship, pledging abstinence cast the temperate as model citizens who performed respectability through public restraint – or, more radically, sobriety – thus entitling them to a political voice. Temperance functioned as a powerful form of identity politics that deliberately challenged the supposed authority of male drinkers and increasingly made respectable morality, not fraternal conviviality, the test of political responsibility. I therefore understand temperance as both an instrumental and symbolic political movement, one focused on a specific (if utopian) social reform, but simultaneously a performative assertion of social status, and both aspects illustrate the democratic British political imaginary.

Below, I offer a short history of the international, British, and colonial temperance movements, illustrating a general pattern of development and the specific form it took in New South Wales. I demonstrate the scale and importance of organized temperance and its close connection to the spread of democracy as a powerful and effective political lobby. In particular, I emphasize a crucial shift in temperance logic: from persuading the drunken sinner to pledge their abstinence, to restricting or prohibiting public access to liquor.

The Global Temperance Movement

Temperance and its campaign against alcohol problems was perhaps the largest social movement of the nineteenth-century English-speaking world. Despite enormous variety within the movement and across the century, an extraordinary number of men and women were united by one central idea: that alcohol was the leading cause of social problems. The word "temperance," as one of Plato's four cardinal virtues, had a long association with moderation and from the sixteenth century onward began to acquire a specific connection with food and especially drink. Religious criticism of excessive drinking was common, especially after the Reformation, and organized campaigns for temperance evolved from earlier efforts to improve morals and manners. Philanthropic and reforming associations like the Proclamation Society sought to reform public behaviour in general and preached moderate use of alcohol and the avoidance of sins like drunkenness.[9]

The first dedicated temperance societies drew from this longer tradition of philanthropic reform and its concern with drunkenness as a symbol and cause of larger evils but were specifically focused on the drinking of spirits, and advocated abstinence as the only cure. The first society to call for members to pledge abstinence was the American Temperance Society, founded in 1826, and by the early 1830s, their success had inspired the formation of similar temperance societies throughout Britain. On both sides of the Atlantic, these early societies emphasized securing the financial support and patronage of prominent leaders and using their influence to persuade drinkers to sign the pledge and abstain from spirits.[10]

By the mid-1830s a more radical and egalitarian temperance was emerging that would rapidly overtake the earlier form. Total abstinence societies attracted a mass membership from the respectable middle and working classes, required their members to renounce all forms of alcohol (teetotalism), and increasingly called for legislative restrictions aimed at abolishing the "demon drink." This shift in temperance thinking is clearly captured in the report of the 1834 Select Committee on Drunkenness, chaired by a leading advocate of temperance, James Buckingham. The report considered a wealth of largely partisan evidence on this "National evil," asserted that "the right to exercise legislative interference ... cannot be questioned," and called for stricter regulation toward the "ultimate" solution of a total prohibition on spirits. Though still conceived within the anti-spirits frame, the radical solutions proposed by the Buckingham Committee would inspire the temperance movement in Britain and New South Wales for much of the remainder of the century.[11] Brian Harrison situates this shift within the wider radical politics of the 1830s, arguing that respectable temperance supporters were deliberately "gaining allies for the radical attack on privilege, deference, corruption and violence – grooming working men to add their numbers to the energy and righteous indignation of the radical middle class."[12] By 1840, teetotallers were the dominant temperance force, and in 1848 the last anti-spirit society in Britain folded.

Thus, the earliest temperance societies married an exclusive focus on spirits to traditional means of reform. They relied on the "benevolent paternalism" of the social elite, and insisted on the "voluntary principle," rejecting any efforts to compel sobriety in favour of "moral suasion." But the new teetotal movement rejected not only this hypocritical tolerance of wine drinking but also the methods of earlier reformers. They attracted a mass membership by "dramatizing social mobility" at their meetings and fostering a sense of community through marches, tea parties, and concerts, and increasingly they lobbied the government for legislative enforcement of temperance.[13] This distinction between what I will term patronizing and populist temperance, and the related distinction between persuasion and compulsion, were also at stake in New South Wales.

The Temperance Movement in New South Wales, 1830–60

There had always been concern about drunkenness – especially among convicts – in New South Wales, so when news of the new temperance movement reached the colony in 1830 it was met by a receptive audience. In 1832, the Quaker missionaries James Backhouse and George Walker founded a series of temperance societies in Van Diemen's Land that helped inspire Sydney activists.[14] Even before this, John Dunmore Lang had taken pledges of abstinence in Sydney Harbour from the emigrant mechanics he brought to the colony in 1831. Lang's project of promoting free emigration was intended to encourage a "moral revolution" in Sydney by offering sober competition for the "drunken ticket-of-leave men" who formed the colony's labour force.[15]

A similar patronizing desire to improve the labouring classes seems to have driven the first advocates of the New South Wales Temperance Society. A preliminary meeting was held in October 1833, chaired by William Pascoe Crook, a Congregationalist missionary and pastor, and the men who formed the Provisional Committee as well as the initial subscribers to the Temperance Society were all from the upper levels of New South Wales society. I have not identified any convicts or emancipists among their number, and those who can be traced were largely clergy, missionaries, merchants, and professionals, especially lawyers and government officials.[16] Notably, none of Lang's sober mechanics joined.

By December, the society had one hundred and fifty pledged members, was meeting regularly in the house of the cabinetmaker Edward Hunt, and had secured the chief justice, Francis Forbes, to act as president. At the first public meeting in May, Forbes praised the cause to a "numerous and highly respectable" crowd as "a great moral engine" to redeem the colony from drunkenness, "the parent and nurse of crime in New South Wales."[17] The inaugural committee was dominated by legal and religious leaders and their preliminary report setting out the rules of the society required members to pledge to "relinquish the use of ardent spirit" and avoid "excess" of other alcoholic beverages. Members met quarterly to discuss the problems of intemperance in the colony, and in order to spread their message they organized public lectures, printed pamphlets and later a newspaper, and funded the missionary work of Saunders, who travelled the rural parts of the colony preaching the evils of alcohol.[18] Their propaganda made many of the familiar arguments against drunkenness but noticeably targeted moderate drinkers, claiming spirit drinking was common "because it is countenanced and supported by YOU ... the respectable moderate spirit drinker."[19] This emphasis arguably reflected Saunders's increasingly populist and radical approach to temperance and foreshadowed the shift to teetotalism.

The society expanded steadily and by its first-anniversary meeting there were four hundred members.[20] In July 1837 the first edition of the monthly *Australian Temperance Magazine* was published, providing a prominent mouthpiece, and by the following year it ran to four thousand copies, nominally the highest circulation of any contemporary journal. However, closer analysis of these figures illustrates the patronizing character of the society. The journal was not sold to the general public but purchased in multiple copies by elite subscribers who then distributed it to the poor for their education and improvement. In Sydney in 1840, when circulation was at its peak, 1,324 copies were printed for only 162 Sydney subscribers, almost half of whom held some form of title, either as gentlemen, clergymen, or military officers. Another 500 were bought by the government and distributed among convict road gangs.[21]

By 1840 the colonial temperance movement was beginning to change. Gipps's support for temperance increased public interest, and perhaps a thousand people attended the annual meeting in 1839, while the following year the popularity of the cause (and the introduction of free postage for newspapers) induced the society to shift from publishing a monthly magazine to a weekly paper, which had 1,100 individual subscriptions by its second number. The official prospectus of *The Temperance Advocate* argued that the object of the Temperance Society was to "produce union among all classes of persons, and of all shades of opinion," and stressed that the cost of an annual subscription (twenty shillings) was "so small as to place the newspaper within the reach of the poor" while also "enabl[ing] the wealthy settlers to take additional copies for their estates in the country." At the packed annual meeting in 1841 hundreds were turned away from the hall of Sydney College in what the somewhat partisan *Temperance Advocate* described as the greatest public meeting ever seen in the colony.[22]

The first teetotal society, the Sydney Total Abstinence Society, was founded in September 1838. It grew rapidly, with over five hundred members by the first anniversary drawn from a broader cross-section of Sydney society, including mechanics and servants. Though membership of these short-lived bodies is difficult to determine, it is notable that subscriptions to abstinence societies were consistently set at much smaller sums, the majority less than six shillings, where most benefactors to the Temperance Society gave several pounds. Also noticeable is the dominance of dissent within the movement, with meetings often held in Nonconformist chapels, Dissenting clergy prominent among the membership, and, in contrast to the Temperance Society, very little support from the Church of England. Indeed, the church was increasingly hostile toward radical temperance, arguing that the movement challenged established religious authority.[23]

The teetotal pledge, copied from England, demanded complete abstinence from all intoxicating beverages, and this message was actively promoted to the working classes. Regular tea parties, processions, and festivals helped to make the society popular, as did the more frequent weekly meetings, which were relatively informal with speakers drawn from the floor and reformed drunkards encouraged to relate their conversion to the cause. Teetotallers also organized a workers' benefit society, a form of mutual insurance with sober members paying an annual subscription in exchange for sick benefits and funeral costs.[24] This approach had rapid and dramatic success. There were overflowing meetings held each week in the hall of the Sydney Mechanics' School of Arts and almost two thousand signed the pledge in 1841–42.[25] More importantly, the meetings were not just popular but *populist* – they actively sought a broad membership and immersed their supporters in a social world to rival that surrounding the public house with regular meetings and events that catered to the whole family. This approach is captured in the processions and festivals that dotted the temperance calendar, during which members publicly celebrated their abstinence, reinforced their sense of virtue, advertised their growing numbers, and attracted new converts with music, food, and sober conviviality.[26] But they were also increasingly radical in their approach. Inclusivity was predicated on a new understanding that restraining the influence of the "demon drink" required a universal commitment to sobriety backed by legislative enactment.

The early 1840s were the high point of early Sydney temperance. At the annual meeting of the original Abstinence Society in September 1842, over a thousand attended the Victoria Theatre, the largest public room in town, while the Boxing Day meeting of the St Patrick's Total Abstinence Society, a new teetotal group linked to the Catholic Church, drew seven hundred.[27] But, in an echo of the British and American patterns, as the abstinence societies grew, support for the Temperance Society declined, and this shift toward more radical and populist temperance was symbolized by the collapse of *The Temperance Advocate* and the rise in its place of a new paper, *The Teetotaller*.[28]

However, in New South Wales, teetotal triumph was short-lived. Personal animosity and power struggles between rival leaders, disagreement over tactics, and cultural and ideological differences led to the fracturing of the movement. By the end of 1843, there were four separate teetotal societies, and the last vestiges of the Temperance Society, competing for support and divided in their respective approaches.[29] The growing radicalism of the movement contributed to a loss of elite patronage, which in turn hurt membership and fundraising efforts. By 1844, ongoing donations from the governor and the few remaining passionate supporters had failed to clear the Temperance Society's debts. In a telling gesture, for the first time since his arrival in New South Wales, Gipps did not attend the annual meeting, instead holding a ball at Government House, and the society seems to have folded within the following year.[30]

These struggles were also experienced by teetotallers. Their newspaper, *The Teetotaller*, suffered "four quarters of loss" in its first year of operation, experienced continually declining subscriptions, and folded for good in September 1843.[31] This loss of an organized public voice for temperance was compounded by the departure of Governor Gipps from the colony in 1846; indeed, it is notable that the largest temperance meeting in Sydney after 1843 was called to thank Gipps for his support before his departure.[32] Lacking a figurehead and the financial backing of the colonial elite, the movement also became increasingly divided, both between moderates and radicals and on sectarian lines. In particular, the prominence of Catholic temperance, and the way that the St Patrick's Society became a focus for Irish Catholic cultural identity, led to sectarian resentment and fears of Irish political power. Embodying these divisions, Lang – who was personally sober and far more politically radical than most temperance supporters – claimed that "teetotalism has ... become a mere device for exhibiting the physical force of the Irish Roman Catholics ... in ostentatious and frequent processions."[33] Following a sectarian riot in Melbourne on the anniversary of the Battle of the Boyne, processions by denominational temperance societies were made illegal if they celebrated an anniversary "connected with any religious or political difference" or carried "any banner, emblem, flag or symbol ... calculated to provoke animosity."[34] Indeed, the St Patrick's Society fell afoul of this legislation in 1847, and was required to publicly apologize to the Catholic attorney general, John Plunkett, to avoid prosecution.

This sectarian politicization also contributed to the decline of temperance in the colony, such that most temperance and teetotal societies struggled to survive through the 1840s. Regular reports of annual meetings come to an end in the middle of that decade, and in 1853 a *Herald* editorial contrasted the thriving temperance movement in Melbourne with its absence in Sydney. Thus, the pattern of early New South Wales temperance diverges from that of England and America, and, for that matter, from other parts of the Australian colonies in the 1840s and early 1850s.[35]

Resurgent public concern about alcohol problems contributed to the gradual revival of the movement in the 1850s. The end of the depression and the gold rushes led to growing prosperity, rising consumption of alcohol, and a moral panic about the newly enriched working classes. all of which provided fertile ground for temperance anxieties. But equally important was the 1851 passage of the so-called Maine Law, an early version of prohibition. This American legislation inspired the formation of the UK Alliance for the Suppression of the Trade in Alcohol, which in turn encouraged the revival of temperance activism in New South Wales.[36] In a series of letters to *The Herald* in 1853, the Anglican minister William Lumsdaine noted the terrible damage caused by drunkenness and called for efforts to "resuscitate the cause" of temperance in New South Wales, and the formation of a Maine Law League in Melbourne soon inspired local imitators under the leadership of a retired naval officer, Lieutenant Richard Sadlier.[37]

A newly revived total abstinence society prepared a petition to the legislature with over seven thousand signatures calling for a complete ban on the legal sale of alcohol, and this revived activism fed into the 1854 Select Committee on Intemperance. Presenting the petition, Sadlier demonstrated some sympathy with the voluntary principle, stressing that prohibition required popular support and calling for a campaign of public education followed by a referendum. But he also justified the resort to legislation, arguing that the earlier movement had failed because "any good we may do is counteracted; for one convert we may reclaim, twenty new drunkards are created by public houses."[38] These tactics were widely criticized, with *The Herald* calling for "reason and persuasion, backed by example," but although the petition was never acted on, the mid- to late 1850s saw a broader revival of the temperance movement throughout New South Wales.[39]

The first bands of hope, societies dedicated to indoctrinating children in the temperance cause, were formed in 1855 and soon spread across the colony. This movement, again inspired by British precedents, sought to "combine instruction with entertainment," securing pledges to abstain from drinking, publishing a magazine for children, and teaching moral lessons to young teetotallers, and it would play an important role in the spread of temperance support in the final quarter of the century.[40] Bands of hope emphasized the feminine sphere of children and homes, and a closely related development was the first temperance society explicitly for women. Despite substantial female support for temperance in the 1830s and '40s, the short-lived Ladies Total Abstinence Society was only founded in 1856. Nonetheless, it illustrates the connections between temperance and feminism that marked a shift toward female dominance of the temperance movement in the late nineteenth century.[41] The period also saw the formation of a series of temperance "alliances" that sought to unite the heavily divided movement. The first of these, an "unsectarian and non-Political" organization, did not take a formal position on prohibition, though many of its members supported the 1854 petition, but it did play an important role in the development of a political temperance lobby, creating a forum for internal temperance debate and organizing the construction of Sydney's first dedicated temperance hall.[42]

Over the remainder of the nineteenth century, the organized movement steadily grew in strength and influence. Fraternal societies aimed at working men and women like the Sons and Daughters of Temperance, the Good Templars, and the Rechabites gained large memberships, providing benefit clubs for workers and social activities for their families. Meanwhile, the Women's Christian Temperance Union was a key feminist lobby that pushed women to the forefront of temperance and played a critical role in securing a political voice for women in Australian society. A series of tours by American and British advocates, backed up by intercolonial and international conferences, also helped to unite the movement.[43] So did the increasingly politicized New South Wales Alliance for the Suppression of Intemperance, which lobbied the government for a so-called permissive law, a means of introducing prohibition by local popular vote. The campaign was finally successful with the 1882 Licensing Act, which introduced a limited form of local option – each electorate voted to veto any new licences. This was a significant measure that further politicized the drink question by mobilizing temperance forces during elections and led to a stricter form of local option in 1905. The movement climaxed in the twentieth century with its campaigns around two referenda: success for six o'clock closing in 1916, and failure for full prohibition in 1928. From then, organized temperance declined into its recent insignificance, though its impact on the social understanding of alcohol remains profound.[44] This longer history of temperance after 1860 is more obviously democratic, with its explicit connections to women's suffrage, electoral lobbying, and referenda. But the early movement is nonetheless revealing of the political imaginary, as I explore in the next chapter.

7

Imagining a Sober Public

TEMPERANCE AS A DEMOCRATIC IDEAL

Even during the mid-nineteenth century, temperance was a democratic ideal. Radical temperance helped to promote a rival vision of citizenship from the drunken fraternity of the public dinner, with performative sobriety serving as a means of social mobility. By engaging their members in an active social movement, and increasingly a campaign for legislative reform, teetotal societies also helped to politicize a wider public, teaching them to be agentive citizens in a democratic society. But temperance was more than a social movement; it was also an influential set of ideas about alcohol, and these ideas had a life beyond the organized societies. As a result of movement activism that began in the late 1830s, the radical temperance view that alcohol was inherently dangerous – a structural cause of social problems – became widely accepted, with far-reaching consequences for alcohol regulation and wider implications for democratic governance into the twentieth century.

Ironically, the very fact that the organized temperance movement was weaker in mid-nineteenth-century New South Wales than in many other places – notably England and Victoria – helps strengthen my argument for the importance of temperance as an idea. Even as temperance societies declined in the colony in the mid-

1840s, temperance advocates were pointing to the broader impact of the movement on the public understanding of alcohol. Speaking at the meeting to bid farewell to Gipps in 1846, Rev. Robert Ross, a Congregational minister, argued that temperance "had exercised a powerful influence on multitudes who had never joined [a] society," suggesting that health, wealth, and even "civil and political liberty" depended upon public temperance and, by implication, not on the declining membership of temperance societies.[1] Indeed, average alcohol consumption declined significantly in New South Wales from the late 1830s (notwithstanding a short but rapid increase that accompanied the gold rush), and temperance certainly influenced this change in behaviour.[2]

More profoundly, the understanding of alcohol in the social imaginary – always highly politicized – was transformed by temperance, and by the 1850s alcohol was increasingly understood as a problem substance requiring a political solution. The 1854 Select Committee on Intemperance illustrates this clearly. Ignoring the central importance of alcohol to the economy and society, it was called to "inquire into the cause of the alarming increase of Intemperance ... and to report what remedies can be applied for this growing evil." The witnesses, committee members, and indeed the Legislative Council and the press more broadly all took the evil for granted; debate solely concerned the appropriate remedy and was conducted in terms framed by temperance.[3] Irrespective of the power of the movement, temperance had profound influence as an idea.

Indeed, by the late nineteenth century temperance advocates often addressed a wider public beyond the membership of temperance societies. In a very influential lecture in 1869, later published as a pamphlet, the chief justice of the New South Wales Supreme Court, Alfred Stephen – who was himself a restrained drinker and not a teetotaller – noted that the observer of colonial drunkenness, while he might not wish to join a temperance society, must nevertheless "cease to consider [temperance] a fitting subject for banter ... [and] will no longer dare to fold his arms in apathy." The movement itself understood temperance as a universal and existential concern, "a great and noble cause," a contest against "mighty evils ... so great and formidable as to constitute a vast moral pestilence, more destructive than the ravages of war or the horrors of famine."[4] From at least the 1840s, the "drink problem" was consistently one of the leading issues in the public sphere, widely debated beyond the temperance movement itself, largely due to the influence of temperance as an idea.

My interpretation builds on existing scholarship that links temperance to a broader cultural politics of respectability that cut across class lines and served as a means of social mobility.[5] In particular, Brian Harrison draws attention to the nineteenth-century distinction between "rough" and "respectable," arguing that the aspirational working poor embraced temperance and respectability willingly – they were not suffering from false consciousness or compelled by patronizing masters – because they believed that performative sobriety, as a symbol of respectable manners, would lead to respectable status. As he argues, respectability, symbolized in the Protestant virtues of temperance, thrift, industry, decency, and character, cut across class barriers opposing the vices of both the rough (and drunken) working classes and the decadent (and drunken) rich.[6]

Harrison also emphasizes the way the movement helped to politicize people who were otherwise outside organized politics by encouraging supporters to exercise a public voice as part of a broader attack on traditional authority, teaching them methods of organizing and lobbying. He argues that such politicization mattered even when the movement failed to achieve its most radical social reforms because temperance was at its core a form of "liberating protest" that judged success in symbolic terms: through public defiance of authority, "assert[ing] the worth of a distinct [respectable] culture," and "eas[ing] the consciences" of supporters.[7] In this sense, temperance is evidence of a democratic political imaginary, through its promotion of a sense of political agency among supporters who were taught to believe that they could reform society.

Michael Roe makes similar arguments for colonial Australia in relation to his concept of a moral enlightenment that transformed political culture in the Victorian age, and more recently, Anne Marie McAllister has interpreted the mass mobilization of radical temperance as a collective performance on the public stage of British urban centres.[8] Following these authors, I likewise read temperance as a performative politics of respectability, and as a meritocracy that sought to educate, enrich, and improve its supporters while promoting their political agency. Scholars including Harry Levine, Marianna Valverde, Virginia Berridge, James Nicholls, and Harry Yeomans also link temperance to the expansion of government in the second half of the nineteenth century.[9] In addition to promoting social mobility and democratic participation, temperance also transformed the public understanding of alcohol, influencing and reflecting a larger revolution in British government, with the assumption of responsibility for positive liberty by the state.

Respectability and Social Mobility

One way in which temperance was democratic was through its emphasis on social mobility. Patronizing temperance sought to improve drinkers and their social conditions through education and urban reform. Though it was often objectifying, temperance always aimed to make drinkers into better people and, implicitly, better citizens: more sober, healthier, wealthier, wiser, more moral. In contrast, populist temperance sought more explicitly to empower supporters, to provide them with the means and opportunity for self-improvement: to performatively make themselves respectable. From this perspective, temperance was a kind of Weberian Protestant ethic, a worldly "calling" to responsibility that encouraged followers to strive for virtue so as to attain greater status and material success.[10] Regardless, all forms of temperance endorsed, more or less explicitly, a vision of a larger respectable public whose morals and demeanour entitled them to civic participation.

Temperance grew out of a much longer tradition of elite philanthropy that sought to improve and assist the poor. But from the earliest days of the movement in New South Wales, this patronizing tradition had democratic implications. In the first temperance pamphlet printed in the colony, the Temperance Society described habitual drunkards as "poor deluded creatures who are the slaves of this vice," and yet the society was also concerned with the consequences for these victims, noting that intemperance led to "neglect of education" as well as wider social harms. Their pamphlet focused on the benefits for the reformed drinker, educating readers about the damage spirit drinking caused to their health, and the money they could save on drink – "in short how you may live more morally, peaceably, and happily." Though condescending, the society's claim that the reader's "moral welfare and worldly comfort" were their main concern was arguably true.[11]

This patronizing ethic was always central to temperance, and even radical temperance arguments often adopted a condescending tone toward drinkers. In a classic example, John Dunmore Lang publicly refused to support the revived temperance movement of the 1850s, claiming that it failed to address "the real causes of the alarming prevalence of intemperance," which in his view was "the system in operation for the management, or rather mismanagement of the waste lands of the colony." Lang's somewhat confected though strikingly radical argument was that the poor squandered their savings on drink because they were prevented from buying land, a view that spoke to the democratic settler-colonial imaginary, in which the fantasy of an unoccupied continent would allow Australia to become a working-man's paradise. In making his case, Lang contrasted his ideal of a sober citizenry with the reality in which "hundreds and thousands of families [were] reduced to the low-huckstering, public-house-keeping, and public-house-frequenting condition of the lower classes of a town population." Lang depicted these working-class drinkers as passive victims of their situation, but he also understood drunkenness as a symptom and not a cause of poverty, and argued for reforms that would create greater opportunities for working men and hence a larger public of "thriving and independent proprietors."[12]

The temperance movement also had practical ideas about how to help drinkers improve themselves, grounded in the long-standing association of sobriety with wealth, health, and morality. But importantly, temperance increasingly reversed the flow of causation, arguing that improved education would lead men to become sober.[13] The importance of education, not merely about the dangers of alcohol, but more broadly as a means of individual and social improvement, was a pervading theme of colonial temperance advocates from the origins of the movement. As Nicole Starling has shown, this was a key theme in Saunders's writing, as he consistently linked temperance to a broader "project of social and individual improvement."[14] In an editorial aiming to boost morale among teetotallers, Saunders argued that "tens of thousands [of former drunkards] are now in a state of moral and intellectual improvement" thanks to the movement, along with "millions" of moderate drinkers, and described the Temperance Society as "in effect an education society."[15] And indeed, temperance societies did seek to educate their members and a wider public, organizing lectures on all manner of improving subjects, setting up lending libraries, and closely associating with other forms of self-improvement like Sunday schools and schools of arts. Similarly, they consistently promoted "rational amusements," forms of recreation for the working classes that did not involve alcohol.[16]

The clearest examples of this connection were the bands of hope that formed in the 1850s with their specific focus on children. At the inaugural meeting of the Bathurst Street Band of Hope in June 1855, it was described as "an association of the rising generation for spiritual and intellectual improvement, and instruction in the principles of 'teetotalism,'" and early meetings advertised lectures on such subjects as "the Acquisition of Knowledge," "Working," "Ambition," and "Slavery." The movement flourished and in early 1856 helped establish a "magazine for children [as] a medium of interest and instruction to them" by publishing "a pure and healthy general literature … whatever tends to expand and strengthen the intellect and enlarge knowledge, while it corrupts not." In a later article, the magazine's editor defined education broadly as including "the teaching of manners, habits, and customs … the formation of habits, the foundation of character, the improvement of disposition, the cultivation of tastes."[17] This was a program of moral enlightenment that assumed all children could become responsible adult citizens.

These ideas were not merely taught, they were also enacted in the spread of temperance benefit and mutual aid societies. The St Patrick's Total Abstinence Society organized one of the earliest, with a small annual subscription providing sick benefits and funeral costs, but with membership restricted to pledged teetotallers.[18] Temperance advocates were convinced – and may have been right – that restricting membership to the temperate made such mutual aid more successful since the members were necessarily healthier "owing to their sober habits."[19] A short story in the *Band of Hope* journal, "Life Insurance," illustrates the broader message at stake in such projects of self-improvement. The story's hero, John Newman, explains to his wife how, since taking the pledge, he has "made so much better use of my money," renting a pew, donating to worthy charities, buying books and subscribing to the *Band of Hope* itself, paying his children's school fees, and buying a life assurance policy to protect his family.[20] Education and mutual aid were both concrete manifestations of the temperance conviction that, through sobriety, people, and indeed society as a whole, could be made better.

Temperance and Political Participation

Temperance supporters, at least in the more radical and populist forms of temperance, actively performed this democratic ideal. The first well-reported meeting of the Sydney Total Abstinence Society, held on Tuesday, 21 May 1839, in the School of Arts, is an excellent illustration. The chair, William Rowe, who worked for the Australian Gas-Light Company, announced the rapid growth of the society from eight pledged members in September to over two hundred in May. Speakers included a blacksmith named Walton who recounted how drunkenness had ruined him in the past, and a "labouring man" named Nichols who spoke about his improved health and temper since he took the pledge, claiming his wife and children used to hide from him when he came home drunk, but now they ran to greet him. Nichols went further: "he earnestly entreated all the working men to join the Society, and by educating their children make them equal to the children of the rich … for there is more money spent in public-houses than would give all the children in Sydney a first rate education." William Jeffrey gave an entertaining speech that included a "facetious report of an imaginary Anti-temperance society," a rendition of a Scottish temperance air, and a proposal to banish the "four great rascals" from New South Wales: rum, gin, brandy, and fermented liquor. Two former publicans, Mr Bancroft, and Mr Lewis, both spoke about how they had abandoned the trade, Bancroft describing the desperation of his former customers, stealing and pawning their goods to buy drink, and Lewis speaking about how he had ruined himself through drinking with his patrons. Rowe concluded the meeting by referring to a new teetotal benefit society that would shortly open its books exclusively to teetotallers.[21]

While the basic form of the meeting – a chairman, speakers, an audience – remained the same, its character was very different from the meetings of the earlier New South Wales Temperance Society. Speakers were drawn from among the audience and from all ranks of society, they spoke to their own experiences with alcohol, and sought to empower and improve themselves and men like them, putting temperance rhetoric into action. This kind of genuinely open meeting was powerfully democratic, even radical; but it was also resented and belittled by critics. *The Gazette* claimed to be unable to report on the May meeting since its reporter was "not a teetotaller," and instead reprinted *The Herald*'s article.[22] By June these scruples seem to have been abandoned and the paper printed a scornful account of the "exceedingly motley" company, claiming only the table and front rows were filled by "persons of respectable appearance," while the main body of the meeting comprised "persons having the look of artisans," a few of whom smelled of rum, and the back of the hall was filled with an "unruly colony of small fry, who kept up a constant hubbub."[23] Of course, this was necessarily the case for a genuinely democratic assembly: working men and women often had to bring their children to meetings, and it was impossible to convert drunkards without exposure to them. Indeed, in a strikingly different report, *The Herald* had the chairman, Rev. McKaeg, a Presbyterian preacher, claiming that there were "upwards of a hundred persons in the room who were formerly as great drunkards as any in Sydney, and who are now sober men."[24]

Radical temperance was not content with public meetings, however. Its adherents insisted on regular processions that publicized the movement and its message as widely as possible in a demonstration of strength that created solidarity among members and attracted converts.[25] On 27 December 1841 – not coincidently, the day after the Boxing Day holiday, when many workers were doubtless nursing hangovers – the combined membership of the flourishing total abstinence and benefit societies marched through Sydney. According to the secretary of the Total Abstinence Benefit Society, John White, they aimed to "muster all our Teetotal forces, to shew the inhabitants of Sydney ... that we are as respectable a class of men as are in Sydney, and that we are doing much towards bringing about a reformation in the manners of the people." The various societies raised funds to pay for a marching band, decorations, and uniforms through a subscription dinner in the Sydney markets that concluded the march.[26]

The procession itself was carefully scripted, with the Sydney Total Abstinence Society and the linked Benefit Society meeting at Vercoe's coffee house and marching to the courthouse, where they met the members of the St Patrick's Society, after which at least six hundred teetotallers processed together through the city. Juvenile members marched in front with special banners and blue flags; then adults wearing white scarfs and rosettes; the Benefit Society members, who wore aprons with a formal coat of arms "representing industry, plenty, truth, and union, supported by the kangaroo and emu"; and, finally, the St Patrick's members. The latter bore a banner with an image of Saint Patrick trampling the demon of intemperance, a portrait of Father Mathew, the Irish temperance leader, and the text of the total abstinence pledge. Other banners and flags carried similarly symbolic messages, including "Sobriety," "Domestic Comfort," "Advance Australia," "Train Up a Child in the Way He Should Go," "Drunkenness Kills More than the Sword," and "This Is Not the Cause of Party or of Faction, but Every Lover of His Country."[27] The public display of these messages was an overt effort to boost morale and convert observers to the cause, illustrating the way in which populist temperance politicized its members, who performatively displayed their sobriety.

This public mobilization contrasted starkly with the patronage model of the original Temperance Society, who proudly emphasized the status of their members and depended upon a paternalistic elite to spread the discourse of reform. In its founding documents, the society emphasized "correspondence ... with Ministers, Medical Gentlemen and other influential persons" as well as printing material "addressed to different classes of persons," and it aimed "to encourage especially, the formation of Associations on similar principles amongst the labouring classes."[28] It is telling that they envisaged working-class temperance as separate and distinct, and that no such societies ever developed on moderate principles. Like the Proclamation Society, the Temperance Society sought moral reform through elite patronage of the poor, not solidarity in a shared respectability: moral reform without social reform.

Unsurprisingly, given the toasting culture of the time, much of the colonial elite were ambivalent about, if not opposed to, temperance. Even before the establishment of the movement in New South Wales, a letter to *The Australian* alleged that overseas experience showed that temperance societies lowered the social tone by reducing conviviality, and this attitude underlay an upper-class disdain for personal temperance, if not the movement in general.[29] High society continued to be lubricated by alcohol, and the governor and chief patron continued to participate in public toasts, but the Temperance Society was ideologically and financially dependent upon this hypocritical elite.

Gipps's leadership was seen as crucial for patronizing temperance because it made the movement fashionable and "must increase public approval" for the cause.[30] Gipps was aware of this, noting in 1841 "the marked increase in the attendance of persons of weight and influence" since he first chaired the society's annual meeting.[31] But such fashionable support was also ephemeral. In his speech the following year Gipps commented on "the respectable appearance [of the room] ... which might lead a stranger to suppose this society is well supported" while noting that in fact their debts had doubled. At the same meeting, Chief Justice Stephen quoted an unnamed "friend" who refused to subscribe, claiming that "Temperance Societies do no good. Your Temperance people are a set of fashionables who go yearly to a large hall to hear the Governor make a speech."[32]

The social elite on whom the society was financially dependent were mostly not devoted to temperance.

Teetotallers were aware of this weakness and increasingly attacked the Temperance Society for its hypocrisy. In 1839, McKaeg argued that "the old Temperance Society is not sufficient to reclaim drunkards ... [because] it forbids one kind of intoxicating liquor but allows others" and claimed the lack of converts to the cause showed that it was a failure. This disdain for rival approaches was mutual: as the Temperance Society went into terminal decline, its conservative supporters largely refused to transfer allegiance to more radical organizations.[33] Similarly, *The Herald*, under the editorship of Kemp and Fairfax, was a strong supporter of the Temperance Society, but regularly criticized teetotallers for what it perceived as overly ostentatious and "political" demonstrations. In December 1841 an editorial described a march by teetotallers in Wollongong as "scarcely compatible with the peace of society" because they carried banners associated with the Irish Catholic politician Daniel O'Connell. Noting the planned procession on Boxing Day, it argued that "many who esteem and admire [temperance] will turn from it in disgust when thus painted and gilded for the sake of effect."[34] In essence, the temperance movement, much like the colony in the 1840s, was divided between a largely conservative elite and a wider and more enthusiastic public.

Certainly, as reported in the press, temperance societies only briefly and occasionally took radical form – democratic temperance, like democracy itself, was elusive. Indeed, after the initial surge of teetotalism (ca 1838–43) even total abstinence became increasingly dominated by a respectable elite.[35] The St Patrick's Society had a diverse membership but its association with the Catholic Church meant that its leaders were invariably clergy who set the tone of the meetings. The banning of processions in the late 1840s can be seen as further evidence of the way the most radical and democratic forms of temperance were repressed, and the movement brought under the control of the respectable middle classes. The revived temperance movement of the 1850s, while it called for radical legislative reform, resembled the original Temperance Society in its organization, with an elite membership running meetings to a tightly controlled agenda packed with exclusively respectable speakers. The first colonial temperance alliance was founded by twenty gentlemen, who decided on the rules and elected the committee of twelve in advance of the first public meeting.[36] To the extent that radical working-man's temperance continued, it happened at a local scale, in small meetings that passed unreported in the increasingly commercial public press.

But even mainstream, respectable, and bourgeois temperance illustrates the democratic political imaginary, as well as its limitations. Though they sought to limit active participation, advocates like Lang and Saunders were anxious to promote social mobility, precisely because it would entitle the temperate to a public voice. In an especially clear illustration, Rev. McEncroe, a teetotaller who also struggled with alcoholism and was president of the St Patrick's Society, spoke at the farewell to Gipps, where he argued that even Gipps's noble leadership was useless "in a dissipated community, where the only law acknowledged was the law of appetite." Comparing the governor to Lycurgus, the legendary founder of Athenian democracy, he argued that by promoting temperance, Gipps had shown his foresight because "the well being and order of society" depended upon temperance and "free institutions could only be appreciated and upheld by temperate people."[37] All temperance sought to make people sober so that they could responsibly participate in a democratic society.

These views were also reflected in debates about legislative reform that were consistently framed in terms of public opinion. Critics of the Maine Law often argued that, while they favoured the reform in principle, they felt it was impractical until it had majority public support. For example, *The Herald* argued that "laws opposed simply to the will of a majority of the people required to obey them are rarely efficacious; laws opposed to the HABITS of the majority, never." Appealing to a wider constituency of public opinion, the editor argued that, "before such a law can exist and be carried out, the bulk of the community must have become staunch Teetotallers," and that it was therefore incumbent on the temperance movement to "enlighten, persuade, [and] convince the masses" before attempting to change legislation.[38]

Importantly, advocates for a Maine law accepted this democratic principle. They organized a series of public meetings, leading to a petition, signed by seven thousand people, that stressed their desire for "some legislative measures" to suppress intemperance, specifically for repeal of the licensed sale of liquor, and asked to be heard before the ongoing Select Committee on Intemperance. Richard Sadlier, speaking on behalf of the petitioners, told the committee that it was too soon for the legislation they proposed since "public opinion is not sufficiently informed," but that they would "proceed by spreading information among the people" in preparation for a poll, as had happened in Maine.[39] Defending the petition in the press from ill-informed criticisms, Sadlier stressed that there were "frequent precedents" for such restrictions on public behaviour, that the proposal was "neither coercive nor unconstitutional," and that the petition had been developed at "a regularly constituted public meeting."[40] Even as its radical energies were tamed, temperance remained a fundamentally democratic movement. Indeed, its evolution toward increasing bureaucracy and respectability illustrates the elusive nature of popular democracy.

Alcohol as a Problem Substance: The Causal Logic of Temperance

This failed campaign for a Maine law also shows the role of temperance in shifting the public understanding of alcohol and defining it as a problem substance. Over the course of the nineteenth century, ideas about alcohol underwent a striking transformation among experts and lawmakers, reflecting the popular imagination. From an eighteenth-century world in which drinking was ubiquitous and unconsidered and drunkenness common and generally tolerated, the twentieth century began with abstinence from alcohol widely regarded as an ideal, habitual drunkenness viewed as a form of insanity, and a vast body of new regulations that increasingly restricted access to alcohol and the manner in which it was consumed.

7.1 George Cruickshank, *Fearful Quarrels and Brutal Violence …* (1847).

The temperance movement was both a symptom of, and a catalyst for, these changes.

Drunkenness was condemned long before the temperance movement, and alcohol, or at least unrestrained drinking, was often seen as a cause of social problems, as for example in *Gin Lane* (see chapter 1, figure 1.1). But Hogarth's images are complex and ambiguous, offering a conservative moral economy in which restrained drinking after labour is idealized and idle drunkenness is its own punishment. In contrast, a key distinguishing feature of temperance over its earlier analogues was its exclusive focus on alcohol as *the* cause of social problems. Another famous series of moralizing images, George Cruickshank's *The Bottle* (figure 7.1), published in London at the height of the early temperance movement in 1847, illustrates the causal logic of temperance.

Cruickshank's prints were modelled on another of Hogarth's series, *A Rake's Progress*, a proto-temperance narrative in which alcohol is a symbol of Tom Rakewell's decline from idle inherited wealth to impoverished madness.[41] In contrast, Cruickshank focuses not on the sins of the protagonist, but on the substance that causes them, with the eponymous bottle featuring prominently throughout. Tellingly, the series begins with affluence, a happy and prosperous working-class home in which "the Bottle is brought out for the first time [and] the husband induces his wife 'Just to take a drop.'" Over the remaining images, the possessions that mark the family's respectable status gradually disappear as the husband loses his job as well as his youngest child (the latter to "cold, misery and want"), kills his wife (with the bottle itself!) "in a state of furious drunkenness," and is confined as "a hopeless maniac." In a sequel, *The Drunkard's Children*, the surviving son turns to crime, is transported for life, and dies of the effects of his "early dissipation," while the daughter – described with typical Victorian squeamishness – "is driven on in that course which ends in misery" and "commits self-murder."[42] Both Hogarth and Cruickshank tell a story of the wages of sin, but there is a subtle shift of emphasis between the two: for Hogarth, the bottle symbolized Rakewell's dissipation; for Cruickshank, it caused the downfall of a respectable family.

This point is clarified in other, similar temperance narratives produced in New South Wales. In 1849, Francis Belfield's play *Retribution, or The Drunkard's Curse*, was first performed in Melbourne, then still part of New South Wales. Later republished as *The Bottle, or The Drunkard's Curse*, presumably due to the popularity of Cruickshank's work, it was a typical Victorian melodrama with an overwrought story and a moral foreshadowed by the title.[43] George Melville begins the play describing drinking as "my only antidote, 'tis an enemy to care ... promotes good fellowship ... [and] gives zest to existence." But encouraged by a ne'er-do-well friend, Watson, he drinks more and more, abuses his wife and neglects his son, and is justly condemned by his brother-in-law, Alfred, as "now callous grown a drunkard and a fool." George stumbles around the stage unable to recognize his friends, loses all his money carousing with Watson, and causes his wife to die from heartbreak. The second act finds George a drunken vagrant, begging and stealing to support his habit, but Alfred takes pity on him, helping him to locate his son and beg God's mercy before his death from the effects of drink. Alfred's concluding speech is a classic statement of temperance logic and its implications: "The Bottle has done its fiendish work, this, this is the fulfilment of the Drunkard's Curse! Frederick, intemperance was your father's only crime, millions have been doomed to the same retribution beware! Oh, drink – drink! thou man-destroying, God-dishonouring, *elixir* of hell ... Oh that Governments were wise, to banish the poison from our land; nor longer license a pernicious traffic more deadly in its effects than wars or plagues!"[44] Since alcohol is the cause of all these evils, prohibition is necessary and just.

A similar narrative, told from a female perspective, was a feature of many of Australia's first literary publications, such as "Susan's Dream," from Mary Vidal's 1845 collection *Tales for the Bush*. Susan and her husband, Tom, are doing well on their bush block until he begins drinking at a sly grog shop. He comes home "in a dreadful state of intoxication," and this soon becomes a habit as he neglects his family and his farm "in idleness and drinking." In the climactic episode, Susan wakes from a prophetic dream and prays for her husband, and Tom's life is then saved by a providential accident. He is immediately sobered and "taught his duty," pledging abstinence and recommitting himself to his family while begging forgiveness from God. Even this explicitly Christian narrative treats alcohol as a cause. Susan's dream and her piety are the means of redeeming her family, but their downfall is the fault of her husband's weakness for the bottle.[45]

The extensive influence of this causal logic also informed temperance historiography. For writers like Lang, alcohol was a key factor in the country's early history: for example, Bligh's efforts to control the rum trade caused the Rum Rebellion. Working-class drunkenness was a symptom of political impotence, inevitable while men were crowded into towns and denied access to land. In this reading, alcohol was an opiate of the masses used to exploit workers.[46] This logic is also illustrated by the work of the 1854 Select Committee on Intemperance, which similarly assumed that alcohol caused the problems associated with it. Once alcohol was understood as a poison, harmful for the individual drinker and for society in general, demands for stricter controls were an obvious response.

Prohibition and Big Government

The temperance movement of the 1850s became increasingly focused on lobbying governments for such restrictions, and this kind of overtly political temperance would become the public face of the movement by the later nineteenth century, arguably to the detriment of its message.[47] But these calls for intervention were always based on an understanding of the colony as a democratic polity and were thus framed in democratic terms. Both as an interest group and as an idea, temperance contributed to the broader revolution in government that saw the responsibilities of the state expand substantially in the late nineteenth century.[48]

Calls for government intervention were a constant source of controversy within the movement. When Gipps spoke at his first meeting in 1838 he argued that solving alcohol problems "depends less upon the exertions of the legislature than it does on the exertions of individuals," a view closely aligned with patronizing temperance.[49] He supported plans before the Legislative Council to include wholesale dealers under the Licensing Act but cautioned that "excessive legislation defeats itself," arguing that high duties or import bans would only promote smuggling. Instead, he called on the audience to "use your utmost influence both by example and precept, and bring the force of public opinion to bear." Many prominent supporters of the Temperance Society shared Gipps's aversion to what they deemed "politics," opposing any call for greater regulation of alcohol.[50]

But increasingly radical temperance was demanding greater political intervention, even submitting an (unsuccessful) petition for prohibition to the council in 1841.[51] The conflict over regulation is well illustrated by Saunders, who walked a difficult line as both the long-time secretary of the Temperance Society and an active teetotaller. In an editorial in the *Temperance Magazine* Saunders argued for restrictions on the sale, import, and production of spirits, but claimed that, "connected as we are with the Temperance Society, we do not call for legislative enactment; but we have no hesitation in saying, that such an enactment, and a very wide and very strong one, would be beneficial."[52] This distinction between a "call for legislative enactment" and a strongly expressed opinion in its favour seems very fine indeed. But it was echoed in the first edition of *The Teetotaler*, where Saunders claimed that while the paper and teetotal societies in general were "non-political," he reserved the right to comment on "questions involving the social interests, or the political rights and privileges of the community at large."[53] What this forced language demonstrates is the growing tension between Saunders's own views and those of his elite patrons, between the radical aspirations of passionate temperance advocates on the one hand and the much more conservative approach demanded by the movement's elite funders on the other. It also shows that legislative temperance was still a minority view.

But by the 1850s, Saunders's position was normal, and government intervention of some form was widely accepted as the solution to the drink problem. One feature of the public debate over a Maine law in New South Wales was that practically all participants accepted that stronger regulation was needed to combat the problems caused by alcohol. Both daily papers, *The Empire* and *The Herald*, editorialized against prohibition, but they both supported the principle and hedged their opposition with calls for what they deemed more practical regulation. *The Empire* approvingly described the reforms as "the beginning of a radical change in the moral system of governments ... [by] setting the laws and the executive to keep watch and ward over the causes instead of the effects" of social evils, while *The Herald* explicitly endorsed proposals for committing habitual drunkards to asylums.[54] A similar endorsement of government intervention was a feature of the 1854 Select Committee. While the witnesses disagreed about the practical details, almost all endorsed stricter liquor laws. Temperance ideas were a significant contributor to the expansion of government in the later nineteenth century.

8

Drinking as a Gendered Performance

On 13 August 1857, a letter from Sarah Sands was published in *The Sydney Morning Herald*. Describing the recent banquet for electoral reform, a typical "public" dinner of men, she claimed that "the ladies of Australia deem it a very equivocal honour to have their healths drank by the Electoral Reform League."[1] This league was the latest in a series of democratic organizations formed in New South Wales since the mid-1840s devoted to expanding the franchise and voting rights on broadly Chartist principles.[2] But, as was typical of the period, their campaign was concerned solely with the rights of men and centred on a demand for universal male suffrage. Indeed, universal suffrage was typically assumed to refer solely to men.[3]

At the banquet Sands referred to, held at the Lyceum Theatre, over a hundred gentlemen dined in the theatre itself, but the boxes in the dress circle were reserved for ladies to observe the proceedings; this is presumably where Sands acquired her first-person account. William Arnold, a newly elected member of the Legislative Assembly, gave the toast in question, and in his speech, he noted that it had been "sneeringly remarked" that the logic of the league's arguments would result in granting the franchise to women. Rather than denying such an obvious absurdity, he suggested that women already had considerable political power and called on his female listeners to refuse to hear suitors who were not enfranchised, arguing that this would "enlist a powerful body of reformers" and lead to universal male suffrage. Returning thanks on behalf of the silently observing ladies was William Benbow, the honorary secretary of the league. According to Sands, Benbow said that "women are not mentally inferior to men ... [but] their mission is to shine, and, by their influence, aid in moulding the aspirations of man, harmonising discord, and civilizing mankind."[4]

Sands was unconvinced. Describing the gesture as "a buttered toast" devoid of real loyalty or "gallantry," she argued that the only women the league was concerned with were those "whose sympathies may be entrapped by drinking to or 'treating' them," asking, "Is it not enough, that they should debar us from the franchise, but that they should also seek to deprive us of what little influence we have in the social scale?" She noted an earlier speech Benbow had given in which he suggested that "men of property" wasted money on "fine dresses their ladies wear," while working men lived in poverty.[5] Sands's acerbic response was to suggest that it was impossible for women to execute their mission to "shine" if they were denied such finery. The league could not speak on behalf of women or claim loyalty to the Queen since "where there is loyalty to rank there is also loyalty to ... the female sex."[6]

Unfortunately, Sands cannot be definitively identified, and her motivations are accordingly difficult to unpack.[7] Assuming she was a female spectator at the dinner – and this seems likely given the focus of her letter and the fact that she quoted from a speech that was otherwise unreported – she can be understood as a frustrated radical, infuriated by the hypocrisy of colonial democracy. She declined to have a league devoted to securing an exclusive male privilege speak on her behalf. But more was at stake here than a question of female honour, of political influence, or even of female suffrage – the political question that would increasingly concern the emerging feminist movement. Beyond Sands's explicit concerns, the practice of toasting the ladies embodied the gendered nature of political society and the ways this was evoked through alcohol. As we have seen, toasting at public dinners was a central political ritual in democratizing New South Wales, and the exclusion of women from these occasions mirrored and symbolized their exclusion from the public sphere more broadly. Reinforcing the patriarchal ideology of separate spheres, the excessive and reverential praise of "the ladies," largely in their absence, had become an obligatory toast, one that celebrated an ideal of respectable domesticated womanhood, at once objectifying and patronizing women.

A year earlier, at the "National Banquet" held to celebrate responsible government, another dinner organized so that the public tables of dining gentlemen could be discreetly observed by fashionable ladies in the privacy of the dress circle, Justice Dickinson proposed a toast to "Lady Denison and the Ladies of New South Wales." In an exemplary display of the form, he decried the reserving of this toast for the end of the evening, but deemed it the place of honour, and argued, to loud applause, that "the existence in every community of refined ladies was of higher interest and political importance than any constitution, however perfect, or any form of Government however responsible ... Equal laws would always produce heroes, statesmen, poets, and philosophers, but the society of refined ladies, alone could fashion and produce gentlemen." He stressed the unparalleled "elegance and refinement" of the colonial ladies "presided over by Lady Denison," praising her exemplary virtues, benevolence, "influence and zeal in good works," and "unaffected grace."[8] Such hyperbole was a backhanded compliment. If public dinners were a stage for an emerging colonial democracy, then women were imagined as its scenery, an adornment necessary to the plot, but denied a speaking part. As Marc Baer has argued of political dinners in England, though they were often "politically radical," in their gender politics they were "culturally conservative," while Rémy Duthille notes that women were treated "as objects, not subjects of toasting."[9]

And yet, Dickinson's insistence on the political importance of women was not entirely disingenuous. In the passive role imagined for them, as an ideal, an inspiration, and a source of morality, women were essential to colonial politics. Indeed, another feature of the British political imaginary as it evolved in colonial New

South Wales was the distinctive importance it placed on feminine exemplars, especially aristocratic wives like Lady Denison. The celebration of women either, as a passive audience or in their absence, symbolizes their deliberate exclusion from citizenship in the emerging democracy. Any deviation from the ideal scripted through such toasts branded women as vicious whores or unfeminine scolds, while complying with it meant accepting the doctrine of separate spheres, which the toasts embodied and scripted. However, women had more agency in practice than such ideals might imply. In particular, women like Sands could – and did – legitimately enter the public sphere by deferring to gendered expectations about women's interests and concerns. Though required to watch from the gallery, Sands felt empowered to attack the male speakers, focusing specifically on their lack of gallantry. Public debate about feminine concerns like manners, morality, family rights, education, and health were potentially, and increasingly, open to female voices.

Toasting can thus illustrate the gendered nature of colonial democracy; and alcohol more generally illustrates the gendered British political imaginary. By analyzing the performative construction of masculinity and femininity in relation to the potent cultural symbol of drinking, I unpack both elements of Joan Scott's explicitly historicizing definition of gender: the "perceived differences between the sexes" that serve as a legitimating signifier of "relationships of power."[10] The ideology of separate spheres, which was so essential to the emerging respectable democratic society, was performatively constituted through gender-segregated drinking rituals.[11]

Drinking was imagined differently for men and women, in ways that intersected with other forms of identity, notably status, and class.[12] Dominant forms of masculinity in eighteenth- and nineteenth-century Britain operated in a symbiotic relationship with fraternal drinking cultures. The capacity to hold one's drink often served as a test of manliness, empowering men to speak and act authoritatively. Even where the dominant form of masculinity rejected drunkenness, elite men often performed other subordinate or even subversive masculinities that celebrated unrestrained alcoholic excess.[13] The men who first colonized New South Wales came from a culture that celebrated an ideal of gentlemanly politeness and chivalry, even as such gentlemen often performed their manliness in displays of restrained but excessive drinking.[14] This dialectic of masculinity, in which sobriety and drunkenness – or restraint and release – were in productive tension, helped to form the political authority of the gentleman, and in so doing, reinforce the gendered political imaginary that coded participation in the public sphere as masculine.

From the 1830s onward the new temperance movement was at the vanguard of an Evangelical and humanitarian culture that emphasized respectable domesticity – a key element of Roe's "moral enlightenment" – and attacked male drunkenness as idle and irresponsible.[15] However, most respectable and otherwise domesticated men were not strictly sober; they continued to drink with other men, and such fraternal drinking remained a powerful imaginative space. As John Tosh argues for Britain, men of all classes – but especially the middle classes – measured themselves against an ideal of patriarchal domestic authority as husband and father, but also celebrated homosociality, often centred on drinking, which could function as "a means of reinforcing gender privilege."[16] The performance of restrained self-control, including while drinking, became a metaphorical test of citizenship, even for respectable domesticated men, in a democratic society. Ward's "legendary" masculinity and its celebration of drunken freedom was a subversive response to the dominant culture of restraint if not sobriety, but similarly reflects the broader dialectic.[17]

For respectable British women, regardless of their class, public drunkenness was always shameful and unfeminine, and drinking was only acceptably restrained when conducted in private, among equally respectable company, and chaperoned by men. While women like Sands contested the public sphere and politicized their femininity, they could only do so by performing scrupulous sobriety, a key symbolic marker of the dominant feminine ideal.[18] In contrast, plebian drinking culture was much more tolerant of female drinking, drinking practices were more genuinely egalitarian – not simply fraternal – and the carnivalesque inversion of norms associated with popular culture often celebrated women's sexuality and drunkenness.[19] But precisely for this reason, female drunkenness was a symbol of deviance, especially sexual immorality, and the figure of the female drunkard was an obsession of moral reformers and temperance advocates, on the front line of a colonial culture war. Anne Summers has influentially depicted colonial women as trapped between two invidious cultural roles, as "damned whores [or] God's police," condemned to either be objectified as guardians of domestic morals or shamed for failing to achieve this impossible ideal, and alcohol was a symbol of this invidious distinction.[20] Subsequent feminist scholarship has helped to restore the agency of colonial women in the face of such limited stereotypes, notably in relation to their active involvement in both the liquor trade and, by the later decades of the century, the temperance movement.[21] However, in the mid-nineteenth-century public sphere women were rarely active participants, but were instead largely scripted as servants, wives, and mothers, and drunkenness challenged these idealized roles.[22]

The ratio of the sexes was a key influence on the development of these gender roles in colonial New South Wales. Throughout the nineteenth century, men outnumbered women: at the first colonial census in 1833, just over a quarter of the New South Wales population was female; by 1861, it was 43 per cent; parity was only reached in the mid-twentieth century.[23] While some imbalance was typical of frontier societies, the levels in the early colony were often extreme, making it unlikely that most colonial men could find a female partner. As scholars have observed, this decisively shaped early gender relations in the colony and likely encouraged an emphasis on homosocial bonding (and homosexual relations), often over alcohol, and sharpened concerns about female morals. Even at the time, commentators were aware of the disparity and saw it as both politically significant and implicated in drinking practices. Lonely bachelors were understood as more likely to get drunk, and the domesticated home was consistently promoted by social reformers, and the state, as a means of reducing crime and immorality, and producing reliable citizens.[24]

I begin here with an account of the gendered nature of toasting in the British world and colonial New South Wales, showing how it served to script a hegemonic masculinity that grounded political authority in restrained comportment and self-control, while idealizing demure and virtuous femininity. I also explore the complex relationship between drinking and masculine competition at different social levels, especially in terms of drunken violence. I then turn to women's drinking, analyzing how the more liberated drinking of convict women served as a symbol of their immorality and exacerbated the construction of female public drinking as shameful and unfeminine. Finally, I show how the respectable femininity associated with temperance was a key means of politicizing women, even as the movement reflected the times in its male leadership.

Toasting and the Performance of Masculinity

The toasting ritual at the centre of my argument was a stereotypically male affair. With rare exceptions – notably some Chartist dinners – women were excluded from public toasting, and even in private contexts, where women could sometimes participate, it was a highly gendered practice that performatively scripted ideals of masculinity and femininity.[25] Rémy Duthille interprets toasting as a ritual that reinforced the hegemonic masculinity of polite gentlemen, both through the gendered celebration of female beauty and virtue, and as a substitute for violence, sublimating masculine competition into rhetoric and drinking capacity.[26] Two distinct and likely apocryphal stories about the etymological origin of toasting illustrate these distinct gendered meanings.

In 1709, Joseph Addison claimed that toasting originated in a witticism by a "gay fellow half fuddled" that allegedly "gave foundation to the present honour which is done to the lady we mention in our liquors, who has ever since been called a toast."[27] Citing this account Duthille suggests that toasting, as distinct from healthing, was a new fashionable practice, "a male homage to female virtue," confined to the male urban elite, that emerged in the early eighteenth century and was linked to the rise of gentlemen's clubs.[28] In this form, echoes of which continued into the nineteenth century, men in private company competed to offer the most eloquent toast to the most fashionably beautiful ladies, a practice that was potentially humiliating for the women named – since their virtue was implicitly drawn into question – as well as for those ignored, since they were implicitly deemed insufficiently attractive. But as Newman argues, what originated as a "misogynistic" and sexualized practice increasingly reinforced bourgeois domesticity by idealizing women as "a curb to masculine excess."[29]

In contrast, later in the century, William Brand reported that the saying "I'll pledge you" originated out of a need for the drinker to be guarded against a surprise attack while they drank.[30] This rival account illustrates what Duthille terms the "undercurrent of violence" that was always latent in homosocial drunkenness. Toasting, with its emphasis on restrained self-control while intoxicated and its competitive displays of rhetoric, channelled such violence into a socially acceptable form "between barbarity and effeminacy." As Charles Ludington argues, in Regency England, drinking was bound by rules that "ensured that everyone's manhood was tested fairly and equally," and, specifically, that "less than full glasses [were] deemed unmanly and disrespectful."[31]

One key space in which toasting took on these gendered features was male-only clubs, which proliferated in the eighteenth century at every social level, from the exclusive gentlemen's clubs of Mayfair to working men's drinking societies.[32] Valérie Capdeville argues that clubs polarized separate spheres by reifying the idea that topics like politics were reserved for men, and that women were an "obstacle to masculine sociability and liberty," in stark contrast to French salons of the same period.[33] Similarly, Anya Taylor shows how Romantic writers framed such fraternal, convivial drinking as manly, in opposition to effeminate dandies, celebrated homosocial bonding over heterosexual love, and resorted to outright misogyny in drunken boasting about their sexual conquests, often while neglecting their wives.[34] Ironically, a preference for masculine company protected English men from their fears of being seen as effeminate. Classic toasting sentiments, deployed in such homosocial environments, helped to reinforce gender roles. A telling example is the following conservative toast: "May he who has neither wife, mistress, nor estate in Britain, never have a share in its government."[35] Patriarchal mastery of women was a test of masculine authority, celebrated in drink.

Even in private company, where women could drink with men, their drinking practices were highly gendered. John Trusler, in his guide to the *Honours of the Table*, published in the 1790s, suggested that during dinner it was "unseemly in ladies" to ask for wine, and called for gentlemen to display their chivalry by ordering their wine and drinking with them in a reciprocal toast marked with a bow. More importantly, he suggested that, "Habit having made a pint of wine after dinner almost necessary to a man who eats freely, which is not the case with women, and as their sitting and drinking with the men, would be unseemly; it is customary, after the cloth and desert are removed and two or three glasses of wine are gone round, for the ladies to retire and leave the men to themselves."[36] This expectation that ladies would withdraw after the meal allowed them to avoid any disreputable association with drunkenness, and the gentlemen to toast, drink, and discuss "public" affairs deemed unsuitable for women.[37] But the practice was unusual in wider European society and the subject of frequent comment by foreign observers.[38]

From the turn of the nineteenth century, and gathering strength in the Victorian era, there was an increasing resistance to male drunkenness after dinner, associated with the rise of respectable and domestic manners and the growth of the middle classes. The *Royal Toast Master* described withdrawing as a "brutal custom" that led to "boisterous and illiberal mirth," contrasted Britain unfavourably with the "refinement and delicacy in … manners which is the boast of neighbouring nations," and framed its collection of sentiments as "calculated to banish indecency – to introduce the fair sex to their original right of partaking in all our pleasures." Importantly, the author stressed that ladies should only participate in a manner "consistent with that modesty which so eminently distinguishes our British fair," suggesting they could toast "over their tea and chocolate."[39] Even when women were present, they were not imagined as equal participants in the ritual, which continued to ascribe political authority to male speakers and drinkers. More commonly, fashionable etiquette still saw women leave the table first, but it was increasingly seen as unchivalrous for gentlemen to leave the ladies waiting, and the drawing room where they joined them was a feminine space in which drunkenness was disgraceful and especial restraint required.

This elite British drinking culture was brought to New South Wales by the earliest colonists. Joseph Holt, a political prisoner, was exiled for his role in the Irish Rebellion of 1798. Once in the colony, he established himself as a farmer, and his later memoirs illustrate the importance of drinking among colonial gentlemen.[40] In a typical episode, shortly after his arrival he met the famed pickpocket turned police officer George Barrington in company with the judge advocate, Richard Atkins, and was invited back to the latter's house. There, "[a] bottle of rum was produced, and some pleasant conversation about Ireland passed. At length I wished to retire, but Mr Atkins said he never allowed any bottle off his table till he saw it emptied. We finished the half-gallon bottle [ca 25 standard drinks each!], and were of course not a little elevated, being each of us as full of chatter as a hen magpie in May." Condemned by his wife on his return home, Holt was able to reassure her that "the hotter the climate, the more spirits might be drank, which I afterwards found to be the case."[41] Such drinking was extreme – indeed, Atkins's drunkenness was notorious, even for New South Wales – but it typifies both the importance of alcohol to sociability and the way that drinking to excess while maintaining a nominally restrained comportment served as a test of manliness for gentlemen, but a test that only took place in unmixed male company.[42] While such excess became increasingly unfashionable over the course of the century, drinking remained associated with manliness.

In early New South Wales mixed-gender dining was rarer than in England, largely because women – especially women of status – were rarer. The viceregal circle took on particular importance as the centre of the social scene and the main space where such fashionable dining could occur. The Macquaries, Lachlan and Elizabeth, sought to establish a more traditional "society" in the colony, and from their arrival there were increased opportunities for respectable socializing between elite men and women. But such occasions only illustrate the disproportionate ratio between the sexes, made particularly acute by scruples about feminine respectability, that prevented the governor's wife from dining with anyone not deemed a lady.[43] At the traditional viceregal dinner to celebrate the King's birthday, there were only four women among the seventy-two guests invited in 1811; none were invited in 1812 because Lady Macquarie was unwell; and, from 1813, a separate mixed supper was held after the gentlemen dined on their own.[44] Balls were a more obviously mixed social occasion and sometimes involved a supper at which toasts were given with ladies present (though never speaking); but often this part of the evening was segregated, with the ladies withdrawing from the toasts. On such occasions, press reports often indulged in a clichéd celebration of "the triumph of Venus over Bacchus," as the men made haste to rejoin the ladies.[45]

Accounts of Sydney life from the 1820s onward – when numbers of non-convict women were increasing – show the transition from a bachelor society to one in which fashionable ladies and gentlemen could socialize over alcohol. In the 1820s, Peter Cunningham noted that much socializing was confined to men, but stressed that etiquette and fashion were crucial among the elite, and the "usual routine" involved "dinners among the gentlemen ... followed up by tea or coffee, evening parties and *petits soupes* (to include the attendance of the ladies) ... [with] dancing and music winding up the entertainments."[46] A London paper published observations on the colony in 1834, claiming that "among the higher circles at Sydney, too, we understand the habits of French society are generally introduced. – At dinner parties, the rule is to drink what you please during dinner; but after the ladies have retired, but two glasses are allowed before they are joined in the drawing room by the gentlemen."[47]

By the 1840s, elite masculinity was increasingly domesticated and respectable feminine manners predominated in society. Louisa Meredith, the wife of a squatter and magistrate in the 1840s, published an account of the colony in which she ruthlessly identified the failings of colonial manners; even still, she stressed that "English customs and fashions are carefully followed" and confined her complaints about dining to the lack of good conversation and the impossibility of finding good servants.[48] Mary Vidal, in her novel *Bengala*, loosely based on her experiences as the wife of an Anglican clergyman and farmer in the 1840s, gave an account of such domestic toasting at a family picnic, illustrating that even when integrated, the ritual remained a performance of separate gender roles. She reports her female heroine's "dismay" when a drunken Mr Budd, rising to toast plans for a new bridge and church in the district, "swung his glass round his head and waved himself to and fro in delight." When an opponent of the project began a rival toast in opposition, he was interrupted and told it was "unfitted to the occasion [and] hardly fair to the ladies," and the toasting ceased entirely when another gentleman was prevailed upon to sing.[49]

The toasting of the new monarch, Victoria, who came to the throne in 1837, illustrates how the ritual remained highly gendered, even as the performance was increasingly restrained. As we have seen, under male monarchs, the toast to the King was a proud display of loyalty, associated with the manly political virtues on which Britain's greatness was thought to depend. In contrast, the toast given by Governor Gipps at the first colonial celebration of the Queen's birthday in 1838 – a ball for six hundred guests at Government House – referred to the virtues of earlier English queens, namely Elizabeth and Anne, and praised Victoria's "amiable disposition and extensive acquirements." His speech was in turn praised by the editor of *The Gazette* for handling the topic "with much feeling and chasteness of expression" and demonstrating "the superior character of the British nation … in regard to the estimation in which it holds the female sex."[50]

At public dinners, like those described above, women were increasingly able to attend and witness if not participate in the ritual. When such dinners were held on a smaller scale, ladies might even remain at the table for the toasts, as they sometimes did during balls. At a dinner of the Goulburn Circuit Court in 1848, married gentlemen were accompanied by their wives and elder daughters so that, of the forty guests, ten of those named in the press were women. They remained at the table for the six formal toasts, including the first to the Queen, given by Attorney General John Hubert Plunkett, who stressed that it should be undertaken with even "greater enthusiasm" since they were "honoured by the presence of so many of her most gracious Majesty's own sex." Demonstrating how rare this was, he told the company that "we even expect to hear the sweet voices of our fair friends mingled with our own, in the usual honours to the toast."[51] In the democratic era, women were occasional witnesses to and even participants in toasting, but it remained a fundamentally masculine performance, and one that reinforced the ideology of separate spheres.

Competitive Drinking: Men, Alcohol, and Violence

While plebian drinking – and the drunken comportment associated with it – lacked the formal, rule-bound restraint of the toasting ritual, it also functioned as a competitive performance of masculine authority. In an early example, David Collins reported an incident on Christmas Eve 1797 in which two young settlers, "boasting of their respective abilities in drinking ... challenged each other to a trial of their skill," which resulted in the death of one and severe injury to the other from alcohol poisoning.[52] More typically, competition was sublimated but could still explode into violence, which often ended in court. Henry Butler was convicted of the manslaughter of Benjamin Davis in 1821, despite the fact that "the most friendly terms had subsisted between them." After a two-day bender that left them both "stupidly drunk," they planned a threshing contest, with Butler telling Davis, "I'll soon wind you," and then suddenly, unaccountably, and fatally attacking him.[53] Sometimes such fights were bound by a code of unofficial rules, and juries were often sympathetic to this. James Carty was tried for the manslaughter of James Ingram in 1853 after the two began drinking together and an "altercation ensued as to who was the best man, and the deceased challenged the prisoner to fight." Witnesses reported that the fight was "fair," since both men had seconds, they fought in rounds, and had both willingly stood up, and though Carty was committed for trial, he was found not guilty.[54]

Especially for convicts, alcohol encouraged assertions of independence and freedom from rules. In 1789, in an early case before the judge advocate's bench, Samuel Barsby was charged with drunkenly abusing and striking two marines, refusing to obey their orders, and challenging their "having any authority over him."[55] Refusing to drink could also serve as an insult linked to the fraternal solidarity drinking created. For convicts, whose drinking was potentially punishable by flogging, it could be interpreted as a sign that the sober man was a class traitor who might inform on the drinkers. In a complex murder case in 1814, George Atkinson reported that he was forced to join a toast with the accused, with his drinking taken to indicate complicity in their violent plot.[56] Similarly, in 1848 Thomas Wood was indicted for assaulting Samuel Schofield; he claimed in his defence that Schofield had "asked him to take some liquor" and picked a fight when he refused.[57]

Of course, much alcohol-related violence occurred between genders, and here, too, it illustrates the ways that masculine authority was tested when men drank. Husbands and partners often used violence to assert their authority. As Paula Byrne argues, reflecting the patriarchal assumptions of the time, domestic violence was "unlikely" to be brought to court unless it was "extreme," repeated, or directly witnessed, and she suggests that intoxication was often raised as an exonerating factor, but only when both partners were drunk.[58] In 1839, a convict, Mary Dunlop, sought police protection from her husband, a "low drunken blackguard" who frequently caused her to flee the house in fear. The court found her husband was already awaiting trial for drunkenness and disorderly conduct, but the only protection it could offer her was a return to the Female Factory.[59] On the same day, James Duff, an emigrant worker "of good family and acquirements" but frequently before the courts since he arrived in New South Wales, was charged with an assault that left his wife – unfortunately though perhaps revealingly unnamed in the sources – in a critical condition. John McGrath, their landlord, gave evidence that "his conduct to her was outrageous; he was constantly intoxicated and ill-treating her," while Duff's lawyers produced a surgeon's certificate that cast "considerable doubt [on] whether the man has been of sane mind for some time," the direct result of "habitual drunkenness."[60] Her injuries prevented her testimony and the case was deferred and never resumed, suggesting that she refused to prosecute him despite her ill-treatment. The frequency of such drunken violence against women contributed to their strong support of the temperance movement.

A rare incident from 1844 in which the conduct of drunken gentlemen came before the courts illustrates how restrained comportment – and specifically self-control over violence while drinking – functioned as a test of responsibility. To celebrate the election of new members, Sydney Municipal Council held a dinner on 12 December 1844 at Petty's Hotel. In the early hours of the next morning, William Moir was regaling the remaining company with a Scottish air when Thomas Ryan, heavily intoxicated and apparently regarding the song as a sectarian insult, hurled his tumbler of whiskey at his fellow councillor, slicing open his head. Following the unprovoked attack, Ryan collapsed insensible in his chair, at which point two magistrates, Alderman Wiltshire and Police Commissioner William Augustus Miles, ordered his arrest. Once at the police office, Moir declined to prosecute the case against a fellow gentleman, and Ryan was never formally charged. However, despite the latter writing a letter of apology and offering to pay medical bills, the two parties could not reach an agreement, and Moir eventually pursued a civil remedy in the Supreme Court. In evidence, it appeared that Ryan rarely drank, could not hold his liquor, and was probably unaware of his actions at the time, but the jury found for Moir and awarded him fifty pounds damages and costs.[61]

This incident is highly revealing of elite masculinity and its changing associations with drinking. Moir and Ryan were both part of an emerging colonial middle class and as such they likely felt considerable pressure to perform the part of gentlemen – including attending public dinners and toasting, which all but necessitated drunkenness. In a particularly clear example of this obligation, the incoming mayor and president of the Australian Total Abstinence Society, George Allen, felt compelled to attend public dinners, including this one, despite the fact that he refused to drink, proudly performing his lonely sobriety. Allen repeatedly attacked traditional upper-class drinking practices in his private journal while noting that "gentlemen seem astonished that any one [*sic*] can deprive themselves of the precious fluid."[62] In the case of the 1844 dinner, despite protests by some witnesses that the members of the party, Ryan excepted, were sober, the evidence provided by the hotel's owner showed that in addition to the seven cases of wine that had accompanied the dinner, those who remained had consumed nine bottles of brandy.[63] In effect, these assertions of sobriety were not about the amount of alcohol consumed; rather, they represented a claim to have performed restrained comportment – to have maintained self-control while intoxicated – as befitted a respectable gentleman, a test that Ryan clearly failed.

Equally, the way the affair was resolved also illustrates a distinct and closely related gentlemanly code of honour that, like the competitive drinking of the toasting ritual, was a means of disciplining potential violence.[64] All witnesses agreed that Ryan was drunk, and though he subsequently claimed to have no memory of the event, his assault was certainly a police matter. But Ryan sought a resolution by offering his "unfeigned regret" and to "make ... any other concession and reparation within my power, which you may require at my hands." *The Chronicle* endorsed this extra-judicial approach to an insult between gentlemen, calling for Mr Ryan to make "whatever apology or atonement" two gentlemen, one appointed by each party, should recommend, and for Moir to accept it. The civil court proceedings that concluded the affair were thus a consequence of the breakdown of the informal system that gentlemen used to resolve their disputes. Summing up the case, the new chief justice, Alfred Stephen, regretted that it had ever come to trial and described the affair as "in some degree disgraceful to all parties concerned."[65] In an earlier era, the incident might well have ended in a duel, but by the mid-nineteenth century, respectable gentlemen increasingly defined themselves by avoiding violence and conducting themselves with restraint.

Such respectable masculinity in turn inspired an increasingly self-conscious defence of free-thinking, free-drinking manhood, a culture war that Marilyn Lake saw as decisive in the late nineteenth century. Some men reacted against the domestic ideal of restraint by marginalizing their critics as "wowsers" – effeminate, sanctimonious, and boring. While the term itself was a later coinage, the idea of temperance as a form of hypocritical cant or humbug preached by sanctimonious do-gooders who frequently failed to live up to their own values, emerged alongside the movement itself.[66] This often took the form of satirical mockery, and one frequent target of such humour was George Allen, who attracted particular attention as a notable teetotaller holding public office. *Bell's* described him as "sleek-haired Allen" and devised a mock inscription for his house: "A large cellar with no beer, / A large house with no cheer."[67]

Louisa Atkinson, an early colonial novelist, published a short story entitled "Be a Man" in 1857, a kind of temperance tale in which drinking leads to moral and physical disaster. It can serve as a particularly vivid illustration of what was at stake in this contest over masculinity at different social levels.[68] The narrator attends a respectable family dinner at which, after the ladies had "left the table" – in this "simple country family" by simply withdrawing to another part of the dining room – the son, Henry (Hal), was encouraged to drink by his father through the titular phrase "be a man!" The call is "several times repeated by others round the table," and when Hal rises, having drunk reluctantly, "his bright eyes, were red, and his cheeks glazed" in drunkenness. The dinner guests then visit a shearing shed where the working-class shearers beg an extra glass of spirits "to drink the ladies' health." Becoming drunk, they send Robert, the youngest shearer, out to buy more spirits and then taunt him to "be a man" and join their drinking party, the resulting drunkenness causing them to fail to complete the shearing before the arrival of a storm. The narrator visits the family again a few years later and hears them condemn their drunken workers, over their own wine, while learning that Robert has died in a drunken accident. Hal has now become a drunkard himself, and his father again calls on him to "be a man," now meaning for him to control his drinking. The narrative concludes with the much-quoted (at least by the temperance movement) biblical verse that "Wine is a mocker; strong drink is raging; and whosoever is deceived thereby is not wise" (Proverbs 20:1).[69]

This fascinating story reveals much about gender roles – and their intersection with social class – through the medium of alcohol. Hal fails the test of respectable masculinity twice: first by declining to drink with other men, and subsequently in his lack of manly self-control and restraint. Robert is also undone by the pressure for men to drink, which sets him on the road to his drunken fate. Atkinson's story also implicitly condemns the hypocrisy of the land-owning family and contrasts the restrained but toxic drinking of the gentlemen with the disorderly and idle drunken celebration of their workers. Interestingly, she reserves her strongest condemnation, though subtly delivered, for Hal's mother, who fails to prevent his initial drinking, and is drinking wine herself as she reports Robert's death, which foreshadows her own son's likely fate. The story captures the contested importance of alcohol as a test of citizenship in a masculine democracy. Male citizens had to display restrained or sober comportment – by masterful drinking or performative abstinence – and their failure to do so was a symbol of their incapacity for self-government. But for women, any public drinking was shameful, especially as it undermined the respectable domesticity of the feminine home, and their symbolic guardianship over morality.

Female Drinking and the Stigma of Drunkenness

Integrated drinking between men and women was common but usually deviant in early New South Wales. Ann Davis was the first woman hanged in the colony, condemned after she was found guilty of breaking and entering to steal clothing. In her defence she claimed to have been drinking "a considerable quantity of grog" with two other convict women and three sailors from the *Sirius*, though the other women denied drinking, and the sailors denied providing the alcohol.[70] While Davis took full responsibility for the crime at the gallows – and was also drunk as she was executed, probably as a mercy – it seems likely that she was part of a mixed drinking party. Accounts of mixed drinking are rare outside of court cases like this one, and the condemnation of moral reformers, but it was clearly a common feature of plebian culture, as it was in late eighteenth-century London, with the men typically treating women who drank with them. Convicts often had at least an ambivalent view of respectable moral codes.

However, the literate elite of the colony typically – though often hypocritically – condemned mixed drinking and especially female drunkenness. The colony's second clergyman, Rev. Samuel Marsden, was a key critic, arguing in 1806 that the spirit trade was responsible for "Many Separations between Husbands and wives," and claiming drunken women bartered away all their family's possessions and turned to prostitution in order to get liquor.[71] As Joy Damousi has shown, such criticisms involved a clear double standard, and the naval surgeon and prison reformer Thomas Reid illustrates her point.[72] He warned convicts that drunkenness was "disgraceful" but "in a woman it is always associated with abandonment and detestation," and argued that due to women's "weaker minds [spirits] may be said to exert a most dangerous influence, injurious to their health and morals, and subversive of good order."[73] Reid made explicit what underlay much of this discourse: the idea that only men had the physical capacity to drink and the requisite rationality to govern their drunken conduct.

As Marsden's arguments show, female drunkenness symbolized a disordered society. In a series of editorials in *The Monitor* in 1830, E.S. Hall argued that the treatment of convict women by the colonial authorities was "much too lenient," in contrast to the excessive severity with which male convicts were flogged. He cited a series of recently arrived women who were assigned to private households as servants, only to be very swiftly arrested for public drunkenness in the company of men and sent to the Female Factory, as evidence that "women sent to this Colony, are much more immoral (having less judgment) than the male convict."[74] As Erin Ihde has argued, Hall's journalism was "at times inconsistent and contradictory." He was deeply concerned about the effect of disproportionate sex ratios on convict men – indeed, he argued that transportation should be made the default punishment for female crime in England, to ensure a steady supply of wives for the colony – but was simultaneously a harsh critic of the morals and conduct of convict women, insisting that female migrants should be "virtuous, industrious, sober and skilful" while condemning female drunkenness.[75] The figure of the drunken convict whore remained a key symbol of the problems with the colony into the 1830s and was widely cited by the hostile witnesses to the 1837 Select Committee on Transportation.[76]

These arguments linked to a long tradition that saw female drunkenness as a threat to public health and focused on drunken mothers neglecting their children, as in Hogarth's *Gin Lane*.[77] Two similar cases in May of 1839 illustrate the trope. Ellen Henry was charged with the manslaughter of her young daughter because she "had given herself up to inebriation, which deadened her maternal feelings, and led to the neglect which caused the death of her child." The surgeon who conducted the autopsy found "want of nutriment" as the cause of death and testified that "ardent spirits taken by the mother would have an injurious effect upon the child at the breast." Henry was subsequently found guilty of manslaughter and sentenced to two years in jail.[78] The next day, Catherine Ward was charged with neglecting her young daughter Eliza. While she and her husband were out drinking, their room caught fire and Eliza had to be rescued by a passing baker. The doctor treating the infant testified that Ward refused to care for her daughter's wounds, contributing to her subsequent death, while several witnesses commented on "the drunken, dissolute habits of the mother, and ... her neglect of the child." Despite this, she was found not guilty and released with a warning from the bench about the "depravity and wickedness of her conduct."[79] Notably, the father's neglect passed without mention.

While male drunkenness was often linked with crime and especially violence, female drunkenness was more typically framed in terms of vice and virtue and seen as a symptom of moral degradation that threatened social order, and both policing and punishment reflect this double standard. In November 1823 the police broke up a drinking party in the Rocks, where they found two men and three women, all "intoxicated." The men, both visiting sailors, were returned to their ship and the discipline of their captain, but the women, who were not convicts but "known ... as the most abandoned of their species," received three months hard labour in the factory at Parramatta.[80] Convicts in particular were subjected to gendered punishments for drunkenness. While female convicts were usually spared corporal punishment, they were instead subjected to imprisonment, sometimes combined with humiliations like head shaving and the withdrawal of privileges, and drunken women were typically confined to the stocks or, if recidivists or convicts, sent to the Female Factory. In 1799 Catherine Evans was charged with abuse and ill-treatment of her master while in a state of "beastly intoxication" and sentenced to sweep the jail for a month wearing an iron collar, a punishment specifically designed to "check the enormities committed by abandoned women whilst in a state of Drunkenness."[81] This system of gendered punishments for drunkenness was codified in the 1830s, with female convicts imprisoned or sent to the factory, while male convicts were flogged or worked on the treadmill.[82]

There is some evidence that convict women were also more likely to be charged with public order offences like drunkenness.[83] By the democratic era, the rare women who drank in public were certainly more likely to be targeted by the police. As I have argued elsewhere, during the 1840s public drunkenness became the key offence for maintaining public order in urban areas among a post-convict population, and women were overrepresented among repeat offenders, regularly highlighted in press reporting of drunkenness, and often among those who received the heaviest sentences.[84] In 1854, only 10 per cent of men but over a quarter of women sent to Darlinghurst jail for drunkenness were jailed three times or more over a six-month period.[85] Given the subjective nature of the offence, and the enormous discretion employed by police and courts in arresting and punishing drunkards, we can interpret such policing as a symbolic enforcement of gender roles. Police specifically targeted a small deviant subculture of women – some of them sex workers, but all labelled "whores" – who were in public, unchaperoned, at night.[86] A notable feature of such cases is the different language used to describe male and female drunkenness. In official records, drunken men were "abusive" and "threatening," while women were "insolent" and "disobedient," or even "depraved and corrupted."[87] Newspapers increasingly published a list of arrested drunkards, naming and shaming offenders, and reporters exercised their imagination on creative insults for such "incorrigible hags."[88]

Respectability, Temperance, and Sobriety

In the light of this discourse and the shaming of female drunkards, it is unsurprising that most women did not drink in public. The convict stain exacerbated the growing cultural distinction between the respectable and disreputable, with women anxious to avoid any association with either convictism or female sexual licence, both of which were symbolically linked to drinking. Performative public sobriety was one important element of respectable femininity as women sought not merely to live up to standards of moral conduct but to be *seen* to live up to them.

One way that elite women performed this kind of sober femininity was through patronage of charities. As Elizabeth Windschuttle has shown, women were actively involved in at least eighteen philanthropic societies in New South Wales in the first half of the nineteenth century, and many of these bodies were actively concerned with female drinking and drunkenness.[89] In the late 1820s, under the patronage of Elizabeth Darling, wife of the governor, a core group of ladies focused on improving plebian women – convict and non-convict – forming a Female Friendly Society that encouraged such women to be sober diligent servants or to marry respectable men.[90]

Elite women's concern with the conduct and virtue of female servants was telling, both about the motives for their philanthropy and their fear of the symbolic taint of drink, and in the democratic era it was widely felt by middle-class wives. Building on Nancy Armstrong's argument for "domestic fiction" as a means to imagine middle-class feminine power, Carolyn Steadman identifies an elite discourse about servants and their failings – often, ironically, addressed to them – that emerged out of the anxieties occasioned by industrialization; and as Babette Smith shows, such anxieties were especially acute in a convict colony.[91] Louisa Meredith described the failings of colonial servants in obsessive detail, focusing especially on their drunkenness. At the inn at Wiseman's Ferry , she was met by "a stupid, dirty, half-dressed, slipshod woman," and this woman's failings embodied the whole household: "Here was a substantial farm-house [and hotel] with the female inmates half-drunk and scarcely out of bed at ten o'clock on a summer's morning, rooms unswept, beds unmade, and the whole establishment telling of plenty, sloth, and drunkenness."[92] Drunken female servants served as a symbol of the wider social disorder in the colony: their appearance and manners were said to be affected by drink, which in turn both embodied and caused a disordered society. Moreover, complaining about the problem and seeking to reform the servant class was a means of performing respectable femininity.

Despite their desire for sober servants, elite women's leadership was a short-lived phase of colonial philanthropy, and the Female Friendly Society seems to have ceased after the departure of Lady Darling. In 1832, *The Gazette* published a series of "Editor's Miscellanies" calling for a renewed "Society of Ladies" to assist and advise female emigrants. Specifically, they should encourage "sobriety" in emigrants, in contrast to convicts, who "are generally given to strong liquors." In calling for "Lady-management" of institutions to help women, the editor cited "delicacy" on the part of Ms Bourke – the unmarried daughter of the recently widowed governor, and by status the First Lady of the colony – as the reason for her declining to promote such a cause, but argued that the wives of other leading colonists should volunteer.[93] His suggestion was not adopted, and married women increasingly avoided any public leadership of colonial philanthropy. As the colony democratized, respectable women increasingly shunned the public sphere because it would expose them to stigmatizing association with working-class men who might well be former convicts.

The temperance movement is both an exception to and an illustration of these trends. Temperance has long been understood as a crucial feminist cause, associated with women's suffrage throughout the British Empire in the late nineteenth century, and specifically in Australia, where the movement successfully argued that women's votes would be crucial to securing prohibition.[94] During the 1840s and '50s, growing female membership and attendance at meetings was matched by greater emphasis on women's crucial role in inspiring temperance, and on the harms experienced by women and children as a result of drink. But even as it became increasingly a movement of and for women, it was consistently led by men.

The first wave of paternalistic temperance focused on high-status women as moral exemplars. At the first general meeting of the Temperance Society in 1834, Justice Forbes noted that "the ladies had the power of doing much good, by endeavouring to rescue by their council those who were falling victim to the dreadful vice of intemperance," and subsequent meetings advertised the provision of seats especially "for the ladies." There were even calls for a dedicated society of "influential ladies" who would promote the cause "by seeking for members amongst all classes of society," though no such female temperance society formed for nearly two decades.[95] In general, the early temperance movement imagined women's political role much as Judge Dickinson would in 1856: supplementing male public advocacy with their moral influence within the home. An important editorial, reprinted in *The Teetotaller* from the *London Temperance Intelligencer*, emphasized "the great and almost irresistible power, which [women] can wield over the other sex … holding, as they do, the reins of the government of social life, and moulding the manners and forming the fashions of domestic scenes." But the author also lamented "the few occasions when females have overstepped the bounds of decorum and stood upon the platform" themselves.[96] Public speaking, even within the temperance movement, ought to be restricted to men.

Governor Gipps and his wife, Elizabeth, embodied this political vision. In 1841, Lady Gipps silently accompanied her husband to the annual meeting of the Temperance Society, and reports attributed the extensive female attendance there to her "power to set the fashion."[97] Her husband noted the "large attendance" of ladies in the audience, but prayed that their support was not simply fashionable and that they were not conniving in male drunkenness or, worse, given to intemperance themselves: "but this could hardly be, for e'er it can arrive, the creature is unsexed, the soft and endearing name of woman shall no longer be applied to her … There is nothing in the whole catalogue of crime, so thoroughly revolting as drunkenness in a woman."[98] In a classic demonstration of Summers's thesis, Gipps insisted that women who did not strive to reform society were betrayers of their angelic sex, and those who fell into drunkenness were beneath contempt, the very devils of society. It was precisely this binary framing that made it so hard for women to act in public.

The governor's fears were borne out by the lack of active female involvement in the society and the rapid decline of temperance. In stark contrast, as Windschuttle has shown, women were much more active in radical temperance, especially middle-class Dissenters.[99] Female members not only attended the regular meetings, along with their families, but also painted and sewed banners and decorations, prepared food, and led musical activities. The limited evidence of membership suggests that women may have made up as much as a third of subscribing teetotallers. Teetotal societies were more popular with women, as well as with men, because they offered entertainment and community, not merely condescension and patronage.[100]

As Windschuttle also shows, the temperance press published the first colonial newspaper column aimed at female readers.[101] But it did so strictly within the framework of separate spheres, emphasizing women's special role as moral guardians within the home. One very early contribution, by "Jemima" (but likely written by Saunders), concerns itself precisely with the reticence respectable women felt about associating themselves with the movement. The author claimed to have been offended by an invitation to a special lecture on temperance for "Ladies only" and the unchivalrous implication that ladies drank too much. She was corrected by her mother, who warned her that even "the loveliest young ladies may be betrayed into the vice of secret drinking." Saunders's editorial echoed this message, offering an argument for women's powerful influence on their husbands, children, and servants, and this ideal of feminine moral influence was a common temperance trope.[102] The column made regular arguments for domesticity, but the only contributions that had a female byline were poems that rehearsed classic temperance sentiments, and respectable colonial women seem to have avoided making public arguments in the press as well as at meetings.[103] More typically, work was anonymous, and in either case it aligned with the gender politics of the movement and the age. A poem on "Women's Part in the Temperance Reformation" called for every woman to use her "still small voice" to "plead" for temperance as "help-meet for man."[104] If this was female temperance advocacy, it was certainly not an argument for a feminine public sphere.[105]

The first dedicated women's temperance society, the short-lived Ladies Total Abstinence Society, while only formed in 1856, is indicative of the growing politicization of women in the movement. An initial announcement invited "all Christian mothers" and "all females, whether young or old," to "join our little band" and "see what females can do."[106] The reported meetings were all chaired by men but featured several female speakers, including a Mrs Roseby, who had been a teetotaller for two decades and had "nursed all her family without the aid of beer, porter, wine, or other alcoholic drinks." She reflected on the history of the Sydney movement, arguing that the reliance on the social elite had caused its decline, and, clearly conscious of separate spheres arguments, offered an "excellent apology for female teaching" grounded in Old Testament examples. Mrs Mullen probably embodied the feelings of her audience when she reported that this was "the first time I ever addressed a public assembly, but seeing the misery and destruction caused by intoxicating drinks, especially to the female part of the community ... I could sit still no longer." A younger speaker, Mrs Leddell, had been a pledged teetotaller since she was five after witnessing how "my mother suffered much from drunkenness [because] my father spent the best part of his earnings in drink," the latter only abandoning the habit after his daughter shamed him with the harm he was causing.[107] These were women with some lived experience, at least of the temperance movement, if not also the harms that alcohol caused women.

The Ladies Total Abstinence Society disappeared from even the temperance press within a year of its establishment, but like Sands's letter, it foreshadowed the growth of female temperance in the decades to come. More typically, at the first annual meeting of the new temperance alliance founded in 1857, every speaker – and every individual named in *Band of Hope*, a journal with a female readership – was male, and women were only mentioned anonymously in a vote of thanks for preparing tea and decorating the hall.[108] In the mid-nineteenth century, women were largely silent supporters of temperance, reflecting the gendered nature of the public sphere. But temperance ideas were increasingly politicizing these women, and outbursts like Sands's would become more common. An important editorial in the *Band of Hope* in 1859, responding to two domestic murders – a drunken husband by his wife, and a wife by her drunken husband – captures the feminist critique of drunken violence that would become so important to the late nineteenth-century flourishing of female temperance. The editor depicted the "Demon of drink," translating the marriage vows of a young couple as "the banns of murder" and warning that the husband's drunken violence would teach his wife "to hate him, to curse the sound of his footfall, to tremble at his angry words, to think him and call him a brute, and at last ... murder him."[109] Even before it became overtly feminist, arguments like these helped politicize women in the face of drunken violence and squandered wages. As the rare examples of female advocacy show, women were well aware that they often bore the burden of male drunkenness.

An anonymous letter to *The Herald* in 1854 captured the increasingly gendered nature of public drinking and the political problem it embodied. The author stressed that men who visited public houses almost invariably drank alone or with other men, and asked rhetorically, "Who has ever seen a man take his wife, his mother, and his sister to the bar of a public-house, and treat her to nobblers ... [or calling for] one to take home to his wife?"[110] But while men drank with other men, women were allegedly drinking alone or with other women at home. The author argued this was because "neither party would like to be seen [by the other] while under the influence," and advocated mixed-gender socializing and non-alcoholic drinks. It is tempting to imagine that this anonymous letter might have had a female author. But even assuming it did not, it points to the way that drinking practices helped to performatively construct a gendered political imaginary. While only men could drink in public, women could not be imagined as equal citizens.

6

Drunken Savagery

IMAGINING ABORIGINAL DRUNKENNESS

The temperance missionary and editor John Saunders was also a passionate advocate of other humanitarian causes, notably the plight of Aboriginal people in the colony. On 14 October 1838, in the wake of the Myall Creek massacre earlier that year, but shortly before the murderers were tried in November, he delivered a powerful sermon on "The Claims of the Aborigines." Saunders's arguments were controversial in the context of an expanding settler colony – he asserted the humanity of Aboriginal people, insisted on their rights to land, called out the brutality by which it was being taken from them, and argued that God would punish the colony – but they were also shaped by his concern for temperance. Among his catalogue of the sins the colonists had committed against the Aborigines, he stressed that "we have brutalised them. We brought the art of intoxication to them – we bribed them to shed the blood of each other in our public streets; and we encouraged them to licentiousness and self-destroying profligacy." He concluded that it was a Christian duty to make recompense for these injuries by converting them to Christianity and stressed the "numerous comforts which flow from it, and which are comprehended in the expressive word civilization."[1]

In a long editorial on "Civilization" in the *Australian Temperance Magazine*, Saunders expanded on these views, using drunkenness as a symbol of barbarism, savagery, and the decadence that threatened colonial progress. He defined civilization as "a high development of the physical, intellectual, social, and moral condition of man," arguing that, for a colony like New South Wales, it could not mean "mere monkey mimicry" of Britain, "or else the black who gets drunk to be 'like murry gentleman' would take a degree in civilization." Citing the examples of drunken settlers and noting the evil influence of spirits on the "South Sea Islands" and in New Zealand, he argued that New South Wales was not civilized while drunkenness prevailed, and that Europeans who corrupted "native" peoples were the real savages.[2]

Saunders was expressing what had become an increasingly prominent view: that alcohol was fundamentally harmful for Indigenous peoples. As European empires expanded, settler colonialism boomed, and European explorers, missionaries, and traders brought the supposed benefits of "civilization" to "native" peoples around the globe, alcohol increasingly became a symbol of the damaging impacts of colonization. More specifically, in New South Wales, by the late 1830s squatters were rapidly expanding their pastoral runs, leading to an almost inevitable cycle of frontier conflict and reciprocal violence between Aboriginal tribes and the shepherds and flocks swarming over their land. The massacre at Myall Creek and the controversial trial of the men involved brought this violence to the attention of the Sydney press at a time when public drunkenness by Aboriginal people in urban areas was increasingly visible and resented. Amid the public discussion of frontier violence and the rule of law, the depiction of Aboriginal people as drunken savages, the helpless victims of alcohol, symbolized their incapacity to govern themselves and hence to qualify for citizenship in the imagined democracy. Notwithstanding his humanitarian arguments, Saunders was convinced that Australian Aborigines were "uncultivated" savages, fundamentally different from the British, who were "required to protect" them accordingly.[3]

Saunders's views were expressed in the context of larger debates about the impact of colonization on Aboriginal people in the British

Empire in general, and New South Wales in particular. The 1837 report of the Select Committee on Aborigines in British Settlements had found that throughout the empire, "their territory has been usurped; their property seized; their numbers diminished; their character debased; the spread of civilization impeded. European vices and diseases have been introduced amongst them, and they have been familiarized with the use of our most potent instruments for the subtle or the violent destruction of human life, viz. brandy and gunpowder."[4] The result of this report was a policy of humanitarian "protection" of Aboriginal peoples, with efforts to "civilize" them through religious education and integration into the settler economy.[5] As a wealth of recent scholarship has shown, humanitarian ideas increasingly influenced conceptions of empire during the nineteenth century at the same time as British settler colonialism accelerated.[6] More specific to Australia, scholars have explored how humanitarianism shaped the control of Indigenous peoples through missions and informed local protection policy, even as such protection was rendered largely meaningless by the violence of the expanding frontier.[7] Throughout the empire, this kind of humanitarian governance helped frame drunkenness among Indigenous people as a result of their apparent helplessness, as well as a consequence of unrestrained colonization.

In New South Wales, this policy of protection was deeply resented by a faction of colonists, led by the squatters, who had the most at stake in the violent expansion of the frontier. In an editorial published the day after Saunders's sermon, *The Herald* claimed to speak for the "true interests" of "settlers ... great and small" in attacking the new protectors of the Aborigines (appointed under this policy) who "will be of no benefit whatever to the Colonists who have to pay [their] salaries." This was a kind of democratic argument against taxation without representation – the salaries were drawn from colonial revenue, but the colonists lacked a parliament, and the appointments were made in Britain – and thus connected to the broader campaign for elected representatives and responsible government. But *The Herald* also called for a larger mounted corps "vested with the power of acting upon martial law" to secure the frontier against "lawless aggression," and for colonists to use "passive resistance" and "do their duty in the jury-box – they must refuse all protection or countenance to public robbers of whatever grade."[8] In the context of the upcoming trial of the Myall Creek murderers, this was an argument for the state to use military force to crush Aboriginal resistance, and for jury nullification in defence of white vigilantes.

As Rebecca Wood has argued, the pro-settler position articulated by *The Herald* – but also implicit in the less splenetic argument of some other newspapers – can be read as an early expression of the racialized settler-colonial nationalism that would become increasingly dominant in the Australian colonies over the remainder of the nineteenth century.[9] But in my terms it was also an expression of the democratic political imaginary. Arguments against protection of Aboriginal people were consistently framed as empowering the colonists to govern themselves in contrast to distant Britain. Saunders's intervention was also made in democratic terms. In an even more forceful speech, delivered at the inaugural meeting of the local branch of the Aborigines Protection Society, he condemned *The Herald* for claiming to speak for the people. He called on the packed meeting to "show its just indignation against sentiments like these ... which if they went uncontradicted would appear to run current in public opinion."[10] In response, the paper belittled "Mr Saunders and the ranting crew who applauded him," claiming such "disinterested philanthropists" were criticizing "the very men who are taxed to support them," and warning that if he did not "keep to his pulpit, and attend to the narrow circle of his own congregation ... we will drive him back to his proper position in society."[11] Here, *The Herald* revealed its Whiggish views on who was entitled to speak in the public sphere: taxpayers, and specifically squatters, on whom the colony allegedly depended.

Both sides of this fraught debate represented themselves as speaking for the colonial public; and both – for very different reasons – presumed that Aboriginal people were incapable of speaking for themselves, necessarily outside of the public sphere. For *The Herald*, and the squatters and their supporters for whom it spoke,

Aboriginal people were dangerous and lawless savages impeding the spread of commerce. For Saunders and his fellow humanitarians, they were victims in need of protection. Either way, they were the objects of imperial concern, whether humanitarian or commercial, and not subject citizens of an imagined democracy.

It is no coincidence that in this moment of fraught debate about the harms of colonization the colony passed some of the first race-conscious legislation in Australian history – namely, a ban on the supply of alcohol to Aborigines. Indeed, the 1837 report quoted above had called for an empire-wide "prohibition" of the sale or barter of spirits to "natives."[12] The 1838 Licensing Act claimed that "the introduction of intoxicating liquors among the aboriginal natives ... is productive of serious evil" and imposed a five pound fine on anyone who supplied an Aboriginal person with alcohol.[13]

This was not the first time Aboriginal people were the specific subject of legal attention. As Lisa Ford has shown there were extensive debates throughout the British Empire about whether Indigenous people were subject to British law, whether they could serve as witnesses, and whether offences against them, and by them, were justiciable.[14] *The Herald*'s call for martial law was justified in precisely these terms, and cited examples of Aboriginal accused who had been released due to an inability to source interpreters, and hence ensure the defendant understood the law, the charges, and could mount a defence.[15] In contrast, the 1838 Licensing Act took the status of Aboriginal people for granted: they were subject to the law but were not full citizens. In the original draft of the act, the relevant clause banned "supplying or giving of spirituous liquors to convicts under sentence and to Aboriginal natives."[16] When these two classes were separated in the final legislation the distinction between them was significant: convicts could be given liquor with their master's permission or for medicinal reasons; Aboriginal people enjoyed no such exception. Like children today – although, interestingly, before age restrictions on drinking were established in New South Wales – Aboriginal people could not be trusted to drink responsibly.[17]

This clause of the Licensing Act – like many others – was largely honoured in the breach. Aboriginal people certainly continued to have access to alcohol in some contexts, no doubt supplied in defiance of the law. Indeed, it seems likely that some Aboriginal people sought alcohol precisely because they understood that it symbolized membership of the political community. But the act demonstrates a British view of Indigenous people that distilled as the colony democratized: they were not seen as citizens or considered subjects within the political imaginary. They were not responsible enough to drink, and failing this test, their voices went unheard.

My argument here builds on recent scholarship exploring the political rights of Indigenous peoples within the democratizing settler colonies. Mark McKenna has examined how Aboriginal people were constructed as primitive and dependent subjects, thereby denying them the imagined birthrights of Britons. Julie Evans and her coauthors show how Aboriginal people were increasingly excluded – in practice if not in theory – from citizenship under responsible government, not least by a franchise linked to ownership of land, and subsequently through clauses designed to exclude vagrants. Naomi Parkinson looks in more detail at how such exclusion worked in early New South Wales elections, drawing attention to the highly ambiguous status of potential Aboriginal voters. Angela Woollacott links arguments for white male citizenship to notions of "manly independence" that emerged from racialized and gendered hierarchies of authority.[18] Ann Curthoys and Jessie Mitchell synthesize this field, arguing that colonial historiography has struggled to reconcile the "tragedy of Aboriginal dispossession and displacement" with a narrative about the achievement of liberal democracy whose "supposed mundanity ... [is] arguably the key to its subtle appeal ... [as] a reassuring history of progress without fuss ... bloodshed, or serious division." As they argue, "in [the] settler imagination Indigenous people were outside society and politics."[19] I argue below that this status as essential outsiders is symbolized in the trope of the drunken savage, unable to drink responsibly.[20]

Given contemporary concern about alcohol problems in Aboriginal communities it is perhaps surprising that there is so little scholarship on the colonial encounter with alcohol.[21] Maggie Brady's work is the key exception.[22] She argues that in early interactions between

European explorers and Aborigines, alcohol was freely offered on the assumption that Aboriginal people were already familiar with it, but that it was increasingly used "as a test of their level of civilisation and as a 'civilising' gesture." As Aboriginal people "learned" to perform public drunkenness they "also absorbed European beliefs ... that alcohol loosens the inhibitions that constrain and excuse bad behaviour" – they learned drunken comportment.[23]

I adapt Brady's views on learned drinking culture, arguing that Aboriginal drinking is politically performative in two senses. First, Aboriginal drinking practices were in part scripted by the culture of public drinking and drunkenness, brought to Australia by British colonists. Second, and more importantly, Aboriginal drinking was increasingly judged by a British audience with reference to a pre-existing trope of drunken savagery, and this judgment and the controls that flowed from it reinforced a distinct drinking subculture that was perceived as problematic. My argument also draws on Marcia Langton's analysis of the "image ... of the 'drunken Aborigine'" as a "colonial construction" that framed "true" Aboriginal people as primitive and natural, thereby justifying the elimination of those corrupted by drink as the inevitable consequence of their encounter with civilization.[24]

Thus, I use perceptions of Indigenous drinking to understand the place of Aboriginal people within the political imaginary. Importantly, I am largely concerned with how the British imagined Aboriginal drinkers, not the reality of how Aboriginal people drank, not least because the nature of our sources makes this reality difficult to interpret. Paul Irish specifically cites drinking as an example of the wider problem posed by the silence or hostility of colonial sources, arguing that it is hard to speak authoritatively about Aboriginal people's experience of alcohol in the nineteenth century.[25] In what follows, I focus instead on what I call the trope of the drunken savage, a colonial narrative that decisively framed perceptions of Indigenous drinking. This trope had a longer and global history but was swiftly applied to Australian Aboriginal people and increasingly dominated public discussion, artistic depictions, and official knowledge. I then explore the political symbolism of this framing by looking in more detail at the government of Aboriginal drinking. As I show, the Licensing Act of 1838 embodied a broader trend of patronizing lenience toward Aboriginal drunkenness, which I argue symbolized their disenfranchisement in a democratizing society.

The Trope of the Drunken Savage

The trope of the drunken savage, deployed by Saunders, originated long before the British colonized New South Wales, notably in relation to Indigenous peoples in the Americas. In early modern thought, the concept of savagery was not explicitly racialized, but was increasingly understood in terms of a hierarchy of development.[26] Accordingly, the absence of alcohol in Indigenous culture – as in Australia – was a symbol of their less civilized society, and the capacity to drink with restraint, in the manner of a gentlemen, could serve as a test of civilization. Peter C. Mancall argues that what he calls the "stereotype of the drunken Indian" in early modern America was inspired by fears about drunkenness and the place of Indigenous people within colonial society.[27] As he shows, by the eighteenth century, colonists consistently saw Indigenous drinking as disorderly and dangerous, and increasingly used this as evidence to support the stereotype of Indigenous people as inferior because uncivilized.[28] By the early nineteenth century, two distinct but related discourses purported to explain the impact of alcohol on the Indigenous people of the Americas, and both were applied to Aboriginal Australians. The first focused on Indigenous people themselves with drunkenness a symbol or symptom of the "supposedly innate depravity and moral weakness of the 'savage'"; the second was causal, focused on the colonists and their use of alcohol as "a sinister tool in the ruthlessly systematic extermination of a rich indigenous culture."[29] In isolation, or when combined, these ideas justified a performative helplessness among colonial observers, since it seemed impossible to prevent colonization, trade, and hence Indigenous drinking and its fatal effects. Regardless of whether it was framed as a symptom or a cause of problems, drunkenness was linked with the uncivilized nature, lack of proper restraint, and supposedly inevitable decline of Indigenous peoples.[30]

Although the trope predated Australian colonization it was not immediately deployed in New South Wales. As Brady has argued, the use of alcohol as a feature of hospitality and gift exchange in early contact between explorers and Indigenous people was often less fraught. Not by coincidence, it was only as colonization forced Aboriginal people from their land and caused them to resort to subsistence on the margins of British settlement that their drinking was problematized and read as drunken.[31] A clear illustration of this transition is Bennelong, a key Eora leader and cultural intermediary in early Sydney.[32] After Bennelong was kidnapped by the British to help them build connections with the local Indigenous people, his enjoyment of wine and ready participation in toasting rituals was often noted by British observers and taken as evidence of his capacity for civilization.[33] Bennelong was taken to London by Governor Phillip in 1792, but on his return he largely withdrew from colonial society, symbolically abandoning his British clothing, and by the time of his death in 1813 he was popularly remembered by the British colonists as a public drunk whose plight embodied the tragic fate of Aboriginal people more broadly.[34]

Bennelong's drinking has attracted the attention of historians. Julie McIntyre has insightfully analyzed his use of wine as a successful performance of both masculinity and civilization, arguing that he understood the importance of the toasting ritual, and used it to build connections with the invaders.[35] Building on this, Brady uses accounts of Bennelong toasting to illustrate her argument for drinking as learned behaviour.[36] More important for my argument, Langton characterizes Bennelong as "the first archetypal 'urban Aborigine,'" whose story helped to reinforce the "historical view of Aborigines as indigent drunks."[37] Emma Dortins focuses on the ways Bennelong's story has been told as the tragedy of a man caught between two worlds, with his drinking a potent symbol of both his boundary crossing and his eventual anomic despair. As Dortins warns, the construction of Bennelong as a tragic "politically and culturally compromised drunkard" who "fails to take responsibility for his fate as a hero ought [to do]," reinforces a colonial narrative in which civilized Europeans must save Aboriginal people from themselves.[38]

However, this tragic narrative, which positions alcohol as a structural cause, seems to have been applied to Bennelong much later in the nineteenth century: only after temperance had transformed the public understanding of alcohol.[39] Contemporary observers of Bennelong's drunkenness framed it as a symptom of his fundamental savagery. Writing in August 1797, David Collins reported that "[Bennelong] was now observed to have become so fond of drinking, that, whenever invited by any of the officers to their houses, he was eager to be intoxicated, and in that state was so savage and violent as to be capable of any mischief."[40] As Dortins notes, impatience with Bennelong's drinking among the officers who produced the literary accounts of the early colony may well reflect the fact that he was now drinking with convicts, not gentlemen.[41] In my terms, due to the company he kept, his drinking comportment was increasingly read as drunken, not restrained.

Whatever the truth of Collins's report, by the early nineteenth century, Bennelong was interpreted as an archetypal drunken savage, with his nudity and drunkenness key symbols of that status. John Turnbull, a merchant sailor who published an account of his voyages in 1806, reported that "[He] is his countrymen in epitome. He is so addicted to drinking that he would scarcely ever be sober could he obtain spirits, and whenever he is intoxicated is intolerably mischievous. On the return of his sobriety he repents, but his repentance has scarcely procured his forgiveness, before the repetition of his offence again exhausts all patience. He is in truth a savage beyond all hopes of amelioration." Turnbull understood Aboriginal people as "the most barbarous on the surface of the globe" precisely because they had proved "physically incapable of civilization." He stressed that they were "wholly without any form of government" and that, as Bennelong's story demonstrated, they rejected civilized comforts in favour of "the enjoyment of their ease and liberty in their own way."[42] This wilful failure to civilize explained why Aboriginal people could not be trusted with alcohol. Unlike British gentlemen, savages could not restrain their consumption or comport themselves properly when drunk. Similar views informed Bennelong's obituary, published in *The Gazette* in 1813, which noted that consistent efforts to "draw him into a relish for civilised life" had been in vain, stressed that his "propensity for drunkenness was inordinate; and when in that state he was insolent, menacing and overbearing," and characterized him as "a thorough savage."[43] During his life, Bennelong's drunkenness was largely understood as a symbol of his savagery and not the cause of it.

In the early colony, this version of the trope predominated, with Aboriginal drunkenness generally understood in secular terms as unsightly and disorderly. A key focus of concern was large gatherings of Aboriginal people in and around British settlements, and forms of ritual conflict associated with these meetings, which were allegedly encouraged by British colonists who incited fights by providing alcohol. Reflecting in 1827 on his two decades in the colony, a correspondent to *The Australian*, "W.G.," reported that when he arrived Aboriginal people frequently begged, or exchanged the clothes they were given for sugar water or "bool" – a drink made from the dregs of sugar bags or rum barrels – which made them "quite tipsey" and caused them to fight, for the entertainment of white spectators.[44] Similarly, the French explorer Jacques Arago described with horror an incident he witnessed in Sydney where a merchant family encouraged two Aboriginal men to fight for bread and brandy.[45]

Supplying Aboriginal people with liquor was increasingly frowned upon even before 1838, and W.G. claimed that Macquarie had largely put a stop to drunkenness and fighting through a series of government orders. The Port Orders of 1810 included the contradictory requirement that "natives of this territory are to be treated in every respect as Europeans," and that "no spirits, wine, beer, or other intoxicating liquor is to be sold or given from on board any vessel to a native."[46] This seems to have been a standard provision, also issued under Governors Hunter and King, to prevent impressment of Indigenous people as sailors.[47] More significantly, in 1816, Macquarie issued a proclamation to the Aborigines forbidding large gatherings and the bringing of weapons into British settlements.[48] Though it did not mention alcohol, *The Gazette* reported that, in addition to protecting British subjects, the proclamation was also motivated by "views of humanity towards a deplorable set of creatures who were disposed, in the moments of intemperance, to hack and hew one another all to pieces."[49] Finally, in 1818, Macquarie was more explicit when he banned "giving Spirits, and the Washings out of Spirit Casks, to the Black Natives." Macquarie claimed the practice was "long since prohibited and discontinued" but recently revived, causing "fighting in the Streets ... and the late disgraceful outrages."[50] As Ford notes, official responses to, and public debate about, urban Indigenous disorder in this period presumed that Aboriginal people were not subject to British law.[51]

At the same time, much as we saw with convicts, the government gave Aboriginal people alcohol, but only in the context of rituals of patronage in which their status as dependents was on full display. At specially organized "conferences," governors would provide blankets, clothing, medals, and food and drink – including alcohol for toasting – to Aboriginal people, who reciprocated by dancing for the assembled audience of colonial officials. Macquarie was the first to introduce the practice as part of a larger suite of policies designed to civilize Aboriginal people, including appointing key men as "chiefs" to act as liaisons with the British.[52] For my purposes, what is most significant about these occasions is the striking contrast in the way Aboriginal drinking was understood when sanctioned by authority. Reporting on an early dinner, *The Gazette* noted that "a large cask of grog lent its exhilarating aid to promote the general festivity and good humour which so conspicuously shone through the sable visages of this delighted congress."[53] Even more striking, in 1832 the attendees were given crockery and cutlery, including glass goblets, and *The Monitor* reported that "the sable feasters drank to the health of 'de new Governor, Major General Bourke,' with three times three, emptying their goblets in their usual off-handed style."[54] This only underscores how the trope of the drunken savage framed Aboriginal drinking as a symbol of their political status. Such drinking was only normalized within the British political imaginary when it was authorized by colonial patrons.

Humanitarian Sympathy and Aboriginal Decline

During the 1820s and '30s, while public fighting among Aboriginal people seems to have been largely driven out of Sydney, drunkenness and complaints about it persisted, leading to calls for stricter regulation and policing.[55] There were regular reports and letters to the press complaining about the "highly offensive" spectacle of drunken gatherings and the public nudity of Aboriginal people, which was, as with Bennelong, another potent symbol of savagery.[56] As Curthoys and Mitchell argue, during this period the idea that Aboriginal people could not be "civilized" became a "foundational assumption in settler society."[57] A letter to *The Australian* in 1827 argued that "the blacks will never civilize themselves," claiming that they could not learn European industry, only idleness, and hence were "all drunkards" and would soon become "extinct."[58] More generous observers leaned on an idealized notion of savagery as a state of nature and consequently of freedom from social obligations. The Austrian explorer Baron Charles von Hügel argued in his travel journals that Aborigines could not be civilized due to "their craving for untrammelled, unlimited freedom which makes them hostile to every aspect of civilization." For von Hügel, the "degraded" state of Aborigines in Sydney was due to their having "acquired from the whites the vice of drunkenness, which brings in its train so many others."[59] However, whether observers were sympathetic or merely disgusted, it was increasingly assumed that it was hopeless to try and civilize Aboriginal people, or, specifically, to teach them how to drink.

Images of drunken savages also began to proliferate in this period, and these reflect both disgust and sympathy.[60] A particularly influential example was Augustus Earle's depiction of Aboriginal people drinking bool in the streets of Sydney (figure 9.1). In the original lithograph, from 1826, a family group of caricatured "native blacks" are centred on a barrel from which two men drink out of a bowl, while a woman sits near them with her breasts uncovered.[61] By the time Earle republished this image in his *Views in New South Wales* (1830), he had added an orderly public house, populated with restrained white drinkers in the background, and discarded rum bottles in the foreground, presumably to make the moral message clearer to the English audience.[62] In a similar image published in 1838, John Carmichael depicted two Aboriginal figures in a mocking

9.1 Augustus Earle, *Natives of N.S. Wales as Seen in the Streets of Sydney* (1830).

caricature, the man holding a bottle and the woman – with an infant bound to her chest, a small, naked child clinging to her leg, and one breast improbably exposed – drinking from another.[63]

An especially significant source is a larger lithograph, presumably by or after Carmichael, which adds two Aboriginal men fighting with waddies. A copy of this print is included in Saunders's manuscript letter book along with an accompanying poem in an unknown hand (figure 9.2). Whoever the original author, the poem embodies the sympathetic trope of drunken savagery that would spread with humanitarianism. It narrates the image, reporting that "the savage leaves the kangaroo ... And comes to have a drunken booze / Where civil white men dwell," but blames this conduct on colonists who "take their ground ... Plunder and poison them with rum," concluding, "Poor savage! Much I mourn thy lot / Made both a beggar and a sot / By men of British name."[64] Regardless of whether Saunders was the author, it certainly fits the themes of his sermons and essays.

9.2 Unknown artist, *Real Life in Sydney* (ca 1838).

This sympathetic version of the trope, in which alcohol caused Aboriginal squalor by way of the bad example and influence of colonists, was increasingly prominent in New South Wales from the 1830s as missionary activity, Evangelicalism, and humanitarianism gained influence. A key figure whose views decisively shaped other Evangelicals was Lawrence Threlkeld, who led the first dedicated mission to Australian Aboriginal people, among the Akwarbal at Lake Macquarie, from the mid-1820s, and who soon began to lament the impact of alcohol on the Akwarbal, even blaming it for his eventual failure to "save" them.[65] In 1839 he reported to his missionary superiors that, despite serving a Christmas dinner accompanied by spruce beer – a patronage ritual analogous to the governor's festival in Sydney – some of the people "gave notice ... that they would leave at Christmas, in order to visit the town, for the sake of spirits."

When he sought to warn them about the sin of drunkenness, they allegedly responded, "if it be really wicked to get intoxicated, why do the Whites sell rum, but that they might drink it? Gentlemen get drunk! Ladies get drunk!! and why should not they?"[66] In another significant example, Threlkeld noted that Biraban (also known as McGill), his closest Aboriginal friend, who often assisted as a court interpreter, had demonstrated his understanding of the meaning of a Bible oath by acknowledging that "he feared he should go to hell when he died, in consequence of his habitual intemperance."[67] In his later *Reminiscences*, Threlkeld argued that Aborigines soon "became adept scholars" of rum drinking, seeing drunkenness "as a kind of accomplishment," and reported an incident where an Aboriginal man was given brine, believing it to be rum, and acted drunk: "Presently he began to say, smacking his lip: 'Rum merry good, me mer[r]y drunk,' and cut all manner of capers, on being asked how he liked it, 'Oh! merry good, merry good, make me merry drunk, me drunk like a gemmem!' (gentleman,) and danced about to the great amusement of his countrymen. It was a fact that he did not know what rum was, but had only heard of its wonderful effects upon those who drank it."[68] Threlkeld understood Aboriginal drinking as a learned sin, or, in my terms, a kind of performative drunken comportment.

Building on his insights, humanitarians increasingly tied the drunkenness of colonists to the failure to convert Aborigines and used the trope to argue for establishing missions well away from British settlements.[69] The Quaker missionaries Backhouse and Walker helped to bring these ideas to a wider audience. While still in Australia they sought to persuade colonists that they had a responsibility to the Aboriginal people because of the "vices which have been introduced among them."[70] More importantly, Backhouse's widely read account of their travels included a version of Threlkeld's story, and claimed that Aboriginal people in Sydney performed drunkenness regardless of whether the bool they were drinking contained alcohol.[71] As Brady notes, such "mimicry of drunken comportment" became a feature of so-called corroborees – celebratory gatherings of Aboriginal people, featuring dances and music, that were performed for white audiences in the second half of the nineteenth century. As she argues, such self-conscious performances demonstrate that, far from being helpless under the effects of liquor, Aboriginal people were often ironically aware of how they were expected to behave around it.[72] But for Backhouse it indicated "the force of example." Relying on the trope, albeit the sympathetic humanitarian version, he understood Aboriginal people as savages who desperately and tragically imitated civilized men. Accordingly, he concluded that "these poor creatures are injured by the profligacy of the white population, who give them drink, till their tribes are fast perishing from the face of the earth."[73]

Increasingly this fatalistic version of the trope of drunken savagery was used to explain the decline – whether real or imagined – of the Aboriginal population upon contact with colonists.[74] The temperance press of the early 1840s – largely edited by Saunders – regularly republished extracts about the harmful effects of alcohol on Indigenous peoples around the world, bolstering the sense that such harms were inevitable.[75] Reporting to Britain on the new protectorates, Gipps noted that Aborigines' interactions with white men "will frequently expose them to temptations, which they may not be strong enough to withstand, the men to the use of ardent spirits, the women to be seduced from their husbands or natural protectors," suggesting that stricter enforcement of prohibition could help address this. In response to this and earlier reports, Lord Stanley replied that it was now clear to the British government that efforts to civilize Aboriginal people had failed, and he saw no prospect of future success.[76] In the colony itself, a series of circular letters to magistrates in the late 1840s asked them to describe and explain the declining Aboriginal population, and while the respondents offered a range of causes, they mentioned drunkenness far more frequently than frontier conflict or loss of land.[77]

A local inquiry, the 1845 Select Committee on the Condition of Aborigines, illustrates this official reliance on the trope, perhaps especially in its treatment of the only Indigenous witness, "Boatswain" Mahroot, a Gameygal man who had made a career serving on sealing and whaling voyages.[78] Asked about the role of alcohol in the decline of his tribe, he allegedly said, "To that degree they took to liquor, at last they went away very fast; it was the only thing that destroyed them." In response to a series of similarly leading questions, he told the committee that he had seen parents give liquor to children, and that women who drank and slept with white men had fewer children. Other parts of his testimony also aligned with the trope. Mahroot reported that when he went on whaling voyages, he earned twenty to thirty pounds, but "went along with the sailors and we threw it away all together [in public houses]."[79] But of course, this was typical of the binge-drinking pattern found in much working-class labour.

Tellingly, the committee were unwilling to listen when his answers contradicted their assumptions. Mahroot was also reported as saying that, more regularly, he made money through fishing, and "threw it away along with my people," spending it on "Clothes, and meat, and flour, and sugar." The chairman, Richard Windeyer, responded that Mahroot should "Tell the truth, did you not buy rum?," to which the latter replied, "I can take a little sometimes."[80] Based on the surviving sources it is probably impossible to say how Mahroot viewed alcohol, or even how problematic his drinking was. But it is clear that the select committee shaped its questions to fit a preconceived narrative in which the observed decline in the numbers of Aboriginal people was an inevitable consequence of contact with civilization, and specifically alcohol.

Governing Aboriginal Drunkenness

The trope also shaped the actions of the authorities in their efforts to manage Aboriginal drinking. During the 1830s there were persistent and growing calls for stricter control of urban Aboriginal people, often linked to their begging for alcohol.[81] An editorial in *The Gazette* in 1837 noted that paper had already "called the attention of the authorities" to the problem, and cited a recent incident in which a labouring man was asked for tobacco and then assaulted and robbed, the paper arguing that "savages should be thrown back upon their native wilds." These calls were echoed in other papers in an increasingly sustained campaign for police action, with *The Monitor* framing this as in the interests of Aboriginal people, claiming "humanity to the Blacks themselves requires interference."[82]

Prior to the 1838 Licensing Act, the only way that police could deal with problem drinkers was to charge them with public drunkenness, and they did so very frequently from the late 1830s onward, making drunkenness the leading cause of arrest. Given the frequent complaints about Aboriginal drunkenness, it is therefore striking that Aboriginal drinkers were rarely arrested and even more rarely punished.[83] While there were occasional arrests, magistrates frequently released Aboriginal drunkards with a warning, especially when Aboriginal leaders appeared in court to plead for them. For example, Simon, "a native well known to the Inhabitants of Windsor," was charged with drunkenness and disorder in 1826 after he violently resisted his removal from a public house, yelling, "I'm a free man!" There are hints here that Simon understood that the right to drink in public was a symbol of political citizenship. But regardless, the lenient response was telling: despite smashing a window and threatening bystanders, he was only placed in the stocks; a convict committing such an aggravated offence would certainly have been flogged.[84] In another such case, Terrebelong was charged with the same offence, but released without punishment after "the Chief of his tribe" came to the court to plead for him.[85]

The unnamed chief in this case was probably Bungaree, an explorer and negotiator, who was probably the Aboriginal individual best known to the British after Bennelong's death. He was designated a chief by Macquarie, and was famous for welcoming visiting vessels to what he termed "his country" – he was actually a Kuringai man from Broken Bay, north of Sydney – by rowing out, climbing on board, drinking the captain's health, and levying a tribute from the ship's pantry. Indeed, like Bennelong before him, Bungaree's drinking was both an agentive performance of restrained gentility that complemented his diplomacy, and widely interpreted by his British audience as a symbol of his drunken savagery. Accounts of Bungaree begging for money and using it to get drunk became key elements of his story, as recounted by numerous visitors to Sydney in the 1820s.[86] In an indicative example, Peter Cunningham described Bungaree's comical dignity in greeting visitors and asking for money in the following terms: "Let it not be supposed, however, that his Majesty condescends to *thieve:* he only solicits the *loan* of a *dump* [a small coin], on pretence of treating his sick *gin* [wife] to a cup of tea, but in reality with a view of treating *himself* to a porringer of 'Cooper's best [spirits],' to which his Majesty is most royally devoted."[87] This reading frames Bungaree as a drunken savage unable to control himself around alcohol.

In contrast, Bungaree was also relied upon as a trusted intermediary. As complaints about Aboriginal drunkenness mounted, Bungaree served as a de facto police liaison, helping the authorities control urban Aboriginal people. In March 1826, the superintendent of police, Francis Rossi, instructed him to warn them that "rioting, drunkenness, and disturbing the quiet of the streets at night, would invariably be followed by the punishment of the tread-mill, or, confinement with hard labour." In September that year, after Davy was arrested for "having been excessively drunk and noisy," Bungaree came to the police office, promised that Davy would not offend again, and had him released into his custody without further punishment.[88]

Even Aboriginal drinkers who did not have a chief to speak on their behalf were often released, or occasionally put in the stocks (or later jail) for want of the money to pay their fines.[89] A report in 1840 claimed that punishing Aboriginal people was "almost impossible" because "they are so inured to the miseries of this life," and called for them to be starved for a day and then deported from Sydney, implying that lack of a civilized sense of shame made British punishments useless.[90] In 1837 the then police magistrate, Colonel Wilson, ordered a larger group of eight Aborigines to be taken to see the treadmill and warned that they would be sentenced to it for a month if they were arrested again.[91] It seems the threat was not acted upon, although at least one of the eight was rearrested: Cora Gooseberry, one of Bungaree's wives, who remained a familiar figure in Sydney after his death, and was sometimes termed "the last of the Sydney tribe."[92] I have located at least five instances where she was arrested for drunkenness and discharged with a warning.[93] Indeed, her name briefly became a signifier of female drunkenness, with reports describing other (white) women as "playing up old gooseberry" when they got drunk. In fact, as Irish has shown, Gooseberry is an example of the kinds of "cross-cultural relationships" that often existed around pubs since she and William Warrell were "regularly hosted" by Edward Borton at his London Tavern in the 1840s.[94] But Aboriginal women found it even harder than men to perform restraint while drinking, in the eyes of a white audience.

Given that police in the 1830s and '40s were encouraged to arrest drunkards because they received half of any fine, the practice of releasing Aboriginal people without punishment, combined with their inability to pay fines, served as a significant disincentive for officers.[95] Indeed, in 1844, after William Annan died of exposure on the Sydney streets, *The Herald* alleged that he had been arrested that night but was released rather than taken to the watch house.[96] Those who argued for arresting Aboriginal drinkers typically framed this as necessary for their own protection, with suggestions that Aboriginal women in particular were vulnerable to assault when drunk on the streets at night.[97] After 1838, complaints increasingly called for action against publicans or white drinkers who supplied Aboriginal people with liquor, but the infrequency of prosecutions suggests that the police only used this new offence when there was heightened public concern.[98] As Irish argues, this system of prohibiting supply, combined with lenience for those arrested for drunkenness, meant that Aboriginal people "had to be treated as victims rather than offenders," needing protection not punishment.[99]

The act of 1838 may not have made much difference in practice, but it symbolized the patronizing emphasis on protecting Aboriginal people from the impact of civilization, which increasingly dominated the colonial imaginary. In a significant court case that year – though before the act was passed – Long Jack, an Aboriginal man, was charged with the drunken murder of his "gin," Mary. The evidence before the court showed that he and his tribe had got "very drunk, by drinking a quantity of 'bull,' given to them by a publican," and that he had beaten her to death. The only defence he offered was his intoxication, but Thomas A'Beckett, who was appointed by the court as his barrister, built on this, claiming Aboriginal people were "not … acquainted with the nature of the liquor … and [were] thus taken by surprise" by its effects.[100] This plea was dismissed by the judge, William Burton (who also sat for both Myall Creek trials), who insisted that Aboriginal people within the colony were fully subject to British law. As Lisa Ford has shown, even before his arrival in New South Wales, Burton was committed to the view that "Indigenous rights ... were best promoted by colonial jurisdiction" and brought this doctrine from the Cape Colony to New South Wales. In his influential decision in another case of drunken murder – R v. Murrell in 1836 – he argued that Aboriginal offenders were subject to British law precisely because their customs were too savage to warrant legal recognition.[101] Regardless of these decisions, both A'Beckett's defence and Burton's legal logic demonstrate the influence of the trope. In practice, Aboriginal drunkenness was regarded differently from the drunkenness of British colonists, and this was reflected in the regular discharge of arrested Aboriginal drunkards and the prohibition on supplying them with alcohol. The trope constructed Aboriginal people as failing the test of self-government posed by drinking.

The Right to Drink

In 1849, in a rare example of a colonist seeing beyond the trope, Robert Nichols challenged the prohibition on supplying alcohol to Aborigines. Nichols, the emancipist and radical politician, had become a leading figure in the Sydney Aborigines Committee, an organization that advocated for urban Aboriginal people.[102] During debate in committee on the new Licensing Act, Nichols suggested that "many of the blacks were industrious, and comparatively civilized, [and] consequently they had a right to equal liberty with the whites."[103] Several (unnamed) members agreed with Nichols, but the amendment was rejected on the casting vote of the chairman and the prohibition remained on the books until the mid-twentieth century in New South Wales.[104]

The context of Nichols's intervention is significant because the Legislative Council was simultaneously in the process of debating the controversial "Aboriginal Natives Evidence Bill." This was one of a series of similar bills that sought to ensure Aboriginal testimony was justiciable, rejected in the 1840s by a council dominated by squatters with long memories of Myall Creek and the supposed injustice done to the executed men.[105] Nichols, as a sympathetic and humane supporter of Aboriginal people who had personal relationships with members of what was then known as the "Sydney tribe," was a key advocate for the Evidence Bill, and his argument about the Licensing Act should be viewed in this light as part of a broader effort to treat Aboriginal people as full citizens. Indeed, his reported remarks point to the wider political significance of prohibition. The right to drink was more than a right to refreshment or even intoxication; it symbolized a right to participate equally in the emerging citizen democracy of New South Wales. As Brady argues, prohibition "represented a state-imposed and maintained racial hierarchy and, as such, it inevitably and eventually became a civil rights issue."[106] While Aboriginal people could and did continue to access alcohol, they could only do so on the sly, not in public, and their ostracism from pubs had a larger political meaning. As Curthoys and Mitchell argue, as the colony democratized Aboriginal people were increasingly framed as the "very opposite to a rational, mature, self-governing subject."[107]

Earlier in 1849, Nichols and the Sydney Aborigines Committee organized a distribution of blankets to the Sydney tribe, and the ceremony was conducted as a kind of public dinner. Mahroot, representing the Aboriginal inhabitants, gave a speech of thanks, in his native language, warning them against selling or trading the blankets, before proposing the health of the Queen, the governor, and the "native people," drunk in bool.[108] Aboriginal people could and did perform the rituals of public drinking and likely understood their political symbolism. But they were only permitted to do so in the context of British patronage. They were not free to drink like merry gentlemen. In the eyes of their British audience, they could only ever mimic such restrained comportment, symbolizing their exclusion from the democratic public.

CONCLUSION

Toasting Democracy

THE NATIONAL BANQUET

In July 1855 the British Parliament passed the New South Wales Constitution Act, which formally established responsible government in the colony.[1] The new constitution came into effect in 1856, coinciding with a by-election for the Sydney Hamlets in which Stuart Donaldson, the first colonial premier, a former squatter turned businessman, and a conservative-liberal ally of William Wentworth, was re-elected. His supporters immediately planned a celebration in his honour, but this plan was soon adjusted in favour of a "National Banquet to celebrate the inauguration of Responsible Government" with the intention that it should have "nothing of a party character."[2]

Although the organizing committee was almost exclusively composed of Donaldson's political allies, they made a public effort to avoid the appearance of partisanship. They chose Dr William Bland, an eminent emancipist surgeon and veteran of the campaign for free institutions, as president, and limited the toasts to fifteen loyal and uncontroversial topics, all announced in advance. Tickets to the dinner, held in the Prince of Wales Theatre on 17 July, cost a guinea – an allegedly "reasonable rate" that would certainly have excluded most working men – but entitled the purchaser to buy two additional ladies' tickets, allowing female friends and relations to observe from the privacy and security of the boxes, for five shillings.[3] The dinner itself was organized on a grand scale, with elaborate patriotic decorations, a military band, and an amateur choir for musical accompaniment, and was probably the largest public dinner in the colony to that date, with six hundred gentlemen dining, and another five hundred ladies looking on.[4]

The toasts themselves were entirely typical of what was now a very familiar colonial ritual, and the speeches were largely conservative in tone, at least in the context of the times. Bland gave "the toast of the evening" to "The Prosperity of New South Wales under Responsible Government" and rehearsed a settler-colonial and Whiggish history of colonial democracy. He saw the new constitution as the fulfillment of a birthright, claiming that "free institutions are a part of every one of us ... interwoven ... from time immemorial ... in the very hearts of our countrymen." He also praised Britain's "perpetual progress" toward liberty, embodied in the motherland's "deed of chivalrous generosity" in granting them responsible government, comparing it to the Reform Act and the abolition of slavery. Responding, the premier took the opportunity to honour Wentworth for his contribution to colonial democracy, hoping that in the future "due recognition will be ... afforded to the aristocracy of talent," a generous reference to Wentworth's "bunyip aristocracy" and the nominated upper house.[5]

More diplomatically, the chief justice and president of the Legislative Council, Sir Alfred Stephen, stressed that the new colonial Parliament was dedicated to "promoting the general welfare of all classes, without preference or distinction of rank, or social position, or employment, or creed, or country, or party."[6] Despite his unelected position, Stephen saw himself as the representative of the colonial public. He was also a temperance advocate, though, like Gipps before him, he was a moderate paternalist, happy to toast in public, but committed to using his prominent position to attack drunkenness. His democratic ideals were morally enlightened and predicated on a reciprocal responsibility between citizens and representatives. Indeed, in his famous public lecture on intemperance in 1869 he told his audience that they were responsible for reforming the colony and its drink laws, since, "[though] we are not all legislators, most of us can, more or less, influence those who are."[7] Similarly, at the banquet itself, Daniel Cooper, the Speaker of the Legislative Assembly, argued that "temperate and religious habits" were essential for responsible citizenship.[8] An anonymous letter to *The Herald* went further, attacking the banquet for promoting drunkenness. The author rehearsed the radical temperance critique of toasting, arguing that public dinners were "temples of moral destruction, spreading poverty and misery" through their bad example.[9]

The performance of democracy at the dinner had other clear limitations. Despite the efforts of the promoters, the dinner was widely seen as partisan and leading radicals and liberals – notably the supporters of "the bunch" – an alliance of radical politicians including John Dunmore Lang – declined to attend, undermining any claim to political unity.[10] Judge Dickinson's effusive praise for "refined ladies" who "alone could fashion and produce gentlemen" was matched by the sentiments of the solicitor general, John Darvall, who rejoiced that "the first fruits of our political freedom" were "sanctioned and adorned by the presence of the fair and virtuous matrons and daughters of Australia."[11] In contrast, the only mention of Aboriginal people was by the premier, who measured the colony's progress from a country "inhabited as it was seventy years ago almost exclusively by the 'blackfellow'" to the current "highly advanced state of civilisation."[12]

Despite these limitations, banquets like this were imagined – scripted and performed – as celebrations of democracy. As with other public dinners described in this book, we know about this event from the extensive press reports, and, in this instance, from a commemorative booklet, published later that year, which sought, somewhat desperately, to claim the banquet as a moment of great historical significance.[13] This booklet is evidence of a broader effort in the 1850s to inspire a historical consciousness in the new settler-colonial democracies of Australasia, in part through an invented tradition of patriotic public dining. In some cases, these events were also recorded in commemorative artwork, and two examples by Samuel Gill, an important commercial artist of the 1850s,

10.1 Samuel T. Gill, *Old Colonists' Festival* (1853).

illustrate how such banquets were conceived.[14] The "Old Colonists' Festival" (figure 10.1), held at the Criterion Hotel in Melbourne in 1853, was restricted to about two hundred gentlemen who had been in Victoria for at least a decade, and Gill depicted this Melbourne dinner as an idealized vision of restrained gentlemanly drinking. Three long tables of men in evening dress sit in parallel lines with glasses in hand, perpendicular to the table of honour, where the committee and guests stand to attention, while the chairman raises his glass in a toast.[15] Ironically, the orderly scene Gill portrayed was largely in his imagination. The actual dinner descended into uproar over a politicized speech, with diners mounting the tables, yelling, and fighting, forcing the stewards to call the police. The conservative *Argus* suggested that future public dinners in Melbourne would have to "be shared by ladies … the true civilisers [whose] presence naturally leads to a species of chivalric disposition for propriety."[16]

10.2 Samuel T. Gill, *Old Colonists' Festival Dinner* (1851).

Public toasting was increasingly respectable, performed to an orderly script, and domesticated by a feminine audience.

The earlier and larger "Old Colonists' Festival" (figure 10.2) – this one for six hundred gentlemen – was held in a pavilion behind the City-Bridge Hotel in Adelaide on 27 March 1851, officially to commemorate the first sale of town land in 1837, but more broadly to celebrate the promise of a new constitution and self-government. Tickets were deliberately set at the much more affordable rate of ten shillings and six pence, and to make the event even more democratic, the following day an oxen was roasted and free beer provided for all, in an exercise of patronage by the local brewers who sponsored the festival.[17] Gill's scene is framed by an ornate border listing the office-holders, organizing committee, and invited guests, and topped with an imagined colonial coat of arms, flanked by an emu and kangaroo, with the motto "Advance Australia." Symbols of

10.3 Samuel T. Gill, *Digger's Wedding in Melbourne* (1852).

maritime trade and agricultural plenty contrast with Aboriginal figures, presumably to show the colony's progress from its "natural" state. The dinner itself fills the pavilion, hung with flags and floral emblems, with a series of long tables surrounding the small, raised table of honour, positioned under the royal coat of arms. But unlike the Melbourne dinner, the diners in Adelaide are a motley crew in varied dress, denoting a mix of social classes, and most of them ignore the distant speaker as they drunkenly talk and celebrate among themselves. In this case, Gill more accurately represented proceedings since reports of the dinner noted that the speakers could hardly be heard, and the chairman constantly struggled to "restore order" amid growing "uproar."[18]

Jim Badger has analyzed Gill's later images of gold rush–era Melbourne as reflective of the anxieties that prevailed in a period when social order seemed under threat from new wealth and egalitarian manners. He focuses on Gill's depiction of a "Digger's Wedding" (figure 10.3) – in which the drunken couple have hired a barouche, and brandish champagne, in a public display of their good fortune – arguing that it was intended to warn viewers of the threat of "horrid democracy."[19] Gill's image of the Adelaide dinner can be read as a similarly acerbic, but affectionate, comment on mass dining in the era of democracy. The democratic public he imagined were less orderly than the Melbourne gentlemen, but united and levelled by drink.

Like Gill's image of Melbourne, the National Banquet was intended as a performance of order; and unlike the reality of the Melbourne dinner, the presence of an audience of ladies – and the absence of partisan rivals – seems to have ensured that the diners remained restrained. Indeed, the banquet was carefully scripted to avoid the kind of lively and freer conviviality that had prevailed in Adelaide. The expansion of the franchise was often imagined fearfully, with plebian drunkenness – like popular sovereignty – seen as dangerous precisely because, as Lang had complained, it empowered drinkers to act as if they were gentlemen.[20]

Later in 1856, when Donaldson lost his seat at yet another by-election, *The Herald* claimed it was the result of his loss of self-control when provoked by an "excited, malignant, distorted, and drunken mob that raged and raved beneath the platform in the interest of Mr John Campbell, and as the hirelings of the Bunch."[21] The paper alleged that this drunken crowd were "brought in omnibuses, primed with liquor, and placed beneath the hustings, for the very purpose of provoking the style of retort which they encountered."[22] Opposition to electoral reform in the late 1850s also centred on such fears. Critics associated the secret ballot with the cowardice of a drunken mob, claiming that "no temperate and industrious man in Australia ... need have any cause to fear giving his vote, *viva voce*, like a man, and an honest man," while suggesting that universal suffrage would enfranchise those who were "either addicted to intemperance or vegetate under the torpid dominion of laziness."[23] Restrained toasting was a performance of citizenship, but drunkenness often symbolized the dangers of democratic freedom.

Above all, the National Banquet illustrates the limits of the democratic political imaginary, and indeed of democracy itself. Donaldson and his supporters scripted a vision of an orderly democracy, much like Gill's Melbourne dinner, a festival of restrained self-congratulation by colonial British gentlemen, settlers who had proved themselves united and free, and were rewarded with a democratic constitution. The audience of ladies were scenic witnesses. Their feminine scruples ensured decorum, but their political endorsement was silent and taken for granted. Colonial progress was contrasted to the assumed savagery of Aboriginal people, who were more radically silenced, excluded, and increasingly ignored, despite the ongoing war of conquest on the colonial frontier.

Increasingly produced in this tightly scripted way, public dinners were a ritual demonstrating the elusive nature of democracy. Even as the dining public expanded, dinners were more strictly organized, limiting who spoke, what they said, and especially how it was remembered. Likewise, democratic politics under responsible government was imagined as restrained, respectable, and orderly. But drunkenness – and sobriety – are potentially radical acts. Popular drinking, especially in pubs – a stage on which the legend of Australian masculinity was performed – taught men to imagine themselves as free citizens, while temperance challenged the chauvinistic limits of this cosy fraternity.

Drink as a Metaphor for Democracy

This interpretation of democracy through drink is significant because it focuses on the political imaginary rather than electoral institutions or even the rare moments when the people had collective power. I have understood democracy as a shared sense of the public as politically authoritative; and shown that the public grew through rituals of restrained sociability that performatively enacted the capacity for self-government and hence the right to a say in public affairs. More specifically, this book intervenes in arguments about the history of sociability and democracy in Britain and especially its

Australian colonies. My concept of restrained comportment helps explain why democracy was persistently – perhaps inevitably – limited. Citizenship was always imagined as gendered and racialized partly because of the ways that authority was performed in public practices like drinking. Building on Lake's fruitful arguments, I trace these limits back further, to the sociable practices through which settler-colonial democracy was first imagined.[24] It also helps explain why democracy was and remains elusive. Our political institutions have never worked the way we imagine democracy should – deliberately, argues Wolin.[25] It is only in moments of collective action – what Butler calls performative assembly – that the public's power can possibly align with its sense of authority.[26]

The book also contributes to the history of alcohol. My focus on restrained drinking as a kind of productive dialectic between drunkenness and sobriety helps explain why the toasting ritual was politically significant, even as masculinity was domesticated and politics reformed. Equally, my reading of temperance as performative sobriety draws attention to the democratic and feminist implications of the movement, while the stigma of feminine drunkenness clarifies the seeming paradox of its male leadership. I also show that, by understanding alcohol as a problem substance, temperance was intimately connected with a broader shift in the political imaginary that underlay the expansion of government in the second half of the nineteenth century.[27]

These findings have implications that go beyond the history of alcohol or colonial New South Wales. Indeed, my argument can certainly be applied to contemporary Australia. When I was learning to drink in the 1990s – under the legal drinking age, as is true of many Australians – a series of iconic adverts for Victoria Bitter, known as "VB," were constantly playing on television, especially during popular men's sport. As I recall them now, they showed a range of legendary Australians – all men – performing manly deeds, while the gravel-voiced narrator certified their right to drink by advising me that "a hard-earned thirst needs a big cold beer, and the best cold beer is Vic."[28] I was younger then, and suitably impressed, I drank my share of VB, although, in strict honesty, I had certainly not earned it.

These ads, too, are politically telling, performative invocations of a democratic political imaginary that, if it is no longer explicitly settler-colonial, is certainly still masculine and white. The hard-earned thirst of these model citizens is precisely the measure of their merit. As the ad closes, and they drink together at a public bar, a fanfare plays to their fraternal mateship, sealed in ritually drained glasses. Young men like me, watching on, were taught that drinking together with other men made us members of a public and symbolized our entitlement to have a say.

Drink was, and remains, a metaphor for democracy.

NOTES

ABBREVIATIONS

HRA – *Historical Records of Australia*
HRNSW – *Historical Records of New South Wales*
NSW – New South Wales
NSWTS – New South Wales Temperance Society
OBPO – *Old Bailey Proceedings Online*
PRO – Public Records Office

INTRODUCTION

1 *Monitor*, 12 November 1827, 6.
2 *Australian*, 14 November 1827, 3; *Gazette*, 5 November 1827, 3; 14 November 1825, 2; Waterhouse and Painter, *Principal Club*, chap. 1.
3 *Monitor*, 12 November 1827, 6; *Australian*, 14 November 1827, 3.
4 *Monitor*, 12 November 1827, 6.
5 *Monitor*, 12 November 1827. See also *Australian*, 14 November 1827, 2, 3.
6 *Monitor*, 12 November 1827, 6. The songs for these last two named toasts are not recorded.
7 *Monitor*, 15 November 1827, 6. For more on the political context, see Fletcher, *Ralph Darling*; Francis, *Governors and Settlers*, chap. 4.
8 *Australian*, 14 November 1827, 2.
9 See the series of dispatches and enclosures in *HRA*, I.13:638–48 and I.14: 356–65. See also *Gazette*, 14 December 1827, 2.
10 *Monitor*, 19 October 1831, 2; *Monitor*, 21 October 1831, 2; *Australian*, 21 October 1831, 2.
11 *Gazette*, 12 November 1827, 2; *Australian*, 14 November 1827, 2–3; *Monitor*, 12 November 1827, 6, and 15 November 1827, 6. Wardell was certainly at the dinner; Hall probably was not but certainly had a direct source on events.

My characterizations of the politics of the Sydney papers are overly simplistic, but broadly accurate. See Walker, *Newspaper Press*, chap. 2.

12 Peter Clark makes similar points about clubs and societies more generally: Clark, *British Clubs*, 251–7.

13 *Australian*, 21 December 1827, 2.

14 On homosociality and eighteenth-century drinking, see Harvey, "Ritual Encounters."

15 *Gazette*, 12 November 1827, 2. She was advertised as a runaway from her husband a week earlier: *Gazette*, 5 November 1827, 1.

16 *Gazette*, 12 November 1827, 2.

17 Gunn, "Analysing Behaviour."

18 Goffman, *Presentation of Self*.

19 Geertz, *Interpretation of Cultures*, 9–10.

20 Gunn, "Analysing Behaviour," 191. On ritual and British governance, see also Gunn, " Ritual"; Cannadine, *Ornamentalism*. On the political nature of rituals, see Kertzer, *Ritual*.

21 Butler, *Excitable Speech*, chap. 4, quotation on 160; Butler, "Performative Acts"; Butler, *Performative Assembly*, chap. 1.

22 See, for example, Epstein, *Radical Expression*; Vernon, *Politics and the People*; Joyce, *Democratic Subjects*; Innes and Philp, eds, *Re-imagining Democracy*.

23 Taylor, *Social Imaginaries*, 23. On the conceptual vagueness of *mentalité*, see Darnton, *Great Cat Massacre*, 250–1; Burke, "History of Mentalities."

24 Strauss, "Imaginary," 331–4; Taylor, *Secular Age*, 170–6. On ideas and imaginaries, see also Castoriadis, *Imaginary Institution*; Gordon, "Charles Taylor," 656–8.

25 Anderson, *Imagined Communities*; Taylor, *Social Imaginaries*, 107.

26 Palti, "Theoretical Revolution," 401–2.

27 Isakhan, "Complex and Contested," 8; Hidalgo, "Concept of Democracy."

28 Tocqueville, *Democracy*; Skocpol, "Tocqueville Problem."

29 Habermas, *Public Sphere*, 28.

30 Landes, "Public and Private," 97–8. For more critical reflection on Habermas's model, see Emden and Midgley, "Public Sphere"; Cowan, "Public Sphere"; Hsueh, "Intoxicated Reasons."

31 Newman, *Romantic Tavern*, 3, 26.

32 Capdeville and Kerhervé, "Introduction"; Cowan, "Sociability."

33 Vernon, *Politics and the People*, 6.

34 Joyce, *Democratic Subjects*, 5.

35 Vernon, *Politics and the People*, 9. On the term, see Gurney, "Democratic Idiom."

36 Wolin, *Fugitive Democracy*, 100, 108.

37 Gollan, *Working Class*; Hirst, *Strange Birth*; McKenna, *Captive Republic*; Pickering, "Popular Constitutionalism"; Irving, *Southern Tree*; Cochrane, *Colonial Ambition*; Scalmer, "Containing Contention"; Jones, *Republicanism*.

38 Irving, *Southern Tree*, 88; Irving, "Liberty Explained." For the importance of public meetings in colonial Australian politics, see Goodman, "Public Meetings.".

39 Atkinson, *Democracy*, xiv, 222–5, 243–9, 316–17.

40 Ward, *Australian Legend*, v, 2, 207.

41 Ward, "Legend Revisited," 175; Davison, "Rethinking."

42 Hirst, "Egalitarianism."

43 Dixson, *Real Matilda*, 57. See also Murphy, "Feminism."

44 Connell, *Gender and Power*; Connell and Messerschmidt, "Hegemonic Masculinity." Note that Connell does not use the metaphor of performance in discussing hegemonic masculinity.

45 Lake, "Mission Impossible," 305, 307.

46 Lake, "Politics of Respectability," 122–6.

47 Lake, "Gendered and Racialised"; Curthoys and Mitchell, *Taking Liberty*.

48 Veracini, "Settler Transition," 302, 307; Veracini, *Settler Colonialism*, chap. 3; Belich, *Replenishing the Earth*.

49 Dietler, "Alcohol," 232, 235, 237, 242; Singer, "Anthropology and Addiction."

50 Barrows and Room, "Introduction," 1.

51 Dietler, "Alcohol," 230.

52 Douglas, "Anthropological Perspective," 3; Gusfield, "Benevolent Repression," 400–1; Wiener, *Reconstructing the Criminal*, introd. For a critical reading of official concern about alcohol, see Gusfield, *Contested Meanings*. For a critique of this aspect of alcohol anthropology, see Room, "Alcohol and Ethnography."

53 Douglas, "Anthropological Perspective," 4; Heath, *Drinking Occasions*, 4. See also Wilson, "Drinking Cultures"; Adler, "Symbolic Exchange."

54 MacAndrew and Edgerton, *Drunken Comportment*. See also Room, "Bad Behaviour"; Fjær and Pedersen, "Drunken Comportment Revisited."

55 MacAndrew and Edgerton, *Drunken Comportment*, 166, 171.

56 For overviews of historical scholarship on alcohol, see Barrows and Room, "Introduction"; Blocker, "Introduction"; Holt, "Introduction."

57 For popular beer history, see, for example, Pearl, *Beer*; Wannan, *Folklore*; Dunstan, *Amber Nectar*. For scholarly treatment of pubs and pub culture, see Freeland, *Australian Pub*; Kirkby, *Barmaids*; Wright, *Female Publicans*; Kirkby, Luckins, and McConville, *Australian Pub*.

58 The best general study is Fitzgerald and Jordan, *Under the Influence*. For a recent popular history of the early crisis, see Gilling, *Grog*. For more scholarly work on Australian alcohol controls, see Room, "Intoxicated Society"; Lewis, *Rum State*. For temperance, see Roe, *Quest for Authority*, chaps 8–9; Beresford, "Anti-drink Movement." For medical concern, see Lewis, "Alcoholism Treatment"; Garton, "Once a Drunkard."

59 For Britain, see Greenaway, *Drink*; Beckingham, *Licensed City*; Yeomans, *Moral Regulation*; Gutzke, "Progressivism." For Australia, see Lewis, *Rum State*.

60 Roe, *Quest for Authority*, 6; Harrison, *Drink*. For a similar view of American temperance, see Gusfield, *Symbolic Crusade*.

61 Smitley, *Feminine Public Sphere*; Barrow, "Teetotal Feminists." For Australia, see Lake, "Politics of Respectability"; Windschuttle, "Women, Class and Temperance"; Hyslop, "Temperance"; Tyrrell, "International Aspects"; Pixley, "Wowser and Pro-woman."

62 For temperance and regulation, see Dingle, *Campaign for Prohibition*; Greenaway, *Drink*, chap. 2. For temperance and the growth of government, see Nicholls, *Politics of Alcohol*, chaps 8–9; Yeomans, *Moral Regulation*; Allen and Thomas, "Problem Substances."

63 Levine, "Discovery of Addiction," 43; Valverde, *Disease of the Will*; Berridge, *Demons*.

64 Capdeville and Kerhervé, "Introduction"; Cowan, "Sociability."

65 On wine and toasting, see Ludington, *Politics of Wine*; McShane, "Political Drinking"; Lemon, "Compulsory Conviviality"; Epstein, *Radical Expression*, chap. 5; Duthille, "Political Toasting"; Duthille, "Toasting and Gender"; Duthille, "Radical Ideas." For literary depictions of drinking, see Taylor, *Bacchus*.

66 Bourdieu, *Distinction*.

67 Ludington, *Politics of Wine*, introd.

68 McIntyre, *First Vintage*.

69 Withington, "Cultures of Intoxication," 15. See also Withington, "Intoxicants and Society"; Herring et al., eds, *Intoxication and Society*.

70 For British pubs and popular drinking, see Clark, *English Alehouse*; Cooke, *Scottish Pub*; Gutzke, "Introduction"; Hands, *Drinking*; Newman, *Romantic Tavern*. For Australia, see Kirkby, *Barmaids*; Wright, *Ladies Lounge*.

71 In general, I use the term "public house" (or, somewhat anachronistically, "pub") as a broad label for *all* spaces that served alcohol to customers. The important distinctions between inns, taverns, and alehouses, and on- and off-licences in English law and drinking culture (and similar distinctions in Australia) are largely irrelevant to my argument. See Clark, *English Alehouse*; Freeland, *Australian Pub*.

72 Levine, "Discovery of Addiction," 43; Valverde, *Disease of the Will*; Berridge, *Demons*.
73 See, for example, McGirr, *War on Alcohol*; Schrad, *Liquor Machine*. Gusfield, *Symbolic Crusade*, is an important exception.
74 Nicholls, *Politics of Alcohol*, 2.
75 Ibid.
76 Stoler, *Archival Grain*.

CHAPTER ONE

1 "Phillip to Dundas," 11 October 1792, *HRNSW*, 1.2:665.
2 "Sydney to Treasury," 18 August 1786, *HRNSW*, 1.2:14–20; Atkinson, *Beginning*, chap. 3; Frost, *First Fleet*.
3 "Admiralty to Sydney," 21 November 1786, *HRNSW* 1.2:29. An Australian standard drink is 10 grams of pure alcohol or 30 millilitres of spirits at 40 per cent strength. Throughout this book, I calculate standard drinks by assuming all spirits are 40 per cent alcohol, all wines are 10 per cent, and all beers 4 per cent, and these were consumed at an average rate across the entire population, while converting imperial measurements into litres. In contemporary Australia, available alcohol is calculated per adult (sixteen years or older), but I employ a cruder per person measure because, at least in the nineteenth century, the assumption that only adults over sixteen drank is flawed. For more detail on these calculations, see Allen, "Temperance Shift," app. 1.
4 Field, *Sea-Soldiers*, 1:134; Moore, *Marines*, 8; "Sydney to Treasury," 18 August 1786, *HRNSW*, 1.2:14–15.
5 "Phillip to Nepean," 2 December 1786; "Memorial," 7 May 1787; "Phillip to Nepean," 8 May 1787, *HRNSW*, 1.2:20, 100–1, 101–2; Moore, *Marines*, 28–9, 44–5.
6 "Sydney to Phillip," 5 May 1787, *HRNSW*, 1.2:94–5.
7 "Phillip to Nepean," 11 May 1787; "Phillip to Nepean," 2 September 1787, *HRNSW*, 1.2:103, 112; "Stephens to Ross," 17 May 1787, *HRNSW*, 2:388.
8 Frost, *First Fleet*, 120.
9 "Phillip to Stephens," 27 December 1786; "Stephens to Phillip," 23 February 1787; "Phillip's Instructions," 2 April 1787, *HRNSW*, 1.2:40–1, 48–9, 86; "Clark to Bedlake," 10 May 1787 in Clark, *Journal and Letters*; Moore, *Marines*, 44–5.
10 "Phillip to Nepean," 18 March 1787, *HRNSW* 1.2:58–9.
11 Howard, *State of Prisons*, 20–1, 49–50, quotation on 76–7. For more on penal reform in this period, see Ignatieff, *Just Measure*.

12 Penitentiary Act (1779); Devereaux, "Penitentiary Act"; Byrnes, "Emptying the Hulks."
13 Atkinson, *Beginning*, 66–72.
14 Burnett, *Liquid Pleasures*, 52–7, 75–80.
15 Wilson, *Alcohol and the Nation*, 331–3.
16 Wilson, *Alcohol and the Nation*, 16; Harrison, *Drink*, 37–9, 88–9; Butlin, "How Many Bottles," 14–15; McCusker, "Business of Distilling"; McKendrick, Brewer, and Plumb, eds, *Consumer Society*.
17 O'Brien, "Taxation in Britain," tab. 5, 11; Warner, *Craze*, 33–4.
18 Clark, *Alehouse*, 181–4; Mathias, "Brewing and Distilling."
19 McCusker, "Business of Distilling," 207, 211, 218–19; McCusker and Morgan, "Introduction"; Mintz, *Sweetness and Power*; Hainsworth, *Sydney Traders*; Steven, *Merchant Campbell*; Holcomb, *Merchant Families*.
20 Lewis, *History of the Navy*, 398–401; Moore, *Marines*, 8; Field, *Sea-Soldiers*, 1:134.
21 Harrison, *Drink*, 38–41; Thompson, "Time," 59–60.
22 "Memorial," 7 May 1787, *HRNSW*, 1.2:100–1.
23 White, *Journal*, 7–8; "Phillip to Nepean," 18 March 1787, *HRNSW*, 1.2:58.
24 See, for example, Trotter, *Drunkenness*; Rush, *Spiritous Liquors*.
25 "Phillip to Nepean," 2 September 1787, *HRNSW*, 1.2:112.
26 Bushaway, *By Rite*, chap. 4.
27 Reid, "Saint Monday."
28 Dunlop, *Drinking Usage*, iii, 2.
29 Thompson, "Time," 76; Reid, "Saint Monday," 79.
30 Place, *Drunkenness – Education*.
31 Harrison, *Drink*, 41–4.
32 Easty journal, Mitchell Library, 5, 13, 29–30.
33 Nagle memoir, Mitchell Library, 75–6, 78–9.
34 Easty journal, Mitchell Library, 8, 27, 30.
35 White, *Journal*, 10.
36 Clark, *Journal*, 62.
37 Easty journal, Mitchell Library, 37, 42, 44.
38 Tench, *Narrative*, 4.
39 Smyth, "Journal of a Voyage," Mitchell Library, 64.
40 Harrison, *Drink*, 46–58, 64–5; Clark, *Alehouse*, chaps 10, 13.
41 Place, *Autobiography*, 27, 37–8, 77; Place, *Drunkenness – Education*, 10, 17.
42 Trial of Elizabeth Dudgeon and Susannah Garth, September 1783, in *OBPO*.
43 Bushaway, *By Rite*, chap. 5; Reid, "Wakes and Fairs"; Storch, "Introduction"; Harrison, *Drink*, 43–4. For the importance of carnival rituals in early modern Europe more broadly, see Bakhtin, *Rabelais*; Burke, *Popular Culture*, chaps 7–8; Davis, *Society and Culture*, chap. 1.

44 Trotter, *Drunkenness*, 158–9, cited in Taylor, *Bacchus*, 15–16.
45 Garrard, *Democratisation*, 262; Rix, "Corrupt Practices."
46 O'Gorman, "Electoral Deference," 399, 411.
47 O'Gorman, "Campaign Rituals," 79, 85–6.
48 Thompson, "Time"; Thompson, "Moral Economy"; Thompson, "Moral Economy Reviewed."
49 Adler, "Symbolic Exchange," 383–4; Harrison, *Drink*, 56.
50 Clark, *Journal*, 41, 46, 50, 55–6, 66, 252, 260.
51 Clark, *Journal*, 80. For a rare example when he did drink (on his wedding anniversary, 24 June 1787), see 21. On gentlemen and drinking, see Ludington, *Politics of Wine*, chap. 10.
52 Clark, *Journal*, 71, 76–7, 79, 86, 89.
53 Ibid., 41, 83.
54 Ibid., 27–8; Trial of Elizabeth Barber, September 1782, in *OBPO*.
55 Colquhoun, *Police*, 324–5.
56 Bernard, "Fasting to Abstinence," 338–42; Hill, *Society and Puritanism*, 124–5, 148–9, chap. 4.
57 Innes, *Inferior Politics*; Innes, "Reform"; Innes and Burns, "Introduction."
58 Davison, "Gin Legislation," 25. See also Clark, "Mother Gin," 73–6; Warner, *Craze*, chaps 4–5.
59 Spirit Duties Act (1736).
60 Wilson, *Spirituous Liquors*; Davison, "Gin Legislation," 35–41; Warner, *Craze*, chaps 4–5, 193–4; White, "Representation of Gin."
61 Hogarth, *Beer Street and Gin Lane*; Wilson, *Spirituous Liquors*, 37–40; Warner, *Craze*, 116, 194–9, 212–13; White, "Representation of Gin," 59–61; Dillon, *Madam Geneva*, 93–9.
62 Innes, *Inferior Politics*, 180–6; Innes and Burns, "Introduction," 7–10; Roberts, *Moral Reform*, 24–33; Atkinson, *Beginning*, 46–55, 66–71.
63 Martin, ed., *Founding*; Frost, *First Fleet*; Atkinson, *Beginning*, chaps 3–4; Ely, "Pains and Penalties."
64 "Phillip's Instructions," 24 April 1787, *HRNSW*, 1.2:90; draft of Phillip's instructions, PRO.
65 Atkinson, *Beginnings*, 176; Stonhouse, *Admonitions*.
66 King, "Remarks & Journal," Mitchell Library, 26 January 1788; Worgan journal, Mitchell Library, 26 January 1788; Phillip, *Journal*, 58; Karskens, *Colony*, chap. 3.
67 Worgan journal, Mitchell Library, 7 February, 9 February 1788; White, *Journal*, 71; Tench, *Narrative*, 65–7; Frost, *First Fleet*, 177–8.
68 Smyth, "Journal of a Voyage," Mitchell Library, 95–6; Aveling, "Gender"; Karskens, *Colony*, 313–15. For a recent recitation see: Fitzgerald and Jordan, *Under the Influence*, 11.

69 Lewis, *History of the Navy*, 398–401; Moore, *Marines*, 8; Field, *Sea-Soldiers*, 1:134.
70 Smyth, "Journal of a Voyage," Mitchell Library, 98.
71 Ibid., 70–1.

CHAPTER TWO

1 Mikaberidze, *Napoleonic Wars*; Frost, *Convicts and Empire*.
2 Armitage and Subrahmanyam, *Age of Revolutions*; McDonnell, "Age of Revolution"; Waterhouse, "Representative Government." The first official inquiry into NSW took place in the aftermath of the Rum Rebellion. See House of Commons, *Report from the Select Committee on Transportation* (1812).
3 Whitaker, *Unfinished Revolution*.
4 Atkinson, "First Plans"; Atkinson, *Beginning*; Neal, *Rule of Law*; Benton and Ford, *Rage for Order*, chap. 2.
5 On the early church and the state, see Fletcher, "Anglican Ascendancy"; Gladwin, *Anglican Clergy*, chap. 5. On early policing and surveillance, see Allen, "Convict Police"; Allen, "Convict Surveillance."
6 Blainey, *Tyranny of Distance*.
7 On colonial networks and lobbying in this period, see Atkinson, "British Whigs." For a more comprehensive analysis in a later period, see Laidlaw, *Colonial Connections*.
8 Fletcher, *Landed Enterprise*; Allen, "Alcohol and Authority."
9 Grimshaw et al., *Creating a Nation*, chap. 1; Bongiorno, *Sex Lives*, chap. 1.
10 Maxwell-Stewart and Quinlan, *Unfree Workers*, 16; Hirst, *Convict Society*, 27–50; Nicholas, "Convict Labour."
11 Gapps, *Sydney Wars*; Karskens, *Colony*.
12 Sargent, "Governors versus Garrison"; McMahon, "Military Insurrection"; Sharp, *Samuel Marsden*, chap. 6.
13 Kercher, *Unruly Child*; Butlin, *Monetary System*. Parsons, "Commercialisation."
14 Ford, *King's Peace*, chap. 5; Waterhouse, "Representative Government"; Allen, "Distilling Liberty."
15 On *amour-propre* and honour, see Sharp, *Samuel Marsden*, 74–7, 184–7.
16 Kercher, *Unruly Child*; Hirst, *Convict Society*.
17 See Allen, "Distilling Liberty."
18 Allen, "Alcohol and Authority."
19 Fitzgerald and Hearn, *Rum Rebellion*; Atkinson, "British Whigs"; Atkinson, *Beginning*, chap. 13; Karskens and Waterhouse, "Property, Liberty"; Benton and Ford, *Rage for Order*, chap. 2; Ford, *King's Peace*, chap. 5.

20 Blair, "Felonry and Free."
21 Grimshaw et al., *Creating a Nation*, chap. 3; Russell, "Gender"; Russell, *Savage or Civilised*; McKenzie, *Scandal*.
22 Curthoys and Mitchell, *Taking Liberty*, chap. 1; Roberts and Ford, "Expansion."
23 Ritchie, *Punishment and Profit*; Ritchie, *Wentworths*; Sharp, *Samuel Marsden*, chap. 19.
24 Karskens, *Colony*, chaps 13–14; Gapps, *Sydney War*.
25 Curthoys and Mitchell, *Taking Liberty*, chap. 3.
26 Castles, *Legal History*, 129–31.
27 Ritchie, *Punishment and Profit*; Benton and Ford, *Rage for Order*, chap. 3; Evans, "Real Terror."
28 Atkinson, "Four Patterns"; Maxwell-Stewart and Quinlan, *Unfree Workers*.
29 Smith, *Defiant Voices*; Damousi, *Depraved and Disorderly*.
30 Fletcher, *Darling*; Walker, *Newspaper Press*, chap. 2; Kercher, "Colonial Settlement"; Neal, *Rule of Law*.
31 Roberts, "Castle Forbes"; Blair, "Felonry and Free."
32 Stoneman, "Church Act"; Hogan, *Sectarian Strand*.
33 Ritchie, "Molesworth Committee"; Hirst, *Convict Society*; Smith, *Birthstain*.
34 Belich, *Replenishing the Earth*, chap. 8; Jones, "Currency Culture"; Maxwell-Stewart and Quinlan, *Unfree Workers*; Hirst, *Convict Society*; Sturma, *Vice*, 1–8, 189.
35 Roberts, *Squatting Age*; Roberts and Ford, "Expansion"; Reynolds, *Frontier*, chap. 4.
36 Lydon and Ryan, *Remembering*; Milliss, *Waterloo Creek*.
37 Curthoys and Mitchell, *Taking Liberty*, chaps 2–4; Jones, "Currency Culture"; Lake, "Gendered and Racialised."
38 Cochrane, *Colonial Ambition*; Hirst, *Convict Society*; Roberts and Ford, "Expansion."
39 Russell, *Wish of Distinction*, chap. 1.
40 Atkinson, *Democracy*.
41 Atkinson, "Self-Government"; Curthoys and Mitchell, *Taking Liberty*, chap. 4; Woollacott, *Settler Society*.
42 Roe, *Quest for Authority*; Russell, *Savage or Civilised*; Russell, "Gender."
43 Irving, *Southern Tree*; Veracini, "Settler Transition."
44 Martin, "Investigating Intemperance"; Allen and Thomas, "Problem Substances."
45 Blainey, "Gold Rushes"; Goodman, "Gold Rushes"; Hirst, *Strange Birth*, chap. 6; Pickering, "Republic."
46 Irving, *Southern Tree*, chap. 6.

47 Irving, *Southern Tree*; Scalmer, "Containing Contention"; Cochrane, *Colonial Ambition*; Hirst, *Strange Birth*; Bongiorno, *Dreamers and Schemers*, 37–8; Brett, *Secret Ballot*, 11–12.
48 Roberts, "Beyond 'the Stain'"; Smith, *Birthstain*, chap. 8.
49 Hamer, *Responsible Government*, chap. 1; Cuthoys and Mitchell, *Taking Liberty*, chap. 9; Jones, *Republicanism*, chap. 10.
50 Irving, *Southern Tree*; Gollan, *Working Class*; Hirst, *Strange Birth*; Cochrane, *Colonial Ambition*.
51 Martin, *Bunyip Aristocracy*; Hirst, *Strange Birth*; Cochrane, *Colonial Ambition*.
52 McKenna, *Captive Republic*; Pickering, "Popular Constitutionalism"; Jones, *Republicanism*.
53 Brett, *Secret Ballot*, 25; Brent, "Returning Officer," chap. 6; McKenna, "Australian Ballot."
54 Irving, *Southern Tree*, 193–7; Pickering, "Popular Constitutionalism"; Scalmer, "Containing Contention."
55 Martin, "Whig View"; Hutchinson, "Civil Religion."
56 Wentworth, *Historical*, 161, 170; Hutchison, "W.C. Wentworth."
57 *Gazette*, 28 January 1826, 3.
58 *Gazette*, 1 February 1826, 3. On Robinson, see Matthews, *Tradition in Exile*; Mackaness, ed., *Odes of Robinson*.
59 White, *Inventing Australia*, chap. 2.
60 On temperance narratives, see Crowley, ed., *Drunkard's Progress*.
61 Lang, *Historical*, 1:81–3, 101–4. For other examples of this temperance framing, see 1:66, 136–7, 141, 167–72, 178–9, 209–11, 420–2; 2:74–6, 219–21.
62 Ibid., 1:283–7.
63 Ibid., 2:377–8.
64 Lang, *Transportation*, 83.

CHAPTER THREE

1 McIntyre, *First Vintage*; Deutscher, *Breweries of Australia*; Parsons, "Colonial Beer"; Allen, "Distilling Liberty."
2 For earlier estimates, see Butlin, "How Many Bottles"; Dingle, "Magnificent Thirst." For more detail on my calculations, see chap. 1, note 3, on page 219.
3 Butlin, *Monetary System*, 19–23; Nicholas, "Convict Labour"; Hirst, *Freedom*, 27–50.
4 Lisle, "Rum Beginnings"; Fletcher, *Landed Enterprise*; Hainsworth, *Sydney Traders*; Steven, *Merchant Campbell*; Holcomb, *Early Merchant Families*; Parsons, "Commercialisation."

5 Allen, "Temperance Shift," chap. 6; Ellis, "Rum Hospital"; Day, *Customs*; Butlin, *Colonial Economy*, 79–81; La Nauze, "Tariffs."
6 Allen, "Temperance Shift," chap. 11.
7 Parsons, "Colonial Beer"; Allen, "Temperance Shift," 108, 199; Dingle, "Magnificent Thirst."
8 McIntyre, *First Vintage*; McIntyre, "Adam Smith."
9 Rowcroft, *Tales*, 30–1.
10 Freeland, *Australian Pub*, chap. 1; Karskens, *Colony*, 179–80.
11 Allen, "Temperance Shift," chap. 7.
12 Cunningham, *Two Years*, 1:49. The term "tavern" seems to have had a broader meaning in colonial NSW than contemporary England. See Clark, *English Alehouse*; Freeland, *Australian Pub*.
13 Harris, *Settlers and Convicts*, 8–10, 36–8; Moran, "Alexander Harris."
14 Harris, *Settlers and Convicts*, 105–6.
15 *Monitor*, 27 March 1827, 2; 1 June 1827, 8. They were forced to abandon the practice when they found that the rewards simply encouraged perjury. See *Gazette*, 1 December 1829, 2.
16 *Gazette*, 6 March 1830, 2.
17 Harbouring Act (1825); Licensed Publicans Act (1826); Publicans Licensing Acts Consolidation (1830); Licensed Publicans Act (1838). For license numbers, see Allen, "Temperance Shift," app. 3.
18 For examples, see Harris, *Settlers and Convicts*, 116–17, 174–6.
19 Freeland, *Australian Pub*, 44, 53–5.
20 Harris, *Settlers and Convicts*, 8.
21 *Sydney Journal*, 10 August 1847, 2; Place, *Drunkenness – Education*.
22 McCombie, *Arabin*; Steer, *Settler Colonialism*, 43, 52–7.
23 McCombie, *Arabin*, 85, 150, 154, 161, 223–6.
24 McCombie, *Arabin*, 122–4. Emphasis in original.
25 MacAndrews and Edgerton, *Drunken Comportment*.
26 On the carnivalesque in colonial Australia, see Franklin, "Carnival."
27 *Monitor*, 12 November 1827, 6.
28 Thompson, "Patricians and Plebs"; Irving and Connell, "Class Structure."
29 Collins, *Account*, 1:392–3.
30 Mann, *Picture*, 53–4.
31 Ibid., 69–71. See also Collins, *Account*, 1:482–3.
32 Harris, *Settlers and Convicts*, 59; Moran, "Alexander Harris," 43–4.
33 Harris, *Settlers and Convicts*, 35.
34 Ibid., 94.
35 *Gazette*, 29 May 1813, 2; 5 June 1813, 2.
36 Karskens, *River*, 398–403, quotation on 402; Karskens, *Colony*, 126–7.

37 *Gazette*, 20 May 1834, 2.
38 Harris, *Settlers and Convicts*, 46–7.
39 Ibid., 8–9.
40 Ibid., 9.
41 Ward, *Australian Legend*.
42 Roberts, "Castle Forbes."
43 Minutes of the inquiry in Mudie, *Vindication*, 7, 12–14, 16, 20, 23, 29.
44 House of Commons, *Report from the Select Committee on Transportation* (1837), 32–5.
45 Roberts, "Castle Forbes"; Blair, "Felonry and Free."
46 *Monitor*, 19 October 1831, 2; 21 October 1831, 2; *Australian*, 21 October 1831, 2.
47 Irving, *Southern Tree*, 184, chap. 15; Cochrane, *Colonial Ambition*, 205–6, 232.
48 Electoral Act (1843). For accusations, see, for example, *Chronicle*, 27 October 1842, 2; *Teetotaler*, 25 January 1843, 1; 1 February 1843, 1; *Herald*, 30 January 1843, 2.
49 *Herald*, 24 October 1848, 2; Electoral Act (1851).
50 See, for example, *Bell's*, 16 February 1850, 2; *Herald*, 24 August 1850, 2.
51 *Herald*, 12 December 1850, 2; 7 June 1851, 3; *Empire*, 28 December 1850, 4; 11 January 1851, 2; 22 February 1851, 2; *Bell's*, 1 March 1851, 2.
52 Mason, *Assigned Convict*, 56.
53 House of Commons, *Report from the Select Committee on Transportation* (1837), 32–5. Lang made similar observations to the committee. See 226, 258–9.
54 *Teetotaler*, 14 May 1842, 3.
55 Ward, *Australian Legend*, 100–2.
56 Weber, *Protestant Ethic*.
57 House of Commons, *Report from the Select Committee on Transportation* (1837), 85–7.
58 *Empire*, 18 April 1857, 2.
59 For other examples, see Mundy, *Our Antipodes*, 96–7; Townsend, *Rambles*, 211–12, 303.
60 *Empire*, 27 September 1855, 2. See also a sequel: 5 October 1855, 3.
61 Howitt, *Land, Labour*, 1:85, 94, 223.
62 Harris, *Settlers and Convicts*, 56, 100.
63 Mundy, *Our Antipodes*, 447–8.
64 Note that the practice has many names, and I generally use "treat" as the most common in the mid-nineteenth century. Fowler reports "stand," "shout," or "sacrifice" as the terms he heard. See Fowler, *Southern Lights*, 52.

65 Fowler, *Southern Lights*, 52. See also Townsend, *Rambles*, 167.
66 Harris, *Emigrant Family*, 124–5.
67 *Bell's*, 22 September 1849, 4.
68 For thefts following a round, see, for example, *Herald*, 7 November 1836, 2; 12 February 1838, 2; 22 October 1855, 4. For violence when a request for a treat was refused, see *Bell's*, 5 May 1855, 2; *Herald*, 15 April 1856, 5.
69 *Star*, 15, 22, 29 November; 6, 13, 20, 27 December 1845.

CHAPTER FOUR

1 The earlier term "health" (and the related term "pledge") was used exclusively for drinking to named individuals ("the King") or groups ("the army and navy"). "Toast" is a broader and later term that includes the former, but also what were sometimes termed "sentiments" (e.g., "the land we live in"), and in general I use the term "toast" for its breadth and because it was used much more commonly in the nineteenth century, even for individual toasts. See also McShane, "Political Drinking," 250; Newman, *Romantic Tavern*, 203–4.
2 Lemon, "Compulsory Conviviality," 381; Nicholls, *Politics of Alcohol*, chap. 2; Ludington, *Politics of Wine*, chap. 1.
3 McShane, "Political Drinking," 248–9.
4 Duthille, "Radical Ideas," 170.
5 Cockburn, *Memorials*, 39–45.
6 Duthille, "Radical Ideas," 176.
7 *Toast Master*, iv–vii, 30–6; Pocock, *Songster*, ii.
8 *Royal Toast Master*, ii–iii.
9 *Complete Toast-Master*, 3–5, 23. While the work is undated, references to Waterloo and George IV, and none to the Reform Act or William IV, suggest a date in the 1820s.
10 Newman, *Romantic Tavern*, 216.
11 Dietler, "Feast," 67–70, 73, 93.
12 Garcia and Pons, "Feasts and Banquets." Emphasis in original.
13 Newman, *Romantic Tavern*.
14 Lloyd, "Pleasing Spectacles"; Hoock, "Artist's Dinner."
15 Brett, "Political Dinners," 540; Newman, *Romantic Tavern*, 219.
16 Duthille, "Political Toasting," 75–7; Duthille, "Radical Ideas," 171.
17 Newman, "Anti-social Convivialist," 226, 234.
18 Dickens, "Public Dinners."
19 *Gazette*, 23 January 1813; 30 January 1813. For regulation of assemblies, see *Gazette*, 27 November 1813, 1.

20 Nichols to Macquarie, 23 January 1817, in Colonial Secretary's Office, main series, 4/1737, 26–8.

21 *Gazette*, 31 January 1827, 2. For other examples of reporting on food and drink, see the contrasting reports on the 1831 anniversary dinner: *Gazette*, 29 January 1831, 2; *Monitor*, 29 January 1831, 2. For the ethnic symbolism of food and drink at dinners, see Tyrrell, Hill, and Kirkby, "Feasting."

22 On the celebration of the anniversary, see Allen, "Imagining a Public."

23 See, for example, *Monitor*, 22 March 1828, 5.

24 *Monitor*, 2 February 1829, 4; *Gazette*, 5 February 1829, 1.

25 Dunlop, *Drinking Usage*, 270.

26 Ludington, *Politics of Wine*, chap. 10.

27 *Monitor*, 12 April 1828, 4.

28 *Hill's Life*, 3 August 1832, 4.

29 Brett, "Political Dinners," 528, 539–44; Duthille, "Political Toasting," 75.

30 O'Gorman, "Campaign Rituals," 80, 82, 100–1.

31 Baer, "Political Dinners," 183–4.

32 Roberts, *Chartism*; Epstein, *Radical Expression*, chap. 5.

33 Brett, "Political Dinners," 528–31, 547–50.

34 Dickens, "Public Dinners."

35 Allen, "Imagining a Public"; Clark, *History of Australia*, 2:55, 66, 72, 80, 97; Ritchie, *Wentworths*, 210–20; Bongiorno, *Dreamers*, 25–7; Liston, "Brisbane," 435–48.

36 Irving, *Southern Tree*, 193.

37 McCormack, "Rethinking Loyalty," 407, 411.

38 Duthille, "Political Toasting," 74, 80; Duthille, "Radical Ideas," 174, 178; Roberts, *Chartism*.

39 Duthille, "Political Toasting," 77–8; Waldstreicher, "Rites of Rebellion"; Powell, "Political Toasting."

40 Epstein, *Radical Expression*, chap. 5. See also Parolin, *Radical Spaces*, 105–6, 125–6, 149; Newman, "Anti-social Convivialist."

41 Pickering, "Hearts of the Million"; Roberts, *Chartism*, chaps 3–4.

42 *True Briton*, 8 January 1798, cited in Duthille, "Political Toasting," 82–3.

43 Anderson et al., eds, *Maritime Radicalism*.

44 "Vice Admiralty Court," 20 August 1798, *HRNSW* 3:455–6.

45 "Evidence of Collins," 22 April 1817, *HRA* I.9:606.

46 Judge Advocate's Bench, 5 March 1800, SZ767.

47 "R. v. O'Dwyer and Others [1807]," in Macquarie, *Colonial Case Law*.

48 Cited in Karr, "Expiring Sedition," 643.

49 Palmer and Skirving, *Narrative*, 31.

50 *Chronicle*, 19 March 1842, 2; *Herald*, 24 July 1846, 2; Pickering, "Popular Constitutionalism."
51 Colley, *Britons*.
52 On what was becoming the national anthem, see ibid., 43–4.
53 Worgan journal, Mitchell Library, 34–5; Collins, *Account*, 1:31–2; White, *Journal*, 169–72, Tench, *Narrative*, 109–10.
54 Atkins, "Journal of a Voyage," 4 June 1791, 18–19. For confirmation of this significance, see "King to Dundas," 10 March 1794, *HRNSW* 3:136.
55 Atkins, "Journal of a Voyage," 4 June 1791, 18–19, and 4 June 1793, 122–3.
56 Macquarie diary, 4 June 1819, in Lachlan & Elizabeth Macquarie Archive; *Gazette*, 5 June 1819, 2. See also *Gazette*, 1 May 1819, 1.
57 *Hobart Town Gazette*, 29 April 1825.
58 *Gazette*, 25 April 1827, 2, and 27 April 1827, 2.
59 *Gazette*, 26 May 1838, 2; *Monitor*, 28 May 1838, 2.
60 *Chronicle*, 28 January 1843, 2; *Sun*, 27 May 1843, 2; *Temperance Advocate*, 31 May 1843, 3.

CHAPTER FIVE

1 *Gazette*, 17 October 1825, 1; 20 October 1825, 1, 2; 24 October 1825, 2–3; *Australian*, 20 October 1825, 4; 27 October 1825, 2. For the full text of the address as delivered and Brisbane's reply, see "Address," 26 October 1825, *HRA* IV.1:627–33.
2 *Gazette*, 27 October 1825, 1; 31 October 1825, 2; *Australian*, 31 October 1825, 2; Liston, "Brisbane," 414, 436–8.
3 *Gazette*, 27 October 1825, 2; *Australian*, 27 October 1825, 2; 3 November 1825, 2.
4 *Gazette*, 10 November 1825, 2; *Australian*, 10 November 1825, 3.
5 "Darling to Bathurst," 10 December 1825, *HRA* I.12:81–3.
6 Liston, "Brisbane," 445. See also Clark, *History of Australia*, 2:55; Bongiorno, *Dreamers*, 26–7.
7 Lang, *Historical*, 1:209–15. He also claimed that the dinner provoked a "selfish and illiberal" reaction by the exclusives and that the growing divides within colonial society undermined the campaign for democracy and delayed its arrival.
8 *Gazette*, 7 October 1825, 2; *Australian*, 7 October 1825, 2. Macarthur, "Names of the Parties," 11 July 1826, Australian Joint Copying Project, CO 201/179.
9 Rowlandson, *The Brilliants*; Ludington, *Politics of Wine*, 206–10.

10 Dunlop, *Drinking Usage*, 3, 240. He also notes similar drinking rules in military messes (253–5).
11 Pocock, *Songster*, ii–v, vii–xv.
12 *Gazette*, 20 March 1830, 2; *Monitor*, 20 March 1830, 3; *Australian*, 19 March 1830, 3.
13 *Monitor*, 21 July 1832, 2.
14 Ludington, *Politics of Wine*, 187.
15 McShane, "Political Drinking," 258.
16 Heath, *Drinking Occasions*, 172–4.
17 Marcinak, "Concept of Gentlemanliness."
18 Sharp, *Samuel Marsden*, 74–7, 184–7.
19 See, for example, Howe, *Pocket Almanack*, 51–3.
20 Russell, *Savage or Civilised*, 122–7, quotation on 122; Cannadine, *Ornamentalism*, 32; McKenzie, *Scandal*.
21 Smith, *Birthstain*, chap. 8.
22 Phillips, *Colonial Autocracy*, 196–201.
23 "Macquarie to Castlereagh," 30 April 1810, *HRA* I.7:276. The four were William Redfern, Andrew Thompson, Simeon Lord, and D'Arcy Wentworth, who Macquarie mistakenly called an emancipist.
24 Macquarie, *Letter to Sidmouth*, 33–49. There were four not mentioned in 1810: Rev. Henry Fulton, Richard Fitzgerald, James Meehan, and Francis Greenway.
25 "Macquarie to Bathurst," 24 August 1820, *HRA* I.10:336.
26 Table plan, Mitchell Library, MLMSS 4199/Item 6.
27 "Macquarie to York," 25 July 1817, *HRA* I.9:441–4.
28 "Molle to Macquarie," 24 June 1817, *HRA* I.9:456; "Charges Intended to Be Preferred," 25 July 1817, *HRA* I.9:460–1.
29 Cunningham, *Two Years*, 2:140.
30 *Gazette*, 28 January 1826, 3.
31 "Darling to Bathurst," 24 July 1826, *HRA* I.12:437–8.
32 *Monitor*, 25 January 1832, 2. For similar arguments, see *Gazette*, 29 January 1820, 3; *Australian*, 20 January 1830, 3; *People's Advocate*, 29 March 1851, 9.
33 *Teetotaler*, 29 January 1842, 1.
34 Sweatman, *Journal*, xiii, xx, xxv, 64, 132.
35 Ibid., 64, 181.
36 *Gazette*, 29 January 1831, 2; *Monitor*, 29 January 1831, 2.
37 *Gazette*, 29 January 1831, 2; *Monitor*, 29 January 1831, 2.
38 *Monitor*, 29 January 1831, and 22 February 1831, 2. See also O'Shaughnessy's private report on the dinner, apparently at the request of the governor, in

which he gives a substantially similar account: O'Shaughnessy, "Holograph Statement," Mitchell Library, Ao 22.

39 *Gazette*, 29 January 1831, 2; *Monitor*, 29 January 1831, and 22 February 1831, 2.

40 *Gazette*, 29 January 1831, 2; 1 February 1831, 2; 8 February 1831, 2; *Monitor*, 2 February 1831, 2. Unfortunately these events are too obscure to be definitively traced, but they probably involve the St Patrick's Day dinner, mentioned above, and the St Andrew's Day dinner of 30 November 1830, on which see *Monitor*, 4 December 1830, 2; Lang, *Historical*, 2:93.

41 *Australian*, 30 December 1826, 2; *Gazette*, 1 January 1827, 2, and 4 January 1827, 2.

42 *Australian*, 6 January 1827, 2.

43 Ibid.

44 Ibid.

45 McCormack, "Rethinking Loyalty."

CHAPTER SIX

1 *Temperance Magazine*, July 1838, 5. See also *Australian*, 12 June 1838, 2.

2 *Temperance Magazine*, July 1838, 5.

3 *Chronicle*, 20 April 1841, 2; *Temperance Advocate*, 21 April 1842, 3.

4 *Australian*, 4 March 1841, 2.

5 *Chronicle*, 20 April 1841, 2.

6 *Temperance Advocate*, 9 June 1841, 2. For other temperance attacks on toasting, see especially Dunlop, *Drinking Usage*, 262–72.

7 For Saunders, see Manley and Coe, *Grace of Goodness*; Starling, "John Saunders."

8 *Temperance Advocate*, 16 June 1841, 1–2.

9 Bernard, "Fasting," 337–41; Hill, *Society and Puritanism*; Roberts, *Morals*; Warner, "Sanctuary of Sobriety."

10 Tyrell, *Sobering Up*, 54–5, 65–8; Harrison, *Drink*, 99–112; Nicholls, *Politics of Alcohol*, 97–9.

11 House of Commons, *Report from the Select Committee on Drunkenness*, vi–vii; Harrison, "Drunken Committee."

12 Harrison, *Drink*, 133. For the abstinence movement, see Harrison, *Drink*, 142–6; Nicholls, *Alcohol*, 97–104; Roberts, *Morals*, 150–2, 165–8.

13 Harrison, *Drink*, chaps 5–6, quotations on 107 and 115.

14 Backhouse, *Narrative*, 33–4, 67, 68, 149; Roe, *Quest for Authority*, 165. For early reference to temperance societies, see *Gazette*, 2 January 1830, 2, and

20 April 1830, 4. For calls for a Sydney society, see *Gazette*, 31 August 1830, 2, 3; 5 June 1832, 2; 10 November 1832, 3; 6 July 1833, 2.

15 Lang, "Declaration," Mitchell Library, MLDOC 1477.

16 New South Wales Temperance Society (hereafter NSWTS), *Provisional Report*, 3, 11.

17 *Gazette*, 26 October 1833, 2; 5 December 1833, 2; 7 December 1833, 2; 17 May 1834, 2; *Herald*, 8 May 1834, 3; *Monitor*, 17 May 1834, 2.

18 *Temperance Magazine*, July 1837, 1–3; NSWTS, *Provisional Report*, 5–6, 10; Saunders, letterbook, Mitchell Library, B 1106, 20 March 1835; Manley and Coe, *Grace of Goodness*, chap. 4; Harrison, *Drink*, 107–8.

19 *Australian*, 9 December 1833, 2. See also *Monitor*, 1 April 1834, 3; *Gazette*, 3 April 1834, 2; NSWTS, *Half an Hour's Reading*.

20 NSWTS, *First Report*, 13.

21 *Temperance Magazine*, October 1838, 62–4, 110–12.

22 *Temperance Magazine*, July 1838, 1–7; *Monitor*, 12 April 1839, 2; *Herald*, 12 April 1839, 2; *Colonist*, 19 September 1840, 3; 24 September 1840, 4; *Temperance Advocate*, 21 October 1840, 1; 21 April 1841, 2.

23 *Teetotaller*, 2 November 1842, 3; *Herald*, 28 April 1842, 2. For Anglican opposition to radical temperance, see *Teetotaller*, 29 January 1842, 2; 5 February 1842, 2; 12 February 1842, 2; 19 February 1842, 2; 26 February 1842, 2; Starling, "John Saunders"; Allen, "Sectarianism."

24 See, for example, *Herald*, 24 May 1839, 2, and 6 September 1839, 2.

25 *Teetotaller*, 26 October 1842, 2.

26 See, for example, *Temperance Advocate*, 22 September 1841, 5; *Chronicle*, 15 October 1842, 2, and 28 December 1841, 2.

27 *Teetotaller*, 7 September 1842, 2, and 19 October 1842, 2. On Catholic temperance, see Allen, "Sectarianism."

28 *Temperance Advocate*, 29 December 1841, 2; *Teetotaller*, 8 January 1842, 2.

29 *Maitland Mercury*, 25 May 1844, 4.

30 *Herald*, 28 April 1842, 2; 29 June 1844, 2; 2 August 1844, 2; *Australian*, 29 June 1844, 2; Allen journal, Mitchell Library, MLMSS 477, 28 June 1844.

31 *Teetotaller*, 21 December 1842, 1, and 27 September 1843, 1.

32 *Herald*, 29 June 1846, 2.

33 Lang, *Popery*, 9.

34 Party Processions Prevention Act (1846).

35 *Herald*, 22 April 1853, 2; *Freeman's Journal*, 31 April 1853, 8. For England, see Harrison, *Drink*, chaps 6 and 9; for the United States, see Tyrrell, *Sobering*, chaps 8–9; for Melbourne, see *Herald*, 22 April 1853, 2; for Hobart, see Roe, *Quest for Authority*, 167. For more detail on this argument, see Allen, "Sectarianism."

36 Tyrell, *Sobering*, chap. 10; Harrison, *Drink*, 182; Nicholls, *Politics of Alcohol*, 113–14.

37 For Lumsdaine and the Victorian example, see *Herald*, 31 October 1853, 3; 28 December 1853, 3; 29 December 1853, 2; 5 January 1854, 3. For the new society in NSW, see *Herald*, 16 February 1854, 5; 2 March 1854, 5; 16 March 1854, 5; *Empire*, 2 March 1854, 2; 17 March 1854, 2s.

38 Legislative Council, "Progress Report from the Select Committee on Intemperance," 619–22; *Herald*, 14 July 1854, 5, and 1 September 1854, 5.

39 *Herald*, 7 January 1854, 4, and 4 March 1854, 4.

40 *Herald*, 15 June 1855, 5; *Band of Hope*, 5 January 1856, 11. For British precedent, see Harrison, *Drink*, 178–80.

41 *Band of Hope*, 5 July 1856, 15–16; 30 August 1856, 15–16; 27 September 1856, 16; *Herald*, 13 December 1859, 11.

42 For the alliance, see NSW Alliance, "Prospectus," Mitchell Library, MLMSS 1810/117, pp. 189–90; *Herald*, 24 February 1857, 8; 27 February 1857, 5. For the hall, see *Herald*, 20 April 1859, 4; *Empire*, 1 May 1857, 4; 15 July 1858, 2.

43 Sons and Daughters of Temperance, *Rules*; *Son of Temperance*, 1 August 1899, 1; Firth, *Good Templarism*; Clark, *Good Templar*; Cole, ed., *Jubilee Celebrations*; Hyslop, "Temperance"; Tyrrell, "International Aspects"; Pixley, "Wowser and Pro-woman"; *Herald*, 10 April 1884, 4; 17 June 1892, 3; 18 June 1892, 11; Meaden, "Temperance in Australia."

44 Licensing Act (1881); Liquor Act (1905); Beresford, "Drinkers"; Wailes and Allen, "Political Temperance"; Fitzgerald and Jordan, *Under the Influence*, chap. 4.

CHAPTER SEVEN

1 *Herald*, 29 June 1846, 2.

2 See chapter 3.

3 *Herald*, 22 June 1854, 5; 23 June 1854, 4; 21 December 1854, 4; *Empire*, 4 September 1854, 4; 2 December 1854; Legislative Council, "Progress Report from the Select Committee on Intemperance." For a broader version of this argument, see Allen and Thomas, "Problem Substances."

4 Stephen, *Intemperance*, 6, 24.

5 Harrison, *Drink*; Gusfield, *Symbolic Crusade*; Roe, *Quest for Authority*.

6 Harrison, *Drink*, 23–7.

7 Ibid., 29–32, 380–3.

8 Roe, *Quest for Authority*; McAllister, "Proud Non-drinker"; McAllister, "Radical Temperance."

9 Levine, "Discovery of Addiction"; Valverde, *Disease of the Will*; Berridge, *Demons*; Nicholls, *Politics of Alcohol*; Yeomans, *Moral Regulation*; Allen and Thomas, "Problem Substances."
10 Weber, *Protestant Ethic*, chap. 5.
11 NSWTS, *Half an Hour's Reading*, 4–6, 8.
12 *Empire*, 18 April 1857, 2.
13 Francis Place was a classic exponent of these views. See Place, *Democracy – Education*; Harrison, "Drunken Committee."
14 Starling, "John Saunders," 387; Manley and Coe, *Grace of Goodness*, chap. 4.
15 *Teetotaller*, 12 February 1842, 1.
16 *Band of Hope*, 7 June 1856, 169; *Herald*, 30 March 1857, 2.
17 *Herald*, 15 June 1855, 5; *Empire*, 21 June 1855, 1; 6 July 1855, 1; 19 July 1855, 1; 9 August 1855, 1; *Band of Hope*, 5 January 1856, 1; 21 April 1860, 184.
18 *Chronicle*, 9 April 1842, 2.
19 *Freeman's Journal*, 6 February 1851, 8.
20 *Band of Hope*, 8 May 1858, 146.
21 *Herald*, 24 May 1839, 2; *Commercial Journal*, 1 June 1839, 4.
22 *Gazette*, 25 May 1839, 2.
23 *Gazette*, 4 July 1839, 2.
24 *Herald*, 5 July 1839, 2.
25 McAllister, "Proud Non-drinker."
26 *Gazette*, 4 December 1841, 3; *Herald*, 10 December 1841, 2, and 16 December 1841, 1.
27 *Sydney Free Press*, 28 December 1841, 3; *Herald*, 28 December 1841, 2; *Chronicle*, 28 December 1841, 2.
28 NSWTS, *Provisional Report*, 6.
29 *Australian*, 20 February 1834, 2. See also *Herald*, 7 February 1834, 2.
30 *Gazette*, 12 June 1838, 2; *Temperance Magazine*, July 1838, 1, and August 1838, 20.
31 *Temperance Advocate*, 21 April 1841, 4.
32 *Teetotaller*, 7 May 1842, suppl., 2.
33 *Herald*, 24 May 1839, 2. See also the series of debates between the two sides: *Temperance Advocate*, 11 August 1841, 8–11, and 18 August 1841, 5–9.
34 *Herald*, 13 December 1841, 2; Allen, "Sectarianism," 386–7.
35 Ian Tyrrell observes a similar pattern in the United States with the decline of Washingtonian temperance: Tyrrell, *Sobering Up*.
36 *Herald*, 24 February 1857, 8.
37 *Herald*, 29 June 1846, 2. On McEncroe, see Starling, "Victims of Intemperance."

38 *Herald*, 30 December 1853, 2; 4 March 1854, 4; 10 March 1854, 4. See also *Empire*, 22 November 1853, 2.
39 Legislative Council, "Progress Report from the Select Committee on Intemperance," 622.
40 *Empire*, 19 August 1854, 3.
41 Hogarth, *Rake's Progress*.
42 Cruickshank, *The Bottle*; Cruikshank, *Drunkard's Children*.
43 Belfield, *Drunkard's Curse*; Belfield, *The Bottle*.
44 Belfield, *The Bottle*.
45 Vidal, *Tales for the Bush*, 253, 269, 277.
46 Lang, *Historical*.
47 Harrison, *Drink*, 16; Wailes and Allen, "Political Temperance."
48 MacDonagh, "Revolution in Government."
49 *Temperance Magazine*, July 1838, 5.
50 *Temperance Magazine*, September 1837, 39.
51 *Temperance Advocate*, 7 July 1841, 1–2; 14 July 1841, 1–2; 18 August 1841, 2.
52 *Temperance Magazine*, August 1838, 20.
53 *Teetotaler*, 8 January 1842, 1.
54 *Empire*, 2 March 1854, 2; *Herald*, 9 June 1854, 4.

CHAPTER EIGHT

1 *Herald*, 13 August 1857, 8.
2 For the origins and purpose of the league, see, for example, *Herald*, 30 June 1857, 4.
3 Oldfield, *Woman Suffrage*, 68–70.
4 *Empire*, 11 August 1857, 2; *Herald*, 11 August 1857, 5; 13 August 1857, 8.
5 For the earlier speech, see *Herald*, 21 July 1857, 4.
6 *Herald*, 13 August 1857, 8. Sands's letter was cited by Marian Quartly (in Grimshaw et al., *Creating a Nation*, 103), but she interprets it as "against democracy" because if "humble men gained political power" ladies of rank would lose influence. I understand the letter differently.
7 Sarah Sands may well be a pseudonym, since this was also the name of a prominent steamship, trading between Britain and the colonies, and a famous Canadian gold nugget.
8 *Empire*, 18 July 1856, 5; *Herald*, 19 July 1856, 7.
9 Baer, "Political Dinners," 201; Duthille, "Toasting and Gender," 38. See also Epstein, *Radical Expression*, chap. 5, where he notes that the active inclusion of women at some radical dinners in the 1820s was politically significant.

10 Scott, "Category of Analysis," 1067.
11 On separate spheres ideology, see, for example, Davidoff and Hall, *Family Fortunes*.
12 On class, gender, and the public sphere, see Clark, *Breeches*; Morgan, *Woman's Place*.
13 Connell, *Gender and Power*; Connell and Messerschmidt, "Hegemonic Masculinity."
14 Cohen, "Manners"; Tosh, "Gentlemanly Politeness"; Harvey, "Ritual Encounters."; Gatrell, *City of Laughter*, chap. 15; Taylor, *Bacchus*, chap. 7.
15 Roe, *Quest for Authority*.
16 Tosh, *Man's Place*, chap. 6, quotation on 126; Tosh, "Masculinities," 335.
17 Lake, "Politics of Respectability"; Tosh, "Flight from Domesticity."
18 For the longer history of this idea, see Warner, "Sanctuary of Sobriety."
19 On women, the carnivalesque, and drunkenness, see Davis, *Society and Culture*, chap. 5; Warner, *Craze*, chap. 3.
20 Summers, *Damned Whores*. See also Sturma, "Eye of the Beholder."
21 Damousi, *Depraved and Disorderly*; Smith, *Defiant Voices*; Kirkby, *Barmaids*; Wright, *Ladies Lounge*; Lake, "Politics of Respectability."
22 Lake, "Gendered and Racialised"; Woollacott, *Settler Society*.
23 Australian Bureau of Statistics, *Historical Population*.
24 Oxley, *Convict Maids*, 180–3; Grimshaw et al., *Creating a Nation*, chap. 3; Summers, *Damned Whores*, chap. 9.
25 Roberts, *Chartist*, 21–3.
26 Duthille, "Toasting and Gender."
27 *Tatler*, 4 June 1709, in *The Tatler*, 71.
28 Duthille, "Toasting and Gender," 40–2; Capdeville, "Gender at Stake."
29 Newman, *Romantic Tavern*, 228.
30 Brand, *Popular Antiquities*, 369. He also cites the account in *The Tatler*.
31 Duthille, "Toasting and Gender," 45–6; Ludington, *Politics of Wine*, 209–10.
32 Clark, *British Clubs*, 226.
33 Capdeville, "Clubs," 18–19; Cohen, "Manners."
34 Taylor, *Bacchus*, 191–205.
35 *Complete Toast-Master*, 5–6, 15, 23–4; *Toast Master*, 33.
36 Trusler, *Honours*, 9–10. For a similar discussion of gendered drinking, reprinted in the colony, see *Herald*, 22 April 1833, 2.
37 Logan, *Victorian Parlour*, 12, 93–4; Tange, *Architectural*, chap. 2.
38 Archenholz, *Picture of England*, 109; Grosley, *Tour to London*, 1:251–2; Le Blanc, cited in Duthille, "Toasting and Gender," 44–5.
39 *Royal Toast Master*, ii–iv; Ludington, *Politics of Wine*, 235–6; Tange, *Architectural*, chap. 2; Tosh, *Man's Place*, chap. 6.

40 For Holt, see Allen, "Distilling Liberty."
41 Holt, *Memoirs*, 2:76–8. On Atkins's drunkenness, see "Macarthur to Hunter," 25 July 1796, *HRNSW* 3:122; John Grant, *Beauteous*, 52–3; Atkins, "Journal of a Voyage," 4 June 1796.
42 See chapter 2; Ludington, *Politics of Wine*, chap. 10.
43 Russell, "Class and Comportment."
44 Macquarie diary, 4 June 1811; 4 June 1812; 4 June 1813, in Lachlan & Elizabeth Macquarie Archive.
45 *Gazette*, 7 June 1807; 25 December 1819, 2; 28 July 1821, 3.
46 Cunningham, *Two Years*, 1:54, 2:120.
47 *Australian*, 19 August 1834, 4.
48 Meredith, *Notes and Sketches*, 51–2, 131, 161–2.
49 Vidal, *Bengala*, 95–6.
50 *Gazette*, 26 May 1838, 2; *Monitor*, 28 May 1838, 2.
51 *Herald*, 17 February 1848, 2.
52 Collins, *Account*, 2:54.
53 *Gazette*, 30 June 1821.
54 *Empire*, 21 January 1853, 2; *Herald*, 21 January 1853, 2; *Maitland Mercury*, 26 January 1853, and 12 February 1853, 2.
55 Judge Advocate's Bench, 20 January 1789, SZ765.
56 *Gazette*, 2 July 1814, 2; Court of Criminal Jurisdiction, minutes, 29 June 1814.
57 *Maitland Mercury*, 12 April 1848, 2.
58 Byrne, *Criminal Law*, 89–103, quotation on 93.
59 *Australian*, 23 April 1839, 2.
60 *Monitor*, 22 April 1839, 4; *Gazette*, 23 April 1839, 2; *Australian*, 25 April 1839, 2.
61 *Chronicle*, 21 December 1844, 2; *Herald*, 15 February 1845, 2.
62 Allen journal, 18 March 1834; 18 April 1836; 29 May 1841; 17 October 1846; 1 June 1847; 2 July 1847.
63 *Herald*, 15 February 1845, 2.
64 Russell, *Savage or Civilised*, 132–4.
65 *Herald*, 15 February 1845, 2; *Chronicle*, 21 December 1844, 2.
66 Lake, "Mission Impossible"; Lake, "Politics of Respectability"; Dunstan, *Wowsers*. For temperance as cant, see, for example, *Australian*, 9 December 1836, 3; *Bent's News*, 4 May 1839, 3; *Bell's*, 11 October 1845, 3. For defences against such charges, see, for example, *Temperance Advocate*, 23 June 1841, 1, 3; *Herald*, 15 September 1845, 2.
67 *Bell's*, 10 October 1846, 2; 4 March 1848, 2; 8 April 1848, 1; 11 November 1848, 2.
68 Crittenden, "Louisa Atkinson."

69 *Band of Hope*, 7 November 1857, 355.

70 Court of Criminal Jurisdiction, minutes, November 1789; Collins, *Account*, 103; Smith, *Defiant Voices*, 75–6.

71 Marsden, "Essays Concerning NSW," Mitchell Library, 3, 22–7. For another example from the period, see Turnbull, *Voyage*, 3:181.

72 Damousi, *Depraved and Disorderly*.

73 Reid, *Two Voyages*, 18, 87, 227–8, 266–7.

74 *Monitor*, 7 August 1830, 3.

75 Ihde, "Manly Men," 125; Ihde, *Manifesto*, 180.

76 House of Commons, *Report from the Select Committee on Transportation*, 60, 148.

77 Warner, *Craze*, chap. 3; Dillon, *Gin*, 93–9.

78 *Monitor*, 17 May 1839, 2; *Sydney Gazette*, 21 May 1839, 2.

79 *Herald*, 17 May 1839, 2.

80 *Gazette*, 27 November 1823, 2.

81 Judge Advocate's Bench, 5, 12 January 1799, SZ767, cited in Golder, *Magistracy*, 22–3.

82 Offenders' Punishment and Transportation Act (1830); Offenders' Punishment and Justices' Summary Jurisdiction Act (1832).

83 Byrne, *Criminal*, 39–40, 161–2. Her sample is not large enough to draw a definitive conclusion.

84 Allen, "Drunkenness and Liberty"; Allen, "Policing Drunkenness."

85 Legislative Council, "Progress Report from the Select Committee on Intemperance," 537–9, 608.

86 Allen, "History of Deviance," 54–61.

87 Sydney Police Office, "Return of Convicts," 10 September 1824.

88 *Australian*, 30 September 1845, 3.

89 Windschuttle, "Women, Class and Temperance," 6. See also Windschuttle, "Public Role."

90 Windschuttle, "Domestic Training"; Fletcher, *Darling*, 202–4; Darling, *Simple Rules*; *Gazette*, 10 December 1828, 2.

91 Armstrong, *Domestic Fiction*; Steadman, *Master and Servant*, chap. 1, 138–45; Smith, *Defiant Voices*, 122–4.

92 Meredith, *Notes and Sketches*, 125.

93 *Gazette*, 18 August 1832, 3; 25 August 1832, 3.

94 Valverde, "Racial Poison." For Australia, see Lake, "Politics of Respectability"; Hyslop, "Temperance"; Tyrrell, "International Aspects"; Pixley, "Wowser and Pro-woman."

95 *Herald*, 20 November 1834, 2; *Colonist*, 1 January 1835, 7; *Herald*, 8 January 1835, 2; 24 April 1839, 2. For futher calls for a female society, see *Temperance Advocate*, 23 December 1840, 4; *Teetotaller*, 26 October 1842, 2.

96 *Teetotaller*, 14 December 1842, 1.
97 *Temperance Advocate*, 21 April 1841, 2; *Chronicle*, 20 April 1841, 2.
98 *Herald*, 19 April 1841, 1; Windschuttle, "Women, Class and Temperance," 8–9.
99 Windschuttle, "Women, Class and Temperance," 9–12.
100 For active participation, see *Chronicle*, 14 September 1841, 2; 28 December 1841, 2; 15 October 1842, 2. For membership, see *Temperance Advocate*, 28 April 1841, 11. For the importance of family, see *Teetotaller*, 23 July 1843, 1.
101 Windschuttle, "Women, Class and Temperance"; *Temperance Advocate*, 7 October 1840, 6.
102 *Temperance Advocate*, 14 October 1840, 1, 4.
103 See, for example, *Temperance Advocate*, 9 June 1841, 8; 29 December 1841, 2.
104 *Teetotaller*, 21 May 1842, 2. See also *Teetotaller*, 2 July 1842, 2.
105 Smitley, *Feminine Public Sphere*.
106 *Band of Hope*, 5 July 1856, 215.
107 *Band of Hope*, 19 July 1856, 231, and 30 August 1856, 279.
108 *Band of Hope*, 24 April 1858, 143.
109 *Band of Hope*, 23 April 1859, 177–8.
110 *Herald*, 11 April 1854, 5.

CHAPTER NINE

1 *Colonist*, 17 October 1838, 3; 20 October 1838, 3; 24 October 1838, 2. For Saunders's Indigenous advocacy, see Manley and Coe, *Grace of Goodness*, chap. 5.
2 *Temperance Magazine*, October 1838, 49–52. In this chapter, I focus exclusively on Australian Aboriginal people, but the trope was deployed throughout the Pacific world. For Maori and Pasifika drunkenness, see Mancall, Robertson, and Huriwai, "Maori and Alcohol"; Nosa, "Pacific Peoples."
3 *Colonist*, 20 October 1838, 2, and 24 October 1838, 2.
4 House of Commons, *Report from the Select Committee on Aborigines in British Settlements*, 5.
5 Benton and Clulow, "Introduction."
6 This is a vast and growing literature, but see Lester and Dussart, *Colonization*; Edmonds and Johnston, eds, "Humanitarianism and Violence"; Skinner and Lester, "Humanitarianism and Empire."
7 Ford, "Protecting the Peace"; Nettelbeck, "Colonial Protection"; Roberts and Ford, "Expansion"; Reynolds, *Frontier*, chap. 4.
8 *Herald*, 15 October 1838, 2. See also *Herald*, 5 October 1838, 2.

9 Wood, "Frontier Violence." For a more comprehensive survey of the press reaction, see Webby, "Reactions."
10 *Colonist*, 31 October 1838, 3.
11 *Herald*, 22 October 1838, 2, and 19 November 1838, 2.
12 House of Commons, *Report from the Select Committee on Aborigines in British Settlements*, 78.
13 Licensing Act (1838).
14 Ford, *Settler Sovereignty*. See also Wright, "Aboriginal Evidence"; Smandych, "Testimony of Others."
15 *Herald*, 15 October 1838, 2.
16 Legislative Council, "Spirit License Act."
17 The first age restrictions on drinking in NSW were enacted in 1882: Licensing Act (1882). Tellingly the clause restricted the sale of liquor to "aboriginals or children."
18 McKenna, "Savage Shores"; Evans et al., *Equal Subjects*, chap. 3; Parkinson, "Impersonating a Voter"; Woollacott, *Settler Society*.
19 Curthoys and Mitchell, *Taking Liberty*, 2, 12.
20 Karskens makes a similar argument in *River*, 445–8.
21 For contemporary concern and anthropology, see, for example, D'Abbs, "Problematizing Alcohol"; Krien, "Booze Territory"; House of Representatives, *Inquiry into Alcohol*; Brady, *Indigenous Australia*.
22 See, for example, Brady, *Teaching*; Brady, *Indigenous Australia*.
23 Brady, *Teaching*, chap. 1, quotations on 6–7, 22. On wine, toasting, and the test of civilization, see also McIntyre (whose work is discussed below), "Bannelong."
24 Langton, "Rum," 196–99.
25 Irish, *Hidden*, 10.
26 Fullagar, "Savages," 212–13; Hudson, "Nation to 'Race'"; Wheeler, *Complexion of Race*; Russell, *Savage or Civilised*, 32–43.
27 Mancall, *Deadly Medicine*, 13. For American debates about Indigenous drunkenness, see Ishii, *Bad Fruits*, introd.
28 Mancall, *Deadly Medicine*, chap. 1.
29 Warner, "Firewater Legacy," 109.
30 Stevens, *Poor Indians*, 169–78. On the "dying native fantasy" in Australia, see Rowse, "Indigenous Heterogeneity."
31 Brady, *Teaching*, chap. 1.
32 For convenience, I will refer to this individual as Bennelong although his name is often recorded or transliterated with different spellings. For his biography, see Smith, "Bennelong."

33 Tench, *Complete Account*, 35, 58, 62, 67; Hunter, *Historical Journal*, 207, 405, 460, 467, 471, 527.

34 On Bennelong in England, see Fullagar, "Bennelong in Britain"; Fullagar, "Savages."

35 McIntyre, "Bannelong"; McIntyre, *First Vintage*, 40–2.

36 Brady, *Teaching*, 8–13.

37 Langton, "Rum," 201, 203.

38 Dortins, "Bennelong's Tragedy," 68.

39 Dortins, *Lives of Stories*, 96–9. The earliest example of Bennelong as a tragic figure is probably Sadleir, *Aborigines*, 25.

40 Collins, *Account*, 2:chap. 5.

41 Dortins, "Bennelong's Tragedy," 67.

42 Turnbull, *Voyage*, 1:61–2, 77–80. Some of this text is duplicated in *The Times*, 29 October 1805, 3, cited in Fullagar, "Savages," 230. I assume Turnbull is the source of this report, though it is possible he copied the newspaper. For other versions of this story, see Mann, *Present Picture*, 46; Lang, *Historical*, 1:36.

43 *Gazette*, 9 January 1813. See also *Gazette*, 29 March 1817, 2.

44 *Australian*, 31 October 1827, 2. The term "bool" was often – as in this report – transcribed as "bull," but I will use the former as a generic term. For more on "bool," see Smith, *King Bungaree*, 113.

45 Arago, *Narrative*, 167–9.

46 "Port Orders," 1 October 1810, *HRA* I.7:656–64.

47 "Further Port Orders," 10 October 1801, *HRNSW* 4:592–3; "Regulations for Vessels," 4 October 1806, *HRNSW* 6:193–7.

48 "Proclamation," 4 May 1816, *HRA* I.9:141–5. For more on these concerns, see Irish, *Hidden*, 25–6, 42. For the legal significance of the proclamation, see Ford, *Settler Sovereignty*, 71–5.

49 *Gazette*, 31 October 1818, 2, and 7 November 1818, 2.

50 *Gazette*, 7 November 1818; Karskens, *River*, 448.

51 Ford, *Settler Sovereignty*, 77.

52 Reece, "Feasts and Blankets."

53 *Gazette*, 4 January 1817, 2. See also Smith, *King Bungaree*, 76, 80, 84–6, 121, 136, 142.

54 *Monitor*, 14 January 1832, 2–3.

55 For calls for bans on Aborigines meeting, see *Australian*, 27 December 1826, 2. For an offence of supplying liquor, see *Monitor*, 13 January 1827, 6; 7 February 1828, 8; *Herald*, 14 December 1837, 2.

56 *Australian*, 27 December 1826. On nudity, see, for example, *Australian*, 31 December 1827, 3; *Monitor*, 2 July 1841, 2.

57 Curthoys and Mitchell, *Taking Liberty*, 39–40. For more on this view and its connections to a wider discourse of idleness, see Lake, "Samuel Marsden."
58 *Australian*, 12 September 1827, 2.
59 Hügel, *New Holland Journal*, 347, 418. For similar views, see McCombie, *Arabin*, 257–8.
60 See Dutton, *White on Black*, 30–2.
61 Earle, *Native Blacks*.
62 Earle, *Views*; Smith, *King Bungaree*, 153.
63 Carmichael, "Black Natives," in Maclehose, *Picture of Sydney*, 164–5, plate 35.
64 "Real Life in Sydney," Mitchell Library. The hand could be Elizabeth Saunders.
65 See, for example, Threlkeld, memoranda of 16 May 1826, in *Reminiscences*, 91–2; report to London, 21 June 1826, in *Reminiscences*, 205–6; seventh annual report, 30 December 1837, in *Reminiscences*, 136–7; tenth annual report, 31 December 1840, in *Reminiscences*, 167. For more on Threlkeld, see Johnston, *Paper War*.
66 Nineth annual report, 31 December 1839, in *Reminiscences*, 159.
67 Eighth annual report, 31 December 1838, in *Reminiscences*, 149–50.
68 Threlkeld, "Employment of the Aborigines," *Christian Herald*, 16 September 1854, in *Reminiscences*, 53–4.
69 *Gazette*, 16 December 1824; 15 February 1831, 2, 3; 1 September 1831, 3.
70 Backhouse and Walker, *Christian Address*, 6.
71 Backhouse, *Narrative*, 327. Though his account is published later, Threlkeld is probably the source of both Backhouse's version of this story and Saunders's reference to it in his editorial on "Civilization" cited above. For later uses of this story, see, for example, *Empire*, 16 September 1853, 2.
72 Brady, *Teaching*, 19–22. See also Parsons, "Tourist Corroboree."
73 Backhouse, *Narrative*, 467.
74 Rowse, "Indigenous Heterogeneity."
75 *Temperance Magazine*, July 1837, 4; August 1837, 26; January 1838, 112; February 1838, 122; October 1838, 52–3; February 1839, 116–17; May 1839, 168; *Temperance Advocate*, 10 March 1841, 2–3; 10 November 1841, 2.
76 Gipps to Russel, 7 April 1841, *HRA* I.21:315; Stanley to Gipps, 20 December 1842, *HRA* I.22:436–9.
77 Legislative Council, "Report from the Select Committee on the Condition of the Aborigines," 964–84; Legislative Council, "Report from the Select Committee on the Aborigines and Protectorate," 449–67.
78 For Maroot, see Smith, "Boatswain Maroot."

79 Legislative Council, "Report from the Select Committee on the Condition of the Aborigines," 944–6.

80 Ibid.

81 On begging, see Cunningham, *Two Years*, 2:20–4.

82 *Gazette*, 4 March 1837, 2; *Monitor*, 31 March 1837, 2. See also *Gazette*, 1 December 1836, 2; *Monitor*, 25 November 1836, 2; *Herald*, 20 November 1845, 3.

83 On the broader and growing concern about drunkenness, see: Sturma, *Vice*, chap. 7; Allen, "Policing Drunkenness."

84 *Monitor*, 9 June 1826, 2. See also *Gazette*, 29 April 1826, 3.

85 *Australian*, 21 July 1825, 3.

86 Smith, "Bungaree"; Smith, *King Bungaree*, 10, 13, 105, 113, 128, 131, 134–5, 142–3, 149–50.

87 Cunningham, *Two Years*, 1:43–4. Emphasis in original.

88 *Gazette*, 25 March 1826, 2; *Australian*, 2 March 1826, 3; *Australian*, 30 September 1826, 3.

89 For release with a warning, see *Gazette*, 4 January 1831, 3; 19 December 1836, 2; *Monitor*, 11 January 1837, 2; *Herald*, 20 April 1837, 2; 30 March 1855, 4; 25 June 1856, 4. For the stocks, see *Gazette*, 14 February 1829, 2; *Monitor*, 10 October 1836, 2; *Herald*, 13 October 1836, 2. For jail, see *Bathurst Free Press*, 31 March 1860, 2.

90 *Gazette*, 21 January 1840, 2.

91 *Herald*, 6 July 1837, 2; *Gazette*, 6 July 1837, 2.

92 *Bell's*, 13 May 1848, 2. On Gooseberry, see Smith, *King Bungaree*, 145–6.

93 *Monitor*, 19 December 1836, 2; *Gazette*, 6 July 1837, 3; *Herald*, 29 December 1843, 2; 15 April 1844, 2; *Bell's*, 13 May 1848, 2.

94 *Bell's*, 28 September 1850, 3; 30 November 1850, 2; 14 June 1851, 3. Irish, *Hidden*, 42.

95 On police and fining, see Sturma, *Vice*, chap. 7; Allen, "Policing Drunkenness."

96 *Herald*, 8 June 1844, 2. For more on this death and its significance in debates about protection, see Curthoys and Mitchell, *Taking Liberty*, 137–40.

97 *Australian*, 30 January 1845, 3.

98 For calls for action against publicans, see *Colonist*, 19 December 1840, 3; *Australian*, 26 October 1842, 3; 23 February 1853, 2; *Chronicle*, 4 February 1840, 2; *Herald*, 9 April 1845, 3. For successful charges, see *Herald*, 29 May 1839, 2; *Colonist*, 29 May 1839, 3; *Herald*, 27 September 1842, 2. For a failed prosecution, see *Empire*, 9 August 1860, 5.

99 Irish, *Hidden*, 42–3.

100 *Australian*, 4 May 1838, 2; *Herald*, 7 May 1838, 2; *Monitor*, 7 May 1838, 2.

101 Ford, *Settler Sovereignty*, 196–203, quotation on 197. Notably the jury disagreed with Burton, and Murrell was acquitted.

102 Irish, *Hidden*, 100–1.

103 *Herald*, 26 July 1849, 2.

104 For the end of prohibition and its consequences, see Brady, *Radical Actions*.

105 Wright, "Aboriginal Evidence," 143; Smandych, "Aboriginal Evidence Acts," 119–20.

106 Brady, "Equality and Difference," 759.

107 Curthoys and Mitchell, *Taking Liberty*, 122–3.

108 *Herald*, 26 May 1849, 2. On a technical reading of the Licensing Act, the committee was guilty of an offence in supplying Aboriginal people with liquor.

CONCLUSION

1 NSW Constitution Act (1855).

2 *Herald*, 18 June 1856, 5; *Empire*, 23 June 1856, 1; 26 June 1856, 4.

3 *Herald*, 2 July 1856, 4; 9 July 1856, 3; 11 July 1856, 5; *Empire*, 2 July 1856, 7.

4 Thompson, *National Banquet*, 13–14; *Empire*, 18 July 1856, 4; *Herald*, 19 July 1856, 6. The one potentially larger dinner was held in honour of Charles Gavan Duffy, in March 1856. On that occasion, *The Herald* and *The People's Advocate* both claimed there were five hundred diners, while *The Empire* said two thousand attended, including "several hundred" ladies. See *Herald*, 12 March 1856, 4; *Empire*, 12 March 1856, 4; *People's Advocate*, 15 March 1856, 5.

5 Thompson, *National Banquet*, 22–8.

6 Ibid., 31.

7 Stephen, *Intemperance*, 6.

8 Thompson, *National Banquet*, 32.

9 *Herald*, 30 July 1856, 5. See also *Herald*, 11 June 1856, 3; 22 July 1856, 2. On "the bunch," see Irving, *Southern Tree*, chap. 16.

10 *Age*, 23 July 1856, 6.

11 *Empire*, 18 July 1856, 5; *Herald*, 19 July 1856, 7; Thompson, *National Banquet*, 42.

12 Thompson, *National Banquet*, 25.

13 Ibid.

14 On Gill, see Morgan, "Gill, Samuel"; Longmire, "S.T. Gill."

15 Gill, *Old Colonists' … Melbourne*; *Argus*, 15 September 1853, 5.

16 *Argus*, 15 September 1853, 5, and 16 September 1853, 4.

17 *South Australian*, 21 February 1851, 2, and 18 March 1851, 4.

18 Gill, *Old Colonists' ... Adelaide*; *Adelaide Times*, 29 March 1851, 2.
19 Badger, "Horrid Democracy"; Gill, *Digger's Wedding*.
20 Lang, *Historical*.
21 *Herald*, 22 October 1856, 4. Due to the electoral system of the time, Donaldson was able to stand for a rural electorate that voted later and retained a seat in the assembly.
22 *Herald*, 22 October 1856, 4.
23 *Herald*, 2 December 1857, 3.
24 Lake, "Gendered and Racialised."
25 Wolin, *Fugitive Democracy*.
26 Butler, *Performative Assembly*.
27 MacDonagh, "Revolution in Government."
28 I have deliberately avoided rewatching the ads, although I know they can be located online, because I am concerned with the political significance of my memory of them.

BIBLIOGRAPHY

ARCHIVES

Allen, George. Journal, 1819–75. Allen Papers. Mitchell Library. MLMSS 477.

Atkins, Richard. "Journal of a Voyage to Botany Bay and South America," 1791–1810. Mitchell Library. MLMSS 737.

Colonial Secretary's Office. Main series of letters received, 1788–1825. Series 897. State Records of NSW.

Court of Criminal Jurisdiction. Minutes of proceedings, 1788–1815. State Records of NSW. 5/1121.

Draft of Phillip's instructions, 20 April 1787. PRO. CO 201/1 ff 29–45v.

Easty, John. Journal, 1786–93. Mitchell Library. SAFE/DLSPENCER. 374.

Judge Advocate's Bench. Proceedings, 1788–1821. State Records of NSW. SZ765–SZ775.

King, Phillip Gidley. "Remarks & Journal Kept on the Expedition to Form a Colony … ," 1786–90. Mitchell Library. Safe 1/246.

Lang, J.D. "Declaration Made by Lang and Others On Board Stirling Castle … 13th October 1831." Mitchell Library. MLDOC 1477.

Legislative Council of NSW. "Spirit License Act." 1838. Tabled papers. Parliament of NSW. 1838/01777–1.

Macarthur, John, Jr. "Names of the Parties Who Gave the Governor a Public Dinner and of the Guests Invited." 11 July 1826. Australian Joint Copying Project. CO 201/179.

Marsden, Samuel. "Essays Concerning NSW, 1807–18—, with List of Females in the Colony." 1806. Mitchell Library. MLMSS 18.

Nagle, Jacob. Memoir, 1775–1802, compiled 1829. Mitchell Library. Safe 1/156.

NSW Alliance for the Suppression on Intemperance and for the Social Moral and Intellectual Elevation of the People. "New South Wales Alliance: Prospectus." John Joseph Therry Papers, 1788, 1807–88. Mitchell Library. MLMSS 1810/117. pp. 189–90.

O'Shaughnessy, Edward. "Holograph Statement ... Respecting the Conduct of G.R. Nichols at the Anniversary Dinner of the Australian Society and His Violent Attack on the Tyranny and Oppression of the Colonial Government." 26 January 1831. Mitchell Library. AO 22.

"Real Life in Sydney." Reverend John Saunders letterbook, 1834–56. Mitchell Library. B 1106.

Saunders, John. Letterbook, 1834–56. Mitchell Library. B 1106.

Smyth, Arthur Bowes. "A Journal of a Voyage from Portsmouth to New South Wales and China in the Lady Penrhyn ... ," 1787–89, compiled ca 1790. Mitchell Library. Safe 1/15.

Sydney Police Office. "Return of Convicts before Magistrates, Jul.–Dec. 1824." Colonial Secretary's Correspondence, Special Bundles 1794–1825. State Records of NSW. 4/6671 pt.

Table plan for a dinner party at Government House, ca 1815. Mitchell Library. MLMSS 4199/item 6.

Worgan, George Bouchier. Letter written to his brother Richard Worgan, 12–18 June 1788, including journal fragment, 20 January 1788–11 July 1788. Mitchell Library. Safe 1/114.

NEWSPAPERS

Note: Some early colonial newspapers regularly changed their titles. In cases where I cite the same paper under similar names, I use a standard title throughout this book, but list all the relevant full titles below.

Adelaide Times. Adelaide: James Allen, 1848–58.

Age. South Melbourne: Francis Cooke, 1854–.

Argus. Melbourne: Argus Office, 1848–.

Australian. Sydney, 1824–48.

Australian Temperance Magazine. Sydney, 1837–40.

Band of Hope: *Australian Band of Hope Review, and Children's Friend*. Sydney, 1856. *Australian Band of Hope Journal*. Sydney, 1857. *Band of Hope Journal and Australian Home Companion*. Sydney, 1858. *Australian Home Companion and Band of Hope Journal*. Sydney, 1859–61.

Bathurst Free Press and Mining Journal. Bathurst, NSW, 1851–62.

Bell's Life in Sydney and Sporting Reviewer. Sydney, 1845–60.

Bent's News and New South Wales Advertiser. Sydney, 1839.

Chronicle: *Australasian Chronicle*. Sydney: Andrew Bent, 1839–43. *Morning Chronicle*. Sydney: Michael D'Arcy, 1843–46. *Sydney Chronicle*. Sydney: Edward John Hawkesley, 1846–48.

Colonist. Sydney: Henry Bull and J. Spilsbury, 1835–40.
Commercial Journal and Advertiser. Sydney, 1835–40.
Empire: Sydney Journal of News, Politics and Commerce. Sydney, 1850–60.
Freeman's Journal. Sydney, 1850–1932.
Herald: The Sydney Herald. Sydney, 1831–42. *Sydney Morning Herald.* Sydney, 1842–.
Hill's Life in New South Wales. Sydney, 1832.
Hobart Town Gazette and Van Diemen's Land Advertiser. Hobart Town, 1821–25.
Maitland Mercury and Hunter River General Advertiser. Maitland, NSW, 1843–93.
Monitor: The Monitor. Sydney: E.S. Hall, 1826–28. *Sydney Monitor.* Sydney, 1828–38. *Sydney Monitor and Commercial Advertiser.* Sydney, 1838–41.
New South Wales Son of Temperance. Sydney, 1899–1917.
People's Advocate and New South Wales Vindicator. Sydney: Edward John Hawksley and Francis Cunninghame, 1848–56.
South Australian. Adelaide, 1844–51.
Star: The Star and Working Man's Guardian. Parramatta, NSW, 1844–45. *Star.* Sydney, 1845–46.
Sydney Free Press. Sydney, 1841–42.
Sun and New South Wales Independent Press. Sydney, 1843.
Sydney Gazette and New South Wales Advertiser. Sydney, 1803–42.
Sydney Journal and Daily Advertiser. Sydney, 1847.
Teetotaller and General Newspaper. Sydney, 1842–43.
Temperance Advocate and Australasian Commercial & Agricultural Intelligencer. Sydney, 1840–41.

PRINTED SOURCES

Adler, Marianna. "From Symbolic Exchange to Commodity Consumption: Anthropological Notes on Drinking as a Symbolic Practice." In *Drinking: Behavior and Belief in Modern History*, edited by Susanna Barrows and Robin Room, 376–98. Berkeley: University of California Press, 1991.
Allen, Matthew. "Alcohol and Authority in Early New South Wales: The Symbolic Significance of the Spirit Trade, 1788–1808." *History Australia* 9, no. 3 (31 August 2012): 7–26.
– "Convict Police and the Enforcement of British Order: Policing the Rum Economy in Early New South Wales." *Australian & New Zealand Journal of Criminology* 53, no. 2 (2020). https://journals.sagepub.com/doi/10.1177/0004865819896398.

– "Distilling Liberty: Reconsidering the Politics of Alcohol in Early New South Wales." *Australian Historical Studies* 50, no. 3 (2019): 1–15.

– "Imagining a Public: Anniversary Dinners and the Democratic Imaginary in Colonial New South Wales, 1788–1842." *Australian Historical Studies* Online prepublication, 11 April 2024. https://www.tandfonline.com/doi/full/10.1080/1031461X.2024.2328094.

– "Policing a Free Society: Drunkenness and Liberty in Colonial New South Wales." *History Australia* 12, no. 2 (2015): 143–64.

– "Sectarianism, Respectability and Cultural Identity: The St Patrick's Total Abstinence Society and Irish Catholic Temperance in Mid-Nineteenth Century Sydney." *Journal of Religious History* 35, no. 3 (2011): 374–92.

– "The Temperance Shift: Drunkenness, Responsibility and the Regulation of Alcohol in NSW, 1788–1856." PhD diss., University of Sydney, 2013.

– "Towards a History of Deviance: Policing Drunkenness in Mid-Nineteenth-Century New South Wales." In *History and Crime: A Transdisciplinary Approach*, edited by Thomas J. Kehoe and Jeffrey Pfeifer, 47–76. Bingley, UK: Emerald Publishing, 2021.

Allen, Matthew, and Natalie Thomas. "Problem Substances: Temperance and the Control of Addictive Drugs in Nineteenth-Century Australia." *Social History of Alcohol and Drugs* 35, no. 1 (2021). http://www.journals.uchicago.edu/doi/10.1086/712581.

Anderson, Benedict R. O'G. *Imagined Communities: Reflections on the Origin and Spread of Nationalism*. Rev. ed. London: Verso, 2006.

Anderson, Clare, Niklas Frykman, Lex Heerma van Voss, and Marcus Rediker, eds. *Mutiny and Maritime Radicalism in the Age of Revolution: A Global Survey*. Cambridge: Cambridge University Press, 2014.

Arago, Jacques. *Narrative of a Voyage Round the World, in the Uranie and Physicienne Corvettes ...* London: Treuttel and Wurtz, 1823.

Archenholz, Johann Wilhelm von. *A Picture of England: Containing a Description of the Laws, Customs, and Manners of England ...* 2 vols. London, 1789.

Armitage, David, and Sanjay Subrahmanyam, eds. *The Age of Revolutions in Global Context, c. 1760–1840*. Basingstoke, UK: Palgrave, 2010.

Armstrong, Nancy. *Desire and Domestic Fiction: A Political History of the Novel*. New York: Oxford University Press, 1987.

Atkinson, Alan. "The British Whigs and the Rum Rebellion." *Journal of the Royal Australian Historical Society* 66, no. 2 (1980): 73–90.

– *The Europeans in Australia: A History*. Vol. 1, *The Beginning*. Melbourne: Oxford University Press, 1997.

– *The Europeans in Australia: A History*. Vol. 2, *Democracy*. Melbourne: Oxford University Press, 2004.

– "The First Plans for Governing New South Wales, 1786–87." *Australian Historical Studies* 24, no. 94 (1990): 22–40.

– "Four Patterns of Convict Protest." *Labour History*, no. 37 (November 1979): 28–51.

– "Towards Independence: Recipes for Self-Government in Colonial New South Wales." In *Pastiche 1: Reflections on Nineteenth Century Australia*, edited by Penny Russell and Richard White, 83–99. St Leonards, NSW: Allen and Unwin, 1994.

– "Women Publicans in 1838." *Push from the Bush: A Bulletin of Social History*, no. 8 (1980): 88–106.

Australian Bureau of Statistics. *Australian Historical Population Statistics, 2008*. Cat. no. 3105.0.65.001. Accessed 17 July 2012. https://www.abs.gov.au/AUSSTATS/abs@.nsf/Lookup/3105.0.65.001Main+Features12008?OpenDocument=.

Aveling, Marian. "Gender in Early New South Wales Society." *Push from the Bush: A Bulletin of Social History*, no. 24 (1987): 30–40.

Backhouse, James. *A Narrative of a Visit to the Australian Colonies*. London: Hamilton, Adams and Co., 1843.

Backhouse, James, and George Washington Walker. *A Christian Address to the Free Inhabitants of New South Wales and Van Diemen's Land*. Sydney, 1837.

Badger, Jim. "The Dangers of 'Horrid Democracy': S.T. Gill's 'Digger's Wedding.'" *La Trobe Journal*, no. 67 (March 2001): 16–23.

Baer, Marc. "Political Dinners in Whig, Radical and Tory Westminster, 1780–1880." *Parliamentary History* 24, no. S1 (2005): 183–206.

Bakhtin, Mikhail. *Rabelais and His World*. Translated by Helene Iswolsky. Bloomington: Indiana University Press, 2009.

Barrow, Margaret. "Teetotal Feminists: Temperance Leadership and the Campaign for Women's Suffrage." In *Suffrage Reader: Charting Directions in British Suffrage History*, edited by Claire Eustance, Joan Ryan, and Laura Ugolini, 69–89. Leicester, UK: Leicester University Press, 2000.

Barrows, Susanna, and Robin Room. "Introduction." In *Drinking: Behavior and Belief in Modern History*, edited by Susanna Barrows and Robin Room, 1–25. Berkeley: University of California Press, 1991.

Belfield, Francis. *Retribution, or The Drunkard's Curse: A Domestic Drama in Two Acts*. Melbourne: 1849.

– *The Bottle, or The Drunkard's Curse: A Temperance Drama in Two Acts*. Hobart: M. Hornsby, 1872.

Belich, James. *Replenishing the Earth: The Settler Revolution and the Rise of the Anglo-World, 1783–1939*. Oxford: Oxford University Press, 2009.

Benton, Lauren A., and Adam Clulow. "Introduction: The Long Strange History of Protection." In *Protection and Empire: A Global History*, edited by Lauren A. Benton, Adam Clulow, and Bain Attwood, 1–10. Cambridge: Cambridge University Press, 2018.

Benton, Lauren, and Lisa Ford. *Rage for Order: The British Empire and the Origins of International Law, 1800–1850*. Cambridge, MA: Harvard University Press, 2016.

Beresford, Quentin. "Drinkers and the Anti-drink Movement in Sydney, 1870–1930." PhD diss., Australian National University, 1984.

Bernard, Joel. "From Fasting to Abstinence: The Origins of the American Temperance Movement." In *Drinking: Behaviour and Belief in Modern History*, edited by Susanna Barrows and Robin Room, 337–53. Berkeley: University of California Press, 1991.

Berridge, Virginia. *Demons: Our Changing Attitudes to Alcohol, Tobacco, and Drugs*. Oxford: Oxford University Press, 2013.

Blainey, Geoffrey. "The Momentous Gold Rushes." *Australian Economic History Review* 50, no. 2 (2010): 209–16.

– *The Tyranny of Distance: How Distance Shaped Australia's History*. Rev. ed. Sydney: Macmillan, 2001.

Blair, Sandra. "The Felonry and the Free? Divisions in Colonial Society in the Penal Era." *Labour History*, no. 45 (1983): 1–16.

Blocker, Jack S., Jr. "Introduction." *Histoire sociale / Social History* 27, no. 54 (1994): 225–39.

Blocker, Jack S., David M. Fahey, and Ian R. Tyrrell, eds. *Alcohol and Temperance in Modern History: An International Encyclopedia*. 2 vols. Santa Barbara, CA: ABC-CLIO, 2003.

Bongiorno, Frank. *Dreamers and Schemers: A Political History of Australia*. Collingwood, Vic.: Black Inc, 2022.

– *The Sex Lives of Australians: A History*. Collingwood, Vic.: Black Inc, 2012.

Bourdieu, Pierre. *Distinction: A Social Critique of the Judgement of Taste*. Translated by Richard Nice. Cambridge, MA: Harvard University Press, 1984.

Brady, Maggie. "Equality and Difference: Persisting Historical Themes in Health and Alcohol Policies Affecting Indigenous Australians." *Journal of Epidemiology and Community Health* 61, no. 9 (2007): 759–63.

– *Indigenous Australia and Alcohol Policy: Meeting Difference with Indifference*. Sydney: UNSW Press, 2004.

– "Radical Actions: Aboriginal and Non-Aboriginal Women's Temperance Activism in Nineteenth- and Twentieth-Century Australia." *Social History of Alcohol and Drugs* 33, no. 2 (September 2019): 286–309.

– *Teaching "Proper" Drinking? Clubs and Pubs in Indigenous Australia*. Canberra: ANU Press, 2017.

Brand, John. *Observations on Popular Antiquities: Including the Whole of Mr Bourne's Antiquitates Vulgares, …* London: J. Johnson, 1777.

Brent, Peter. "The Rise of the Returning Officer: How Colonial Australia Developed Advanced Electoral Institutions." PhD diss., Australian National University, 2008.

Brett, Judith. *From Secret Ballot to Democracy Sausage: How Australia Got Compulsory Voting*. Melbourne: Text, 2019.

Brett, Peter. "Political Dinners in Early Nineteenth-Century Britain: Platform, Meeting Place and Battleground." *History* 81, no. 264 (1996): 527–52.

Burke, Peter. *Popular Culture in Early Modern Europe*. 3rd ed. Farnham, UK: Ashgate, 2009.

– "Strengths and Weaknesses of the History of Mentalities." *History of European Ideas* 7, no. 5 (1986): 439–51.

Burnett, John. *Liquid Pleasures: A Social History of Drinks in Modern Britain*. London: Routledge, 1999.

Bushaway, Bob. *By Rite: Custom, Ceremony and Community in Britain, 1700–1880*. London: Junction Books, 1982.

Butler, Judith. *Excitable Speech: A Politics of the Performative*. New York: Routledge, 1997.

– *Notes toward a Performative Theory of Assembly*. Cambridge, MA: Harvard University Press, 2015.

– "Performative Acts and Gender Constitution: An Essay in Phenomenology and Feminist Theory." *Theatre Journal* 40, no. 4 (December 1988): 519–31.

Butlin, N.G. *Forming a Colonial Economy, Australia 1810–1850*. Cambridge: Cambridge University Press, 1994.

– "Yo Ho Ho and How Many Bottles of Rum?" *Australian Economic History Review* 23 (1983): 1–27.

Butlin, Sydney James. *Foundations of the Australian Monetary System, 1788–1851*. Sydney: Sydney University Press, 1968.

Byrne, Paula Jane. *Criminal Law and Colonial Subject: New South Wales, 1810–1830*. Cambridge: Cambridge University Press, 2003.

Byrnes, Dan. "'Emptying the Hulks': Duncan Campbell and the First Three Fleets to Australia." *Push from the Bush: A Bulletin of Social History*, no. 24 (1987): 2–23.

Cannadine, David. *Ornamentalism: How the British Saw Their Empire*. London: Penguin, 2002.

Capdeville, Valérie. "Gender at Stake: The Role of Eighteenth-Century London Clubs in Shaping a New Model of English Masculinity." *Culture, Society & Masculinities* 4, no. 1 (2012): 13–32.

Capdeville, Valérie, and Alain Kerhervé. "Introduction." In *British Sociability in the Long Eighteenth Century: Challenging the Anglo-French Connection*, edited by Valérie Capdeville and Alain Kerhervé, 1–4. Woodbridge, UK: Boydell and Brewer, 2019.

Castles, Alex C. *An Australian Legal History*. Sydney: Law Book Co., 1982.

Castoriadis, Cornelius. *The Imaginary Institution of Society*. Translated by Kathleen Blamey. Cambridge, MA: MIT Press, 1987.

Clark, Anna. *The Struggle for the Breeches: Gender and the Making of the British Working Class*. Berkeley: University of California Press, 1997.

Clark, C.M.H. *A History of Australia*. 6 vols. Carlton, Vic.: Melbourne University Press, 1963–78.

Clark, G.D. *The Good Templar Movement; Its History and Work: A World View of the Liquor Problem*. Sydney: Grand Lodge of NSW of the International Order of Good Templars, 1928.

Clark, Peter. *British Clubs and Societies 1580–1800: The Origins of an Associational World*. Oxford: Oxford University Press, 2000.

– *The English Alehouse: A Social History, 1200–1830*. London: Longman, 1983.

– "The 'Mother Gin' Controversy in the Early Eighteenth Century." *Transactions of the Royal Historical Society* 38 (1988): 63–84.

Clark, Ralph. *The Journal and Letters of Lt Ralph Clark, 1787–1792*. Edited by Paul G. Fidlon and R.J. Ryan. Sydney: Australian Documents Library, 1981.

Cochrane, Peter. *Colonial Ambition: Foundations of Australian Democracy*. Melbourne: Melbourne University Press, 2006.

Cockburn, Henry [Lord Cockburn]. *Memorials of His Time*. New York: D. Appleton and Co., 1856.

Cohen, Michèle. "'Manners' Make the Man: Politeness, Chivalry, and the Construction of Masculinity, 1750–1830." *Journal of British Studies* 44, no. 2 (2005): 312–29.

Cole, George W., ed. *Jubilee Celebrations: Proceedings of the first Intercolonial Convention* ... Melbourne, 1886.

Colley, Linda. *Britons: Forging the Nation 1707–1837*. 3rd rev. ed. New Haven, CT: Yale University Press, 2009.

Collins, David. *An Account of the English Colony in New South Wales ...* 2 vols. London: T. Cadell Jr and W. Davies, 1798–1802.

"Colonial Case Law." Macquarie University Division of Law. Accessed 12 May 2020. http://www.law.mq.edu.au/research/colonial_case_law/.

Colquhoun, Patrick. *A Treatise on the Police of the Metropolis ...* 3rd ed. London: C. Dilly, 1796.

Complete Toast-Master; a Collection of Toasts and Sentiments. Newcastle: J. Marshall, n.d.

Connell, R.W. *Gender and Power: Society, the Person and Sexual Politics.* Sydney: Allen and Unwin, 1987.

Connell, R.W., and James W. Messerschmidt. "Hegemonic Masculinity: Rethinking the Concept." *Gender & Society* 19, no. 6 (December 2005): 829–59.

Cooke, Anthony. *A History of Drinking: The Scottish Pub since 1700.* Edinburgh: Edinburgh University Press, 2015.

Cowan, Brian. "'Restoration' England and the History of Sociability." In *British Sociability in the Long Eighteenth Century: Challenging the Anglo-French Connection*, edited by Valérie Capdeville and Alain Kerhervé, 7–24. Woodbridge, UK: Boydell and Brewer, 2019.

– "What Was Masculine about the Public Sphere? Gender and the Coffeehouse Milieu in Post-Restoration England." *History Workshop Journal*, no. 51 (2001): 127–57.

Crittenden, Victor. "Louisa Atkinson as a Short Story Writer." *MARGIN: Monash Australiana Research Group Informal Notes*, no. 36 (1995): 20–6.

Crowley, John W., ed. *Drunkard's Progress: Narratives of Addiction, Despair, and Recovery.* Baltimore: Johns Hopkins University Press, 1999.

Cruickshank, George. *The Bottle, a Series of Temperance Themed Illustrations by George Cruikshank, with Poetry by Charles Mackay.* London, 1847.

– *The Drunkard's Children. A Sequel to "The Bottle."* London: David Bogue, 1848.

Cunningham, Peter Miller. *Two Years in New South Wales: A Series of Letters, Comprising Sketches of the Actual State of Society in That Colony...* London: Henry Colburn, 1827.

Curthoys, Ann, and Jessie Mitchell. *Taking Liberty: Indigenous Rights and Settler Self-Government in Colonial Australia, 1830–1890.* Cambridge: Cambridge University Press, 2018.

D'Abbs, Peter. "Problematizing Alcohol through the Eyes of the Other: Alcohol Policy and Aboriginal Drinking in the Northern Territory, Australia." *Contemporary Drug Problems* 39, no. 3 (Fall 2012): 371–96.

Damousi, Joy. *Depraved and Disorderly: Female Convicts, Sexuality and Gender in Colonial Australia*. Cambridge: Cambridge University Press, 1997.

Darling, Eliza. *Simple Rules for the Guidance of Persons in Humble Life: More Particularly for Young Girls Going Out to Service*. Sydney: James Tegg, 1837.

Darnton, Robert. *The Great Cat Massacre and Other Episodes in French Cultural History*. Rev. ed. New York: Basic Books, 2009.

Davidoff, Leonore, and Catherine Hall. *Family Fortunes: Men and Women of the English Middle Class 1780–1850*. London: Hutchinson, 1987.

Davis, Natalie Zemon. *Society and Culture in Early Modern France: Eight Essays*. Stanford, CA: Stanford University Press, 1975.

Davison, Graeme. "Rethinking the Australian Legend." *Australian Historical Studies* 43, no. 3 (2012): 429–51.

Davison, Lee. "Experiments in the Social Regulation of Industry: Gin Legislation, 1729–1751." In *Stilling the Grumbling Hive: The Response to Social and Economic Problems in England, 1689–1750*, edited by Lee Davison, Tim Hitchcock, Tim Keirn, and Robert Shoemaker, 25–48. New York: St Martin's Press, 1992.

Day, David. *Smugglers and Sailors: The Customs History of Australia 1788–1901*. Canberra: Australian Government Publication Service, 1992.

Deutsher, Keith. *The Breweries of Australia: A History*. Port Melbourne, Vic.: Lothian, 1999.

Devereaux, Simon. "The Making of the Penitentiary Act, 1775–1779." *Historical Journal* 42, no. 2 (June 1999): 405–33.

Dickens, Charles. "Public Dinners." In *Sketches by "Boz," Illustrative of Every-Day Life, and Every-Day People*, vol. 1, 288–99. London: John Macrone, 1836.

Dietler, Michael. "Alcohol: Anthropological/Archaeological Perspectives." *Annual Review of Anthropology* 35, no. 1 (2006): 229–49.

– "Theorising the Feast – Rituals of Consumption, Commensal Politics, and Power in African Contexts." In *Feasts: Archaeological and Ethnographic Perspectives on Food, Politics, and Power*, edited by Brian Hayden and Michael Dietler, 65–114. Tuscaloosa: University of Alabama Press, 2010.

Dillon, Patrick. *The Much-Lamented Death of Madame Geneva: The Eighteenth-Century Gin Craze*. London: Review, 2002.

Dingle, A.E. *The Campaign for Prohibition in Victorian England: The United Kingdom Alliance, 1872–1895*. London: Croom Helm, 1980.

– "'The Truly Magnificent Thirst': An Historical Survey of Australian Drinking Habits." *Historical Studies* 19, no. 75 (October 1980): 227–49.

Dixson, Miriam. *The Real Matilda: Woman and Identity in Australia 1788 to the Present*. 4th ed. Sydney: University of NSW Press, 1999.

Dortins, Emma. *The Lives of Stories: Three Aboriginal-Settler Friendships*. Canberra: ANU Press, 2018.

– "The Many Truths of Bennelong's Tragedy." *Aboriginal History* 33 (2009): 53–76.

Douglas, Mary. "A Distinctive Anthropological Perspective." In *Constructive Drinking*, edited by Mary Douglas, 3–15. London: Routledge, 1987.

Dunlop, John. *The Philosophy of Artificial and Compulsory Drinking Usage in Great Britain and Ireland …* London: Houlston and Stoneman, 1839.

Dunstan, Keith. *The Amber Nectar: A Celebration of Beer and Brewing in Australia*. Ringwood, Vic.: Viking O'Neil, 1987.

– *Wowsers; Being an Account of the Prudery Exhibited by Certain Outstanding Men and Women in Such Matters as Drinking, Smoking, Prostitution, Censorship and Gambling*. Melbourne: Cassell Australia, 1968.

Duthille, Rémy. "Political Toasting in the Age of Revolutions: Britain, America and France, 1765–1800." In *Liberty, Property and Popular Politics*, edited by Gordon Pentland and Michael T. Davis, 73–86. Edinburgh: Edinburgh University Press, 2016.

– "Toasting and the Diffusion of Radical Ideas, 1780–1832." In *Radical Voices, Radical Ways*, edited by Laurent Curelly and Nigel Smith, 170–90. Manchester: Manchester University Press, 2016.

– "Toasting and Gender in Great-Britain in the Eighteenth Century." *Zinbun* 50 (March 2020): 37–55.

Dutton, Geoffrey. *White on Black: The Australian Aborigine Portrayed in Art*. South Melbourne: Macmillan, 1974.

Earle, Augustus. *Native Blacks, New South Wales*. Sydney, n.d., ca 1826.

– *Views in New South Wales and Van Diemens Land: Australian Scrap Book 1830*. London: J. Cross, 1830.

Edmonds, Penelope, and Anna Johnston, eds. "Empire, Humanitarianism and Violence in the Colonies." Special issue, *Journal of Colonialism & Colonial History* 17, no. 1 (2016).

Ellis, M.H. "Governor Macquarie and the 'Rum' Hospital." *Journal of the Royal Australian Historical Society* 32, no. 5 (1946): 273–93.

Ely, Richard. "Pains and Penalties: The Religio-Moral Economy of Penal Transportation to New South Wales and Van Diemen's Land." In *Revisioning Australian Colonial Christianity*, edited by Mark Hutchinson and Edmund Campion, 61–96. Sydney: Centre for the Study of Australian Christianity, 1994.

Emden, Christian J., and David Midgley. "Introduction: Changing Perceptions of the Public Sphere." In *Changing Perceptions of the Public Sphere*, edited by Christian J. Emden and David Midgley, 1–12. Oxford: Berghahn Books, 2012.

Epstein, James A. *Radical Expression: Political Language, Ritual, and Symbol in England, 1790–1850*. New York: Oxford University Press, 1994.

Evans, Julie, Patricia Grimshaw, Shurlee Swain, and David Phillips. *Equal Subjects, Unequal Rights Indigenous People in British Settler Colonies, 1830–1910*. Manchester: Manchester University Press, 2003.

Evans, Raymond. "19 June 1822: Creating 'an Object of Real Terror': The Tabling of the First Bigge Report." In *Turning Points in Australian History*, edited by Martin Crotty and David Roberts, 48–61. Sydney: University of NSW Press, 2009.

Field, Cyril. *Britain's Sea-Soldiers: A History of the Royal Marines and Their Predecessors and of Their Services in Action, Ashore and Afloat, and Upon Sundry Other Occasions of Moment*. 2 vols. Liverpool: Lyceum Press, 1924.

Firth, Rev. Frank. *Good Templarism: An Exposition of the Order*. Sydney, n.d.

Fitzgerald, Ross, and Mark Hearn. *Bligh, Macarthur and the Rum Rebellion*. Kenthurst, NSW: Kangaroo Press, 1988.

Fitzgerald, Ross, and Trevor L. Jordan. *Under the Influence: A History of Alcohol in Australia*. Sydney: ABC Books, 2009.

Fjær, Eivind Grip, and Willy Pedersen. "Drinking and Moral Order: Drunken Comportment Revisited." *Addiction Research & Theory* 23, no. 6 (2015): 449–58.

Fletcher, Brian H. "The Anglican Ascendancy, 1788–1835." In *Anglicanism in Australia: A History*, edited by Bruce Kaye, 7–30. Carlton South: Melbourne University Publishing, 2002.

– *Landed Enterprise and Penal Society: A History of Farming and Grazing in New South Wales before 1821*. Sydney: Sydney University Press, 1976.

– *Ralph Darling: A Governor Maligned*. Melbourne: Oxford University Press, 1984.

Ford, Lisa. *The King's Peace: Law and Order in the British Empire*. Cambridge, MA: Harvard University Press, 2021.

– "Protecting the Peace on the Edges of Empire: Commissioners of Crown Lands in New South Wales." In *Protection and Empire: A Global History*, edited by Adam Clulow, Bain Attwood, and Lauren Benton, 153–74. Cambridge: Cambridge University Press, 2017.

– *Settler Sovereignty: Jurisdiction and Indigenous People in America and Australia, 1788–1836*. Cambridge, MA: Harvard University Press, 2011.

Francis, Mark. *Governors and Settlers: Images of Authority in the British Colonies, 1820–60*. Basingstoke, UK: Macmillan, 1992.

Franklin, Adrian. "Carnival Relocated? Popular Culture and the Carnivalesque in Colonial Van Diemen's Land (Tasmania)." *Cultural and Social History* 20, no. 5 (2023): 1–23.

Freeland, J.M. *The Australian Pub*. Melbourne: Melbourne University Press, 1966.

Frost, Alan. *Convicts and Empire: A Naval Question, 1776–1811*. Melbourne: Oxford University Press, 1980.

– *The First Fleet: The Real Story*. Collingwood, Vic.: Black Inc, 2011.

Fullagar, Kate. "Bennelong in Britain. (Woollarawarre Bennelong)." *Aboriginal History* 33 (2009): 31–51.

– "'Savages That Are Come among Us': Mai, Bennelong, and British Imperial Culture, 1774–1795." *Eighteenth Century: Theory and Interpretation* 49, no. 3 (2008): 211–37.

Gapps, Stephen. *The Sydney Wars: Conflict in the Early Colony 1788–1817*. Sydney: NewSouth Publishing, 2018.

Garcia, Lluís, and Enriqueta Pons. "The Archaeological Identification of Feasts and Banquets: Theoretical Notes and the Case of Mas Castellar." In *Guess Who's Coming to Dinner*, edited by Gonzalo Aranda Jiménez, Sandra Montón-Subías, and Margarita Sánchez Romero, 224–46. Havertown, CT: Oxbow Books, 2011.

Garrard, John. *Democratisation in Britain: Elites, Civil Society, and Reform since 1800*. Basingstoke, UK: Palgrave, 2002.

Garton, Stephen. "'Once a Drunkard Always a Drunkard': Social Reform and the Problem of 'Habitual Drunkenness' in Australia, 1880–1914." *Labour History*, no. 53 (1987): 38–53.

Gatrell, Vic. *City of Laughter: Sex and Satire in Eighteenth-Century London*. New York: Walker, 2007.

Geertz, Clifford. *The Interpretation of Cultures: Selected Essays*. New York: Basic Books, 1973.

Gill, S.T. *Digger's Wedding in Melbourne*. Melbourne: Macartney and Galbraith, 1852.

– *Old Colonists' Festival Dinner Held at the Rear of the City Bridge Hotel Morphett St Adelaide South Australia on Thursday the 27th March 1851 …* Adelaide: Penman and Galbraith, 1851.

– *Old Colonists' Festival, Held in the Criterion Hotel Melbourne, 14th Septr 1853*. Melbourne: J.S.

Gilling, Tom. *Grog: A Bottled History of Australia's First 30 Years*. Sydney: Hachette Australia, 2016.

Gladwin, Michael. *Anglican Clergy in Australia, 1788–1850: Building a British World*. London: Royal Historical Society, 2015.

Goffman, Erving. *The Presentation of Self in Everyday Life*. Edinburgh: University of Edinburgh, Social Sciences Research Centre, 1956.

Golder, Hilary. *High and Responsible Office: A History of the NSW Magistracy*. Melbourne: Sydney University Press, 1991.

Gollan, Robin. *Radical and Working Class Politics: A Study of Eastern Australia, 1850–1910*. Melbourne: Melbourne University Press, 1960.

Goodman, David. "The Gold Rushes of the 1850s." In *Cambridge History of Australia*, vol. 1, edited by Alison Bashford and Stuart Macintyre, 170–88. Melbourne: Cambridge University Press, 2013.

– "Public Meetings and Public Speaking in Colonial Australia." *Australian Cultural History*, no. 16 (1997): 107–27.

Gordon, Peter E. "The Place of the Sacred in the Absence of God: Charles Taylor's 'A Secular Age.'" *Journal of the History of Ideas* 69, no. 4 (October 2008): 647–73.

Grant, John. *This Beauteous, Wicked Place: Letters and Journals of John Grant, Gentleman Convict*. Edited by Yvonne Cramer. Canberra: National Library of Australia, 2000.

Greenaway, John R. *Drink and British Politics since 1830: A Study in Policy-Making*. New York: Palgrave Macmillan, 2003.

Grimshaw, Patricia, Marilyn Lake, Ann McGrath, and Marian Quartly. *Creating a Nation*. Ringwood, Vic.: McPhee Gribble, 1994.

Grosley, Pierre Jean. *A Tour to London, or, New Observations on England and Its Inhabitants*. 2 vols. London: Lockyer Davis, 1772.

Gunn, Simon. "Analysing Behaviour as Performance." In *Research Methods for History*, edited by Simon Gunn and Lucy Faire, 184–201. Edinburgh: Edinburgh University Press, 2012.

– "Ritual and Civic Culture in the English Industrial City, c. 1835–1914." In *Urban Governance: Britain and Beyond since 1750*, edited by Richard H. Trainor and R.J. Morris, 226–41. Aldershot, UK: Ashgate, 2000.

Gurney, Peter J. "The Democratic Idiom: Languages of Democracy in the Chartist Movement." *Journal of Modern History* 86, no. 3 (2014): 566–602.

Gusfield, Joseph R. "Benevolent Repression: Popular Culture, Social Structure, and the Control of Drinking." In *Drinking: Behavior and Belief in Modern History*, edited by Susanna Barrows and Robin Room, 399–424. Berkeley: University of California Press, 1991.

– *Contested Meanings: The Construction of Alcohol Problems*. Madison: University of Wisconsin Press, 1996.

– *Symbolic Crusade: Status Politics and the American Temperance Movement.* 2nd ed. Urbana: University of Illinois Press, 1986.

Gutzke, David W. "Introduction." In *Women Drinking Out in Britain since the Early Twentieth Century*, 1–13. Manchester: Manchester University Press, 2014.

– "Progressivism and the History of the Public House, 1850–1950." *Cultural and Social History* 4, no. 2 (2007): 235–59.

Habermas, Jürgen. *The Structural Transformation of the Public Sphere: An Inquiry into a Category of Bourgeois Society.* Translated by Thomas Burger. Cambridge, MA: MIT Press, 1991.

Hainsworth, D.R. *The Sydney Traders: Simeon Lord and His Contemporaries, 1788–1821.* 2nd ed. Melbourne: Melbourne University Press, 1981.

Hamer, David. *Can Responsible Government Survive in Australia?* 2nd ed. Canberra: Centre for Research in Public Sector Management, 2004.

Hamilton, Thomas. *The Youth and Manhood of Cyril Thornton.* Edinburgh: W. Blackwood, 1827.

Hands, Thora. *Drinking in Victorian and Edwardian Britain: Beyond the Spectre of the Drunkard.* Basingstoke, UK: Palgrave Macmillan, 2018.

Harris, Alexander. *The Emigrant Family; or, The Story of an Australian Settler.* London: Smith, Elder and Co., 1849.

– *Settlers and Convicts, or, Recollections of Sixteen Years' Labour in the Australian Backwoods.* London: C. Cox, 1847.

Harrison, Brian. *Drink and the Victorians: The Temperance Question in England 1815–72.* 2nd ed. London: Keele University Press, 1971.

– "Teetotal Chartism." *History* 58, no. 193 (1973): 193–217.

– "Two Roads to Social Reform: Francis Place and the 'Drunken Committee' of 1834." *Historical Journal* 11, no. 2 (1968): 272–300.

Harvey, Karen. "Ritual Encounters: Punch Parties and Masculinity in the Eighteenth Century." *Past & Present* 214, no. 1 (2012): 165–203.

Heath, Dwight. *Drinking Occasions: Comparative Perspectives on Alcohol and Culture.* Philadelphia, PA: Taylor and Francis, 2000.

Herring, Jonathan, Ciaran Regan, Darin Weinberg, and Phil Withington, eds. *Intoxication and Society: Problematic Pleasures of Drugs and Alcohol.* London: Hart Publishing, 2012.

Hidalgo, Oliver. "Conceptual History and Politics: Is the Concept of Democracy Essentially Contested?" *Contributions to the History of Concepts* 4, no. 2 (2008): 176–201.

Hill, Christopher. *Society and Puritanism in Pre-revolutionary England.* London: Secker and Warburg, 1964.

Hirst, John B. *Convict Society and Its Enemies: A History of Early New South Wales*. Sydney: Allen and Unwin, 1983.

– "Egalitarianism." In *Sense and Nonsense in Australian History*, 149–73. Melbourne: Schwartz Publishing, 2009.

– *The Strange Birth of Colonial Democracy: New South Wales 1848–1884*. Sydney: Allen and Unwin, 1988.

Historical Records of Australia. Edited by Frederick Watson. 4 series, 33 vols. Sydney: Library Committee of the Commonwealth Parliament, 1914–25.

Historical Records of New South Wales. Edited by F.M. Bladen. 6 vols. Sydney: Government Printer, 1892–1901.

Hogan, Michael. *The Sectarian Strand: Religion in Australian History*. Ringwood, Vic.: Penguin Books, 1987.

Hogarth, William. *Beer Street and Gin Lane*. London, 1751.

– *A Rake's Progress*. London, 1735.

Holcomb, Janette. *Early Merchant Families of Sydney: Speculation and Risk Management on the Fringes of Empire*. London: Anthem Press, 2014.

Holt, Joseph. *Memoirs of Joseph Holt, General of the Irish Rebels, in 1798 …* Edited by Thomas Crofton Croker. 2 vols. London: H. Colburn, 1838.

Holt, Mack P. "Introduction." In *Alcohol: A Social and Cultural History*, edited by Mack P. Holt. Oxford: Berg Publishers, 2006.

Hoock, Holger. "From Beefsteak to Turtle: Artists' Dinner Culture in Eighteenth-Century London." *Huntington Library Quarterly* 66, no. 1 (2003): 27–54.

House of Commons. *Report from the Select Committee on Aborigines in British Settlements*. London, 1837.

– *Report from the Select Committee on Drunkenness …* London, 1834.

– *Report from the Select Committee on Transportation*. London, 1837.

– *Report from the Select Committee on Transportation*. London, 1812.

House of Representatives, Standing Committee on Indigenous Affairs. *Inquiry into the Harmful Use of Alcohol in Aboriginal and Torres Strait Islander Communities: Alcohol, Hurting People and Harming Communities*. Canberra: Parliament of Australia, 2015.

Howard, John. *The State of the Prisons in England and Wales, with Preliminary Observations and an Account of Some Foreign Prisons*. Warrington, UK: William Eyres, 1777.

Howe, George, ed. *New South Wales Pocket Almanack: For the Year of Our Lord and Saviour*. Sydney: G. Howe, 1806.

Howitt, William. *Land, Labour and Gold, or, Two Years in Victoria: With Visits to Sydney and Van Diemen's Land*. London: Longman, Brown, Green, and Longmans, 1855.

Hsueh, Vicki. "Intoxicated Reasons, Rational Feelings: Rethinking the Early Modern English Public Sphere." *Review of Politics* 78, no. 1 (2016): 27–57.

Hudson, Nicholas. "From 'Nation' to 'Race': The Origin of Racial Classification in Eighteenth-Century Thought." *Eighteenth-Century Studies* 29, no. 3 (1996): 247–64.

Hügel, Baron Charles von. *New Holland Journal: November 1833–October 1834*. Edited by Dymphna Clark. Melbourne: Melbourne University Press, 1994.

Hunter, John. *An Historical Journal of the Transactions at Port Jackson and Norfolk Island …* London: John Stockdale, 1793.

Hutchinson, Mark. "History as Civil Religion: Writing Australian History in the Nineteenth Century." *Journal of Religious History* 16, no. 2 (1990): 185–201.

– "W.C. Wentworth and the Sources of Australian Historiography." *Journal of the Royal Australian Historical Society* 77, no. 4 (1992): 63–85.

Hyslop, Anthea. "Temperance, Christianity and Feminism: The Woman's Christian Temperance Union of Victoria, 1887–97." *Historical Studies* 17, no. 66 (1976): 27–49.

Ignatieff, Michael. *A Just Measure of Pain: The Penitentiary in the Industrial Revolution, 1750–1850*. London: Pantheon Books, 1978.

Ihde, Erin. "'Bold, Manly-Minded Men' and 'Sly, Cunning Base Convicts': The Double Standard of Escape." *Journal of Australian Colonial History* 7 (2005): 123–38.

– *A Manifesto for New South Wales: Edward Smith Hall and the Sydney Monitor*. Melbourne: Australian Scholarly Publishing, 2004.

Innes, Joanna. *Inferior Politics: Social Problems and Social Policies in Eighteenth-Century Britain*. New York: Oxford University Press, 2009.

– "'Reform' in English Public Life." In *Rethinking the Age of Reform: Britain 1780–1850*, edited by Joanna Innes and Arthur Burns, 71–97. New York: Cambridge University Press, 2003.

Innes, Joanna, and Arthur Burns. "Introduction." In *Rethinking the Age of Reform: Britain 1780–1850*, edited by Joanna Innes and Arthur Burns, 1–70. New York: Cambridge University Press, 2003.

Innes, Joanna, and Mark Philp, eds. *Re-imagining Democracy in the Age of Revolutions: America, France, Britain, Ireland 1750–1850*. Oxford: Oxford University Press, 2013.

Irish, Paul. *Hidden in Plain View: The Aboriginal People of Coastal Sydney*. Sydney: New South, 2017.

Irving, T.H. *The Southern Tree of Liberty: The Democratic Movement in New South Wales before 1856*. Sydney: Federation Press, 2006.

– “The Southern Tree of Liberty Explained: Class Struggle, Popular Democracy and Representative Government in New South Wales before 1856.” *Marxist Left Review*, no. 9 (2015): 119–36.

Irving, Terry, and Raewyn Connell. “Scholars and Radicals: Writing and Re-thinking Class Structure in Australian History.” *Journal of Australian Studies* 40, no. 1 (2016): 3–15.

Isakhan, Benjamin. “Introduction: The Complex and Contested History of Democracy.” In *The Edinburgh Companion to the History of Democracy*, edited by Benjamin Isakhan and Stephen Stockwell, 1–26. Edinburgh: Edinburgh University Press, 2015.

Ishii, Izumi. *Bad Fruits of the Civilized Tree: Alcohol and the Sovereignty of the Cherokee Nation*. Lincoln: University of Nebraska Press, 2008.

Jones, Benjamin T. “Currency Culture: Australian Identity and Nationalism in New South Wales before the Gold Rushes.” *Australian Historical Studies* 48, no. 1 (2017): 68–85.

– *Republicanism and Responsible Government: The Shaping of Democracy in Australia and Canada*. Montreal and Kingston: McGill-Queen’s University Press, 2014.

Joyce, Patrick. *Democratic Subjects: The Self and the Social in Nineteenth-Century England*. Cambridge: Cambridge University Press, 1994.

Karr, David S. “‘The Embers of Expiring Sedition’: Maurice Margarot, the Scottish Martyrs Monument and the Production of Radical Memory across the British South Pacific.” *Historical Research* 86, no. 234 (2013): 638–60.

Karskens, Grace. *The Colony: A History of Early Sydney*. Crows Nest, NSW: Allen and Unwin, 2009.

– *People of the River: Lost Worlds of Early Australia*. Crows Nest, NSW: Allen and Unwin, 2020.

Kercher, Bruce. “Colonial Settlement to Colony.” In *The Cambridge Legal History of Australia*, edited by Lisa Ford, Mark McMillan, and Peter Cane, 87–107. Cambridge: Cambridge University Press, 2022.

– *An Unruly Child: A History of Law in Australia*. St Leonards, NSW: Allen and Unwin, 1995.

Kertzer, David I. *Ritual, Politics, and Power*. New Haven, CT: Yale University Press, 1989.

Kirkby, Diane Erica. *Barmaids: A History of Women’s Work in Pubs*. Melbourne: Cambridge University Press, 1997.

Kirkby, Diane, Tanja Luckins, and Chris McConville. *The Australian Pub*. Sydney: University of NSW Press, 2010.

Krien, Anna. “Booze Territory.” *The Monthly*, 1 September 2011.

Lachlan & Elizabeth Macquarie Archive. Accessed 1 June 2023. https://www.mq.edu.au/macquarie-archive/lema/.

Laidlaw, Zoë. *Colonial Connections, 1815–45: Patronage, the Information Revolution and Colonial Government*. Manchester: Manchester University Press, 2012.

Lake, Marilyn. "The Gendered and Racialised Self Who Claimed the Right to Self-Government." *Journal of Colonialism & Colonial History* 13, no. 1 (2012). https://dx.doi.org/10.1353/cch.2012.0011.

– "Mission Impossible: How Men Gave Birth to the Australian Nation – Nationalism, Gender and Other Seminal Acts." *Gender & History* 4, no. (3) (1992): 305–22.

– "Politics of Respectability: Identifying the Masculinist Context." *Historical Studies*, no. 22 (1986): 116–31.

Lake, Meredith. "Samuel Marsden, Work and the Limits of Evangelical Humanitarianism." *History Australia* 7, no. 3 (December 2010): 57.1–57.23.

Landes, Joan B. "The Public and the Private Sphere: A Feminist Reconsideration." In *Feminists Read Habermas: Gendering the Subject of Discourse*, edited by Johanna Meehan, 91–116. Abingdon, UK: Routledge, 2013.

La Nauze, J.A. "Australian Tariffs and Imperial Control (Part 1 of 2)." *Economic Record* 24, no. 1 (1948): 1–17.

Lang, John Dunmore. *An Historical and Statistical Account of New South Wales: Both as a Penal Settlement and as a British Colony*. 2nd ed. 2 vols. London: A.J. Valpy, 1837.

– *Popery in Australia and the Southern Hemisphere; and How to Check It Effectually* … Edinburgh: Thomas Constable, 1847.

– *Transportation and Colonization; or, The Causes of the Comparative Failure of the Transportation System in the Australian Colonies* … London: A.J. Valpy, 1837.

Langton, Marcia. "Rum, Seduction and Death: 'Aboriginality' and Alcohol." *Oceania* 63, no. 3 (1993): 195–206.

Legislative Council of NSW. "Progress Report from the Select Committee on Intemperance …" *Votes and Proceedings of the Legislative Council of NSW* 2 (1854): 517–641.

– "Report from the Select Committee on the Aborigines and Protectorate … " *Votes and Proceedings of the Legislative Council of NSW* 2 (1849): 417–75.

– "Report from the Select Committee on the Condition of the Aborigines … " *Votes and Proceedings of the Legislative Council of NSW* 2 (1845): 937–1001.

Lemon, Rebecca. "Compulsory Conviviality in Early Modern England [with Illustrations]." *English Literary Renaissance* 43, no. 3 (2013): 381–414.

Lester, Alan, and Fae Dussart. *Colonization and the Origins of Humanitarian Governance: Protecting Aborigines across the Nineteenth-Century British Empire*. Cambridge: Cambridge University Press, 2014.

Lewis, Michael. *A Social History of the Navy, 1793–1815*. London: George Allen and Unwin, 1960.

Lewis, Milton James. "The Early Alcoholism Treatment Movement in Australia, 1859–1939." *Drug and Alcohol Review* 11, no. 1 (1992): 75–84.

– *A Rum State: Alcohol and State Policy in Australia, 1788–1988*. Canberra: Australian Government Publication Service, 1992.

Lisle, Philip. "Rum Beginnings: Towards a New Perspective of the Grose Years." *Journal of the Royal Australian Historical Society* 91, no. 1 (2005): 15–28.

Liston, Carol. "New South Wales under Governor Brisbane, 1821–1825." PhD diss., University of Sydney, 1980.

Lloyd, Sarah. "Pleasing Spectacles and Elegant Dinners: Conviviality, Benevolence, and Charity Anniversaries in Eighteenth-Century London." *Journal of British Studies* 41, no. 1 (2002): 23–57.

Logan, Thad. *The Victorian Parlour*. Cambridge: Cambridge University Press, 2006.

Longmire, Anne. "Raciness and Ease? S.T. Gill and the Arm-Chair." *Victorian Historical Journal* 80, no. 1 (2020): 22–44.

Ludington, Charles. *The Politics of Wine in Britain: A New Cultural History*. Basingstoke, UK: Palgrave Macmillan, 2013.

Lydon, Jane, and Lyndall Ryan, eds. *Remembering the Myall Creek Massacre*. Sydney: NewSouth, 2018.

McAllister, Annemarie. "The Alternative World of the Proud Non-drinker: Nineteenth-Century Public Displays of Temperance." *Social History of Alcohol and Drugs* 28, no. 2 (June 2014): 161–79.

– "Temperance Past and Present: Thoughts on Radical Temperance." *Social History of Alcohol and Drugs* 33, no. 2 (September 2019): 164–85.

MacAndrew, Craig, and Robert B. Edgerton. *Drunken Comportment: A Social Explanation*. Clinton Corners, NY: Eliot Werner Publications, 1969.

MacDonagh, Oliver. "The Nineteenth-Century Revolution in Government: A Reappraisal." *Historical Journal* 1, no. 1 (1958): 52–67.

Mackaness, George, ed. *Odes of Michael Massey Robinson, First Poet Laureate of Australia (1754–1826)*. Dubbo, NSW: Review Publications, 1946.

Maclehose, James. *The Picture of Sydney: And Stranger's Guide in New South Wales for 1838*. Sydney: J. Maclehose, 1838.

Macquarie, Lachlan. *A Letter to the Right Honourable Viscount Sidmouth ...* London: Richard Rees, 1821.

Mancall, Peter C. *Deadly Medicine: Indians and Alcohol in Early America.* Ithaca, NY: Cornell University Press, 1995.

Mancall, Peter C., Paul Robertson, and Terry Huriwai. "Maori and Alcohol: A Reconsidered History." *Australian and New Zealand Journal of Psychiatry* 34, no. 1 (2000): 129–34.

Manley, Ken R., and Barbara J. Coe. *The Grace of Goodness: John Saunders Baptist Pastor and Activist, Sydney 1834–1848: A Documentary Biography*. Macquarie Park, NSW: Greenwood Press, 2014.

Mann, David Dickinson. *The Present Picture of New South Wales ...* London: John Booth, 1811.

Marciniak, Marlena. "Blue-Blooded or White-Collared? The Gradual Democratization of the Concept of Gentlemanliness in Selected Examples of Victorian Fiction." *British and American Studies*, no. 21 (2015): 61–9.

Martin, A.W. "Drink and Deviance in Sydney: Investigating Intemperance 1854–5." *Historical Studies* 17, no. 68 (1977): 342–60.

– "The 'Whig' View of Australian History: A Document." In *The Whig View of Australian History and Other Essays*, 1–27. Melbourne: Melbourne University Press, 2007.

Martin, Ged. *Bunyip Aristocracy*. Sydney: Croom Helm, 1986.

–, ed. *The Founding of Australia: The Argument about Australia's Origins.* Sydney: Hale and Iremonger, 1981.

Mason, Joseph. *Joseph Mason: Assigned Convict, 1831–1837*. Edited by David Kent and Norma Townsend. Carlton, Vic: Melbourne University Press, 1996.

Matthews, John Pengwerne. *Tradition in Exile: A Comparative Study of Social Influences on the Development of Australian and Canadian Poetry in the Nineteenth Century*. Toronto: University of Toronto Press, 2019.

Mathias, Peter. "Agriculture and the Brewing and Distilling Industries in the Eighteenth Century." *Economic History Review*, n.s., 5, no. 2 (1952): 249–57.

Maxwell-Stewart, Hamish, and Michael Quinlan. *Unfree Workers: Insubordination and Resistance in Convict Australia, 1788–1860*. Singapore: Palgrave Macmillan, 2022.

McCombie, Thomas. *Arabin; or, The Adventures of a Colonist; with an Essay on the Aborigines of Australia*. London: Simmonds and Ward, 1845.

McCormack, Matthew. "Rethinking 'Loyalty' in Eighteenth-Century Britain." *Journal for Eighteenth-Century Studies* 35, no. 3 (2012): 407–21.

McCusker, John J. "The Business of Distilling in the Old World and the New World during the Seventeenth and Eighteenth Centuries: The Rise of a New Enterprise and Its Connection with Colonial America." In *The Early Modern Atlantic Economy*, edited by John J. McCusker and Kenneth Morgan, 186–224. Cambridge: Cambridge University Press, 2000.

McCusker, John J., and Kenneth Morgan. "Introduction." In *The Early Modern Atlantic Economy*, edited by John J. McCusker and Kenneth Morgan, 1–12. Cambridge: Cambridge University Press, 2000.

McDonnell, Michael A. "Rethinking the Age of Revolution." *Atlantic Studies* 13, no. 3 (2016): 301–14.

McGirr, Lisa. *The War on Alcohol: Prohibition and the Rise of the American State*. New York: W.W. Norton and Company, 2015.

McIntyre, Julie. "Adam Smith and Faith in the Transformative Qualities of Wine in Colonial New South Wales." *Australian Historical Studies* 42, no. 2 (2011): 194–211.

– "'Bannelong Sat Down to Dinner with Governor Phillip, and Drank His Wine and Coffee as Usual': Aborigines and Wine in Early New South Wales." *History Australia* 5, no. 2 (2008): 39.1–39.14.

– *First Vintage: Wine in Colonial New South Wales*. Sydney: University of NSW Press, 2012.

McKendrick, Neil, John Brewer, and J.H. Plumb, eds. *The Birth of a Consumer Society: Commercialization of Eighteenth Century England*. Bloomington: Indiana University Press, 1982.

McKenna, Mark. "Building 'a Closet of Prayer' in the New World: The Story of the 'Australian Ballot.'" In *Elections: Full, Free & Fair*, edited by Marian Sawer, 45–62. Annandale, NSW: Federation Press, 2001.

– *The Captive Republic: A History of Republicanism in Australia 1788–1996*. Cambridge: Cambridge University Press, 1996.

– "Transplanted to Savage Shores: Indigenous Australians and British Birthright in the Mid Nineteenth-Century Australian Colonies." *Journal of Colonialism & Colonial History* 13, no. 1 (2012). https://dx.doi.org/10.1353/cch.2012.0009.

McKenzie, Kirsten. *Scandal in the Colonies: Sydney & Cape Town, 1820–1850*. Carlton, Vic.: Melbourne University Press, 2004.

McMahon, John. "Not a Rum Rebellion but a Military Insurrection." *Journal of the Royal Australian Historical Society* 92, no. 2 (2006): 125–44.

McShane, Angela. "Material Culture and 'Political Drinking' in Seventeenth-Century England." *Past & Present* 222, no. 9 (2014): 247–76.

Meaden, J.W. "Temperance in Australia." In *Temperance in Australia: The Memorial Volume of the International Temperance Convention ...*, 27–36. Melbourne: Temperance Book Depot, 1889.

Meredith, Louisa. *Notes and Sketches of New South Wales: During a Residence in That Colony from 1839 to 1844*. London: J. Murray, 1844.

Mikaberidze, Alexander. *The Napoleonic Wars: A Global History*. New York: Oxford University Press, 2020.

Milliss, Roger. *Waterloo Creek: The Australia Day Massacre of 1838, George Gipps and the British Conquest of New South Wales*. Sydney: University of NSW Press, 1994.

Mintz, Sidney W. *Sweetness and Power: The Place of Sugar in Modern History*. New York: Viking, 1985.

Moore, John H. *The First Fleet Marines 1786–1792*. St Lucia: University of Queensland Press, 1987.

Moran, Andrew. "Alexander Harris: The Man and His Family." *Journal of Australian Colonial History* 1, no. 2 (1999): 30–44.

Morgan, E.J.R. "Samuel Thomas Gill (1818–1880)." In *Australian Dictionary of Biography*. Canberra: National Centre of Biography, Australian National University. Accessed 7 November 2023. https://adb.anu.edu.au/.

Morgan, Simon. *A Victorian Woman's Place: Public Culture in the Nineteenth Century*. London: Tauris Academic Studies, 2007.

Mudie, James. *Vindication of James Mudie and John Larnach …* Sydney: E.S. Hall, 1834.

Mundy, Godfrey Charles. *Our Antipodes: Or, Residence and Rambles in the Australasian Colonies With a Glimpse of the Gold Fields*. London: R. Bentley, 1855.

Murphy, Kate. "Feminism and Political History." *Australian Journal of Politics and History* 56, no. 1 (2010): 21–37.

Neal, David. *The Rule of Law in a Penal Colony: Law and Politics in Early New South Wales*. Melbourne: Cambridge University Press, 1991.

Nettelbeck, Amanda. "Colonial Protection and the Intimacies of Indigenous Governance." *History Australia* 14, no. 1 (2017): 32–47.

Newman, Ian. "The Anti-social Convivialist: Toasting and Resistance to Sociability." In *British Sociability in the Long Eighteenth Century: Challenging the Anglo-French Connection*, edited by Alain Kerhervé and Valérie Capdeville, 219–36. Suffolk, UK: Boydell and Brewer, 2019.

– *The Romantic Tavern: Literature and Conviviality in the Age of Revolution*. Cambridge: Cambridge University Press, 2021.

New South Wales Temperance Society. *First Annual Report of the Temperance Society of New South Wales*. Sydney, 1835.

– *Half an Hour's Reading from the NSW Temperance Society*. Sydney, 1834.

– *Report of the Provisional Committee of the Temperance Society of New South Wales*. Sydney, 1834.

Nicholas, Stephen. "The Convict Labour Market." In *Convict Workers: Reinterpreting Australia's Past*, edited by Stephen Nicholas, 111–26. Cambridge: Cambridge University Press, 1988.

Nicholls, James. *Politics of Alcohol: A History of the Drink Question in England*. Manchester: Manchester University Press, 2009.

Nosa, Vili. "Pacific Peoples and Alcohol: A Review of the Literature." *New Zealand Medical Journal* 134, no. 1529 (2021): 86–96.

O'Brien, Patrick. "Taxation in Britain and France, 1715–1810. A Comparison of the Social and Economic Incidence of Taxes Collected for the Central Governments." *Journal of European Economic History* 5 (1976): 601–50.

O'Gorman, Frank. "Campaign Rituals and Ceremonies: The Social Meaning of Elections in England 1780–1860." *Past & Present*, no. 135 (1992): 79–115.

– "Electoral Deference in 'Unreformed' England: 1760–1832." *Journal of Modern History* 56, no. 3 (1984): 392–429.

Old Bailey Proceedings Online. Version 7.2. Accessed 26 September 2017. www.oldbaileyonline.org.

Oldfield, Audrey. *Woman Suffrage in Australia: A Gift or a Struggle?* Cambridge: Cambridge University Press, 1992.

Oxley, Deborah. *Convict Maids: The Forced Migration of Women to Australia*. Cambridge: Cambridge University Press, 1996.

Painter, Martin, and Richard Waterhouse. *The Principal Club: A History of the Australian Jockey Club*. North Sydney: Allen and Unwin, 1992.

Palmer, Thomas Fyshe, and William Skirving. *A Narrative of the Sufferings of T.F. Palmer, and W. Skirving, during a Voyage to New South Wales, 1794, On Board the Surprise Transport*. Cambridge: W.H. Lunn, J. Deighton, and J. Nicholson, 1797.

Palti, Elías José. "The 'Theoretical Revolution' in Intellectual History: From the History of Political Ideas to the History of Political Languages." *History and Theory* 53, no. 3 (2014): 387–405.

Parkinson, Naomi Gabrielle. "Impersonating a Voter: Constructions of Race, and Conceptions of Subjecthood in the Franchise of Colonial New South Wales, c. 1850–1865." *Journal of Imperial and Commonwealth History* 47, no. 4 (2019): 652–75.

Parolin, Christina. *Radical Spaces: Venues of Popular Politics in London, 1790–c.1845*. Canberra: ANU Press, 2010.

Parsons, Michael. "The Tourist Corroboree in South Australia to 1911." *Aboriginal History* 21 (1997): 46–69.

Parsons, T.G. "The Commercialism of Honour: Early Australian Capitalism, 1788–1809." In *A Difficult Infant: Sydney before Macquarie*, edited by Graeme Aplin, 102–19. Sydney: NSW University Press, 1988.

– "The Limits of Technology, or Why Didn't Australians Drink Colonial Beer in 1838?" *Push from the Bush: A Bulletin of Social History*, no. 4 (1979): 22–9.

Pearl, Cyril. *Beer, Glorious Beer: With Incidental Observations on Great Beer Myths, Pubs and Publicans, Barmaids and Breathalysers, Mum, Flip, Beery Bards, and Beer in the Kitchen, Etc., Etc.* Melbourne: Nelson, 1969.

Phillip, Arthur. *The Voyage of Governor Phillip to Botany Bay: With an Account of the Establishment of the Colonies of Port Jackson & Norfolk Island* ... London: John Stockdale, 1789.

Phillips, Marion. *A Colonial Autocracy, New South Wales under Governor Macquarie, 1810–1821*. London: P.S. King and Son, 1909.

Pickering, Paul A. "'The Hearts of the Millions': Chartism and Popular Monarchism in the 1840s." *History* 88, no. 2 (2003): 227–48.

– "'The Oak of English Liberty': Popular Constitutionalism in New South Wales, 1848–1856." *Journal of Colonial History* 3, no. 1 (April 2001): 1–27.

– "Ripe for a Republic: British Radical Responses to the Eureka Stockade." *Australian Historical Studies* 34, no. 121 (2003): 69–90.

Pixley, Jocelyn. "Wowser and Pro-woman Politics: Temperance against Australian Patriarchy." *Journal of Sociology* 27, no. 3 (December 1991): 293–314.

Place, Francis. *The Autobiography of Francis Place: 1771–1854*. Edited by Mary Thale. Cambridge: Cambridge University Press, 1972.

– *Improvement of the Working People: Drunkenness – Education*. London: C. Fox, 1834.

Pocock, Robert. *Pocock's Everlasting Songster, Containing a Selection of the Most Approved Songs ... Toasts and Sentiments ... To Which Is Added, Original Rules for Behaviour*. London: R. Pocock, 1804.

Powell, Martyn J. "Political Toasting in Eighteenth-Century Ireland." *History* 91, no. 4 (2006): 508–29.

Reece, R.H.W. "Feasts and Blankets: The History of Some Early Attempts to Establish Relations with the Aborigines of New South Wales, 1814–1846." *Archaeology & Physical Anthropology in Oceania* 2, no. 3 (October 1967): 190–206.

Reid, Douglas A. "The Decline of Saint Monday 1766–1876." *Past & Present*, no. 71 (1976): 76–101.

– "Interpreting the Festival Calendar: Wakes and Fairs as Carnivals." In *Popular Culture and Custom in Nineteenth-Century England*, edited by Robert D. Storch, 125–53. London: Croom Helm, 1982.

Reid, Thomas. *Two Voyages to New South Wales and Van Diemen's Land, with a Description of the Present Condition of That Interesting Colony* ... London: Longman, Hurst, Rees, Orme, and Brown, 1822.

Reynolds, Henry. *Frontier: Aborigines, Settlers and Land*. Sydney: Allen and Unwin, 1986.

Ritchie, John. *Punishment and Profit: The Reports of Commissioner John Bigge on the Colonies of New South Wales and Van Diemen's Land, 1822–1823; Their Origins, Nature and Significance*. Melbourne: Heinemann, 1970.

– "Towards Ending an Unclean Thing: The Molesworth Committee and the Abolition of Transportation to New South Wales, 1837–40." *Historical Studies* 17, no. 67 (1976): 144–64.

– *The Wentworths: Father and Son*. Carlton, Vic.: Melbourne University Press, 1997.

Rix, Kathryn. "'The Elimination of Corrupt Practices in British Elections'? Reassessing the Impact of the 1883 Corrupt Practices Act." *English Historical Review* 123, no. 500 (2008): 65–97.

Roberts, David Andrew, ed. "Discussion Forum: Beyond 'the Stain': Rethinking the Nature and Impact of the Anti-transportation Movement." *Journal of Australian Colonial History* 14 (2012): 205–79.

– "Masters, Magistrates and the Management of Complaint: The 1833 Convict Revolt at Castle Forbes and the Failure of Local Governance." *Journal of Australian Colonial History* 19 (2017): 57–94.

Roberts, David Andrew, and Lisa Ford. "Expansion, 1820–50." In *Cambridge History of Australia*, vol. 1, *Indigenous and Colonial Australia*, edited by Alison Bashford and Stuart Macintyre, 121–48. Melbourne: Cambridge University Press, 2013.

Roberts, Matthew. *Chartism, Commemoration and the Cult of the Radical Hero*. London: Routledge, 2019.

Roberts, M.J.D. *Making English Morals: Voluntary Association and Moral Reform in England, 1787–1886*. Cambridge: Cambridge University Press, 2004.

Roberts, Stephen H. *The Squatting Age in Australia, 1835–1847*. Carlton, Vic.: Melbourne University Press, 1964.

Roe, Michael. *Quest for Authority in Eastern Australia, 1835–1851*. Parkville, Vic.: Melbourne University Press, 1965.

Room, Robin. "Alcohol and Ethnography: A Case of Problem Deflation?" *Current Anthropology* 25, no. 2 (1984): 169–78.

– "'An Intoxicated Society?'" In *The World Alcohol Industry with Special Reference to Australia, New Zealand and the Pacific Islands*, edited by John Cavanagh, Frederick Clairmonte, and Robin Room, 147–215. Sydney: University of Sydney Press, 1985.

– "Intoxication and Bad Behaviour: Understanding Cultural Differences in the Link." *Social Science and Medicine* 53 (2001): 189–98.

Rowcroft, Charles (1798–1856). *Tales of the Colonies, or The Adventures of an Emigrant*. London: Saunders and Otley, 1843.

Rowlandson, Thomas. *The Brilliants*. London: Rudolph Ackerman, 1801.

Rowse, Tim. "Indigenous Heterogeneity." *Australian Historical Studies* 45, no. 3 (2014): 297–310.

The Royal Toast Master Containing Many Thousands of the Best Toasts Old and New, to Give Brilliancy to Mirth ... 2nd ed. London: J. Roach, 1791.

Rush, Benjamin. *An Enquiry into the Effects of Spiritous Liquors upon the Human Body and Their Influence upon the Happiness of Society*. Thomas Bradford: Philadelphia, 1790.

Russell, Penny. "The Brash Colonial: Class and Comportment in Nineteenth-Century Australia." *Transactions of the Royal Historical Society*, 6th ser., 12 (2002): 431–53.

– "Gender and Colonial Society." In *Cambridge History of Australia*, edited by Alison Bashford and Stuart Macintyre, 1:462–86. Melbourne: Cambridge University Press, 2013.

– "Ornaments of Empire? Government House and the Idea of English Aristocracy in Colonial Australia." *History Australia* 1, no. 2 (July 2004): 196–208.

– *Savage or Civilised? Manners in Colonial Australia*. Sydney: University of NSW Press, 2011.

– *A Wish of Distinction: Colonial Gentility and Femininity*. Carlton, Vic.: Melbourne University Press, 1994.

Sadleir, Richard. *The Aborigines of Australia*. Sydney: T. Richards, 1883.

Sargent, Clem. "The British Garrison in Australia 1788–1841. Part 2: Governors versus Garrison." *Sabretache* 40, no. 3 (1999): 17–26.

Scalmer, Sean. "Containing Contention: A Reinterpretation of Democratic Change and Electoral Reform in the Australian Colonies." *Australian Historical Studies* 42, no. 3 (2011): 337–56.

Schrad, Mark Lawrence. *Smashing the Liquor Machine: A Global History of Prohibition*. New York: Oxford University Press, 2021.

Scott, Joan W. "Gender: A Useful Category of Historical Analysis." *American Historical Review* 91, no. 5 (December 1986): 1053–75.

Sharp, Andrew. *The World, the Flesh and the Devil: The Life and Opinions of Samuel Marsden in England and the Antipodes, 1765–1838*. Auckland: Auckland University Press, 2016.

Singer, Merrill. "Anthropology and Addiction: An Historical Review." *Addiction* 107, no. 10 (October 2012): 1747–55.

Skinner, Rob, and Alan Lester. "Humanitarianism and Empire: New Research Agendas." *Journal of Imperial and Commonwealth History* 40, no. 5 (December 2012): 729–47.

Skocpol, Theda. "The Tocqueville Problem: Civic Engagement in American Democracy." *Social Science History* 21, no. 4 (1997): 455–79.

Smandych, Russell. "Contemplating the Testimony of 'Others': James Stephen, the Colonial Office, and the Fate of Australian Aboriginal Evidence Acts, circa 1839–1849." *Legal History* 10, nos 1–2 (2006): 97–143.

Smith, Babette. *Australia's Birthstain: The Startling Legacy of the Convict Era*. Crows Nest, NSW: Allen and Unwin, 2008.

– *Defiant Voices: How Australia's Female Convicts Challenged Authority*. Canberra: National Library of Australia Publishing, 2020.

Smith, Keith Vincent. "Boatswain Maroot." *The Dictionary of Sydney*, State Library of New South Wales. 2018. https://dictionaryofsydney.org/index.php/entry/boatswain_maroot#ref-uuid=15838877-0a41-292b-277c-199ca8d95ccf.

– "Bungaree." *The Dictionary of Sydney*, State Library of New South Wales. 2011. https://dictionaryofsydney.org/entry/bungaree.

– *King Bungaree: A Sydney Aborigine Meets the Great South Pacific Explorers, 1799–1830*. Kenthurst, NSW: Kangaroo Press, 1992.

– "Woollarawarre Bennelong." *The Dictionary of Sydney*, State Library of New South Wales. 2013. https://dictionaryofsydney.org/entry/woollarawarre_bennelong.

Smitley, Megan. *The Feminine Public Sphere: Middle-Class Women and Civic Life in Scotland, c. 1870–1914*. Manchester: Manchester University Press, 2009.

Sons and Daughters of Temperance, National Division of Australasia. *Rules and Regulations to Be Observed by the National, Grand, & Subordinate Divisions of the Sons and Daughters of Temperance*. Sydney, 1890.

Starling, Nicole. "'An Auxiliary, Not an Usurper': John Saunders, Temperance, and Secularisation." *Journal of Religious History* 43, no. 3 (September 2019): 380–99.

– "'Victims of Intemperance': Status Politics and Clerical Drunkenness in the Second-Wave Temperance Societies of Colonial Sydney." *Australian Historical Studies* 53, no. 1 (2022): 43–60.

Steer, Philip. *Settler Colonialism in Victorian Literature: Economics and Political Identity in the Networks of Empire*. Cambridge: Cambridge University Press, 2020.

Stephen, Alfred. *Address on Intemperance and the Licensing System*. Sydney: John L. Sheriff, 1870.

Steven, Margaret. *Merchant Campbell, 1769–1846: A Study of Colonial Trade*. Melbourne: Oxford University Press, 1965.

Stevens, Laura M. *The Poor Indians: British Missionaries, Native Americans, and Colonial Sensibility*. Philadelphia: University of Pennsylvania Press, 2004.

Stoler, Ann Laura. *Along the Archival Grain: Epistemic Anxieties and Colonial Common Sense*. Princeton, NJ: Princeton University Press, 2009.

Stoneman, David. "The Church Act: The Expansion of Christianity or the Imposition of Moral Enlightenment." PhD diss., University of New England, 2011.

Stonhouse, Sir James. *Admonitions against Swearing, Sabbath-Breaking and Drunkenness; with Abstracts of the Penal Laws Now in Force against Those Vices*. London: Society for Promoting Christian Knowledge, 1769.

Storch, Robert D. "Introduction: Persistence and Change in Nineteenth-Century Popular Culture." In *Popular Culture and Custom in Nineteenth-Century England*, edited by Robert D. Storch, 1–19. London: Croom Helm, 1982.

Strauss, Claudia. "The Imaginary." *Anthropological Theory* 6, no. 3 (September 2006): 322–44.

Sturma, Michael. "Eye of the Beholder. The Stereotype of Women Convicts, 1788–1852." *Labour History*, no. 34 (1978): 3–10.

– "Police and Drunkards in Sydney, 1841–1851." *Australian Journal of Politics & History* 27, no. 1 (1981): 48–56.

– *Vice in a Vicious Society: Crime and Convicts in Mid-nineteenth Century New South Wales*. St Lucia: University of Queensland Press, 1983.

Summers, Anne. *Damned Whores and God's Police*. Ringwood, Vic.: Penguin, 1994.

Sweatman, John. *The Journal of John Sweatman: A Nineteenth-Century Voyage in North Australia and Torres Strait*. Edited by Frederick James Allen and Peter Corris. St Lucia: University of Queensland Press, 1977.

Tange, Andrea Kaston. *Architectural Identities: Domesticity, Literature and the Victorian Middle Classes*. Toronto: University of Toronto Press, 2010.

The Tatler: With Notes, and a General Index … Complete in One Volume. Philadelphia: J.J. Woodward, 1831.

Taylor, Anya. *Bacchus in Romantic England: Writers and Drink 1780–1830*. Basingstoke, UK: Palgrave Macmillan, 1998.

Taylor, Charles. "Modern Social Imaginaries." *Public Culture* 14, no. 1 (2002): 91–124.

– *Modern Social Imaginaries*. Durham, NC: Duke University Press Books, 2003.

– *A Secular Age*. Cambridge, MA: Belknap Press, 2007.

Tench, Watkin. *A Complete Account of the Settlement at Port Jackson in New South Wales* ... London: G. Nicol and J. Sewell, 1793.

– *A Narrative of the Expedition to Botany Bay with an Account of New South Wales* ... London: J. Debrett, 1789.

Thompson, E.P. "The Moral Economy of the English Crowd in the Eighteenth Century." *Past & Present* 50, no. 1 (1971): 76–136.

– "Moral Economy Reviewed." In *Customs in Common*, 259–351. London: Penguin, 1993.

– "The Patricians and the Plebs." In *Customs in Common*, 16–96. London: Penguin, 1993.

– "Time, Work-Discipline, and Industrial Capitalism." *Past & Present* 38, no. 1 (1967): 56–97.

Thompson, Richard. *Report of the Proceedings at the National Banquet Held at the Prince of Wales Theatre* ... Sydney: Thomas Daniel, 1856.

Threlkeld, Lancelot Edward. *Australian Reminiscences & Papers of L.E. Threlkeld, Missionary to the Aborigines, 1824–1859*. Edited by Niel Gunson. Canberra: Australian Institute of Aboriginal Studies, 1974.

The Toast Master: Being a Genteel Collection of Sentiments and Toasts, ... London: John Abraham, 1789.

Tocqueville, Alexis de. *Democracy in America and Two Essays on America*. Edited by Isaac Kramnick. Translated by Gerald Bevan. London: Penguin Classics, 2003.

Tosh, John. "Gentlemanly Politeness and Manly Simplicity in Victorian England." *Transactions of the Royal Historical Society*, 6th ser., 12 (2002): 455–72.

– "Home and Away: The Flight from Domesticity in Late-Nineteenth-Century England Re-visited." *Gender & History* 27, no. 3 (2015): 561–75.

– *A Man's Place: Masculinity and the Middle-Class Home in Victorian England*. New Haven, CT: Yale University Press, 2008.

– "Masculinities in an Industrializing Society: Britain, 1800–1914." *Journal of British Studies* 44, no. 2 (2005): 330–42.

Townsend, Joseph Phipps. *Rambles and Observations in New South Wales* ... London: Chapman and Hall, 1849.

Trotter, Thomas. *An Essay, Medical, Philosophical, and Chemical on Drunkenness, and Its Effects on the Human Body*. London: Longman, Hurst, Rees, and Orme, 1810.

Trusler, John. *The Honours of the Table, or, Rules for Behaviour during Meals* ... London: Literary-Press, 1791.

Turnbull, John. *A Voyage Round the World, in the Years 1800, 1801, 1802, 1803, and 1804* ... 3 vols. London: R. Phillips, 1805.

Tyrrell, Alex, Patricia Hill, and Diane Kirkby. "Feasting on National Identity: Whisky, Haggis and the Celebration of Scottishness in the Nineteenth Century." In *Dining on Turtles: Food Feasts and Drinking in History*, edited by Diane Elizabeth Kirkby and Tanja Luckins, 46–63. Basingstoke, UK: Palgrave Macmillan, 2007.

Tyrrell, Ian R. "International Aspects of the Woman's Temperance Movement in Australia: The Influence of the American WCTU, 1882–1914." *Journal of Religious History* 12, no. 3 (1983): 284–304.

– *Sobering Up: From Temperance to Prohibition in Antebellum America, 1800–1860*. Westport, CT: Greenwood Press, 1979.

Valverde, Mariana. *Disease of the Will: Alcohol and the Dilemmas of Freedom*. Cambridge: Cambridge University Press, 1998.

– "'Racial Poison': Drink, Male Vice, and Degeneration in First-Wave Feminism." In *Women's Suffrage in the British Empire: Citizenship, Nation and Race*, edited by Ian Christopher Fletcher, Philippa Levine, and Laura E. Nym Mayhall, 33–50. London: Taylor and Francis, 2012.

Veracini, Lorenzo. "Ian Turner's The Australian Dream and Australia's 'Settler Transition.'" *Journal of Australian Studies* 40, no. 3 (2016): 302–18.

– *Settler Colonialism: A Theoretical Overview*. London: Palgrave Macmillan, 2010.

Vernon, James. *Politics and the People: A Study in English Political Culture, c. 1815–1867*. Cambridge: Cambridge University Press, 1993.

Vidal, Mary Theresa. *Bengala, or Some Time Ago*. London: John W. Parker, 1860.

– *Tales for the Bush*. Sydney: D.L. Welch, 1845.

Wailes, Lyn, and Matthew Allen. "The Failure of Political Temperance: The Politics of No-License in Broken Hill, 1883–1914." *Journal of Australian Colonial History* 21 (2019): 121–50.

Waldstreicher, David. "Rites of Rebellion, Rites of Assent: Celebrations, Print Culture, and the Origins of American Nationalism." *Journal of American History* 82, no. 1 (June 1995): 37–61.

Walker, R.B. *The Newspaper Press in New South Wales, 1803–1920*. Sydney: Sydney University Press, 1976.

Wannan, Bill. *Folklore of the Australia Pub*. Melbourne: Sun, 1975.

Ward, Russel Braddock. *The Australian Legend*. Oxford: Oxford University Press, 2003.

– "Australian Legend Re-visited." *Historical Studies* 18, no. 71 (1978): 171–90.

Warner, Jessica. *Craze: Gin and Debauchery in an Age of Reason*. New York: Random House, 2003.

– "The Sanctuary of Sobriety: The Emergence of Temperance as a Feminine Virtue in Tudor and Stuart England." *Addiction* 92, no. 1 (1997): 97–111.

Warner, Nicholas O. "Firewater Legacy: Alcohol and Native American Identity in the Fiction of James Fenimore Cooper." In *High Anxieties*, edited by Janet Farrell Brodie and Marc Redfield, 109–16. Berkeley: University of California Press, 2002.

Waterhouse, Richard. "'… A Bastard Offspring of Tyranny under the Guise of Liberty': Liberty and Representative Government in Australia, 1788–1901." In *Exclusionary Empire: English Liberty Overseas, 1600–1900*, edited by Jack P. Greene, 220–47. Cambridge: Cambridge University Press, 2010.

Webby, Elizabeth. "Reactions to the Myall Creek Massacre." *Push from the Bush: A Bulletin of Social History*, no. 8 (1980): 1–8.

Weber, Max. *The Protestant Ethic and the Spirit of Capitalism*. Translated by Talcott Parsons. London: Unwin University Books, 1930.

Wentworth, William C. *A Statistical, Historical and Political Description of the Colony of New, South Wales …* London: G. and W.B. Whittaker, 1819.

Wheeler, Roxann. *The Complexion of Race: Categories of Difference in Eighteenth-Century British Culture*. Philadelphia: University of Pennsylvania Press, 2000.

Whitaker, Ann-Marie. *Unfinished Revolution: United Irishmen in New South Wales, 1800–1810*. Darlinghurst, NSW: Crossing Press, 1994.

White, John. *Journal of a Voyage to New South Wales*. London: J. Debrett, 1790.

White, Jonathan. "The 'Slow but Sure Poyson': The Representation of Gin and Its Drinkers 1736–1751." *Journal of British Studies*, no. 42 (2003): 35–64.

White, Richard. *Inventing Australia: Images and Identity, 1688–1980*. Sydney: Allen and Unwin, 1981.

Wiener, Martin J. *Reconstructing the Criminal: Culture, Law, and Policy in England, 1830–1914*. Cambridge: Cambridge University Press, 1994.

Wilson, George B. *Alcohol and the Nation: A Contribution to the Study of the Liquor Problem in the United Kingdom from 1800 to 1935*. London: Nicholson and Watson, 1940.

Wilson, Thomas. *Distilled Spirituous Liquors the Bane of the Nation …* 2nd ed. London: J. Roberts, 1736.

Wilson, Thomas M. "Drinking Cultures: Sites and Practices in the Production and Expression of Identity." In *Drinking Cultures: Alcohol and Identity*, edited by Thomas M. Wilson, 1–24. Oxford: Berg Croom Helm, 2005.

Windschuttle, Elizabeth. "Discipline, Domestic Training and Social Control: The Female School of Industry, Sydney, 1826–1847." *Labour History*, no. 39 (1980): 1–14.

– "'Feeding the Poor and Sapping Their Strength': The Public Role of Ruling-Class Women in Eastern Australia, 1788–1850." In *Women, Class and History: Feminist Perspectives on Australia 1788–1978*, 53–82. Melbourne: Fontana, 1980.

– "Women, Class and Temperance: Moral Reform in Eastern Australia, 1832–57." *Push from the Bush: A Bulletin of Social History*, no. 3 (1978): 5–23.

Withington, Phil. "Intoxicants and Society in Early Modern England." *Historical Journal* 54, no. 3 (September 2011): 631–57.

– "Introduction: Cultures of Intoxication." *Past & Present* 222, no. S9 (2014): 9–33.

Wolin, Sheldon S. *Fugitive Democracy and Other Essays*. Edited by Nicholas Xenos. Princeton, NJ: Princeton University Press, 2016.

Wood, Rebecca. "Frontier Violence and the Bush Legend: The Sydney Herald's Response to the Myall Creek Massacre Trials and the Creation of Colonial Identity." *History Australia* 6, no. 3 (2009): 67.1–67.19.

Woollacott, Angela. *Settler Society in the Australian Colonies: Self-Government and Imperial Culture*. Oxford: Oxford University Press, 2015.

Wright, Claire. *Beyond the Ladies Lounge: Australia's Female Publicans*. Melbourne: Melbourne University Press, 2003.

Wright, Nancy E. "The Problem of Aboriginal Evidence in Early Colonial New South Wales." In *Law, History, Colonialism: The Reach of Empire*, edited by Diane Elizabeth Kirkby and Catharine Coleborne, 140–55. Manchester: Manchester University Press, 2001.

Yeomans, Henry. *Alcohol and Moral Regulation: Public Attitudes, Spirited Measures and Victorian Hangovers*. London: Policy Press, 2014.

INDEX

Page numbers in italics indicate a figure.

A'Beckett, Thomas, 201–2
"Aboriginal Natives Evidence Bill," 202–3
Aboriginal people: introduction, 23, 187–8; ban on alcohol sales to, 185–6, 191–2, 240n17, 244n108; Bennelong's experience, 189–91, 240n32, 241n39; Bungaree's experience, 199–200; complaints and pro-settler opposition to, 183–5, 192–3; democratic political imaginary and, 184–5, 187–8, 203; drunken savage trope, 23, 51, 72, 182, 186, 187, 188–92, 193–7, *194*, *195*, 199–200, 202, 239n2; governing Aboriginal drunkenness, 198–202; humanitarian care, 51, 182–3, 185, 194–7; Mahroot's experience, 197–8, 203; Myall Creek massacre and trials, 54, 181, 182, 184, 201, 203; NSW's colonial expansion and, 47, 51, 54–5; patronage-sanctioned drinking, 192, 203; perceived decline of, 197–8; right to drink, 202–3; Saunders on, 181–2; scholarship on, 186–7
Aborigines Protection Society, 184
Addison, Joseph, 160
Adler, Marianne, 34
age restrictions, drinking, 240n17
alcohol: introduction, 21; aboard First Fleet, 24–7, 28–9, 30–1, 34–6; access to and political boundaries, 102; Australian standard drink, 219n3; beer, 27–8, 29, 65–6, 212–13; "bool," 191, 241n44; British drinking culture, 24, 26–7, 27–8, 29–30; democratic political imaginary and, 8–9, 9–10, 13, 15, 33–4, 211–13; drinking age restrictions, 240n17; during establishment of NSW, 42–3; economic importance, 28; gin, 37, 40–1; grog, 67; identity politics and, 22, 69–71, 91, 126; industrialization and, 28, 30, 34; NSW drinking culture, 67–71, 163–6; patronage and, 26, 33, 67, 75, 78–9, 103; as problem substance, 36–7, 137–8, 148–52; public dinners and, 7–8, 94–5; public houses, 19, 31–2, 36–7, 67–8, 69, 76–7, 218n71, 225n15; regulation of, 65, 67, 127–8, 152–3; rum, 25, 28, 47, 49, 61, 64, 66; rural drinking, 29, 66–7, 68–9, 76, 78, 80–1; scholarship on, 15–19; as social lubricant, 32–3, 35; sources and

method, 19–21; spirits, 28, 49, 64–5, 66, 127–8; as stimulant, 29; styles of drinking, 71–3; supply, demand, and consumption in NSW, 64–7; urban drinking, 66, 69, 76–7, 78, 80, 82; wine, 18, 29, 65–6, 72, 124. *See also* Aboriginal people; drunken comportment; drunkenness; plebian drinking; restrained comportment; sober comportment; temperance; toasting; women
Allen, George, 80, 168, 170
American Temperance Society, 127
Anderson, Benedict, 10
Anglican Church. *See* Church of England
Annan, William, 201
anthropology, 15
Arago, Jacques, 191
Argus (newspaper), 207
Armstrong, Nancy, 175
Arndell, Thomas, 35, 36
Arnold, William, 154–5
Aspinall, Edward, 3
Atkins, Richard, 102, 163
Atkinson, Alan, 12
Atkinson, George, 167
Atkinson, Louisa: "Be a Man," 170–1
Australia. *See* Aboriginal people; alcohol; New South Wales
Australia Club, 118
Australian, The (newspaper): on Aboriginal people, 191, 193; on public dinners and fetes, 6, 79, 106, 121; in public sphere, 5, 52; on temperance, 145
Australian Courts Act (1828), 53
Australian Temperance Magazine, 124, 130, 152–3, 182
Aveling, Marian, 42–3
Backhouse, James, 129, 196–7, 242n71
Badger, Jim, 209–10
Baer, Marc, 95, 156
Bancroft, Mr, 143
Band of Hope (journal), 142, 179, 180
bands of hope (children's temperance societies), 134, 141
Bannister, Saxe, 116
banquets, 90. *See also* public dinners
Barber, Elizabeth, 35–6
Barrington, George, 163
Barrows, Susan, 15
Barsby, Samuel, 166–7
Barwell (convict ship), 99
beer, 27–8, 29, 65–6, 212–13
Belfield, Francis: *The Bottle, or The Drunkard's Curse*, 150–1
Benbow, William, 155
Bennelong, 189–91, 240n32, 241n39
Berridge, Virginia, 139
Bigge, John, 51, 52
binge (spree) drinking, 67, 80–2
Bland, William, 204, 205
Bligh, William, 49–50, 61, 151
"bool," 191, 241n44
Bourdieu, Pierre, 18
Bourke, Richard, 53
Brady, Maggie, 186–7, 189, 196–7, 203
Brand, William, 161
Brett, Peter, 95, 96
Brisbane, Thomas, 3–5, 51, 105–8, 116, 121
Britain: British Empire, 8, 12, 28, 45, 183, 185; drinking culture, 24, 26–7, 27–8, 29–30; radical politics, 45, 95, 98–100
Buckingham, James, 128

Bungaree, 199–200
Burn, Simon, 74
Burt, Mary, 8, 20, 216n15
Burton, William, 201–2
Butler, Henry, 166
Butler, Judith, 9, 212
Byrne, Paula, 167, 238n83

Cannadine, David, 114
Capdeville, Valérie, 161
Carmichael, John, 193–4
Carty, James, 166
Castle Forbes revolt (1833), 78
Catholics and Catholic Church, 53, 113, 132, 133, 146
Chapman (ship), 99
children, 134, 141
Chronicle, The (newspaper), 169
Church Act (1836), 53
Church of England, 53, 131
citizenship: Aboriginal people and, 186; restrained comportment and, 7, 19, 72–3, 158, 171, 210, 212
Clark, Manning, 107
Clark, Peter, 216n12
Clark, Ralph, 26, 31, 34–6, 37, 83
clubs, male-only, 161
Cockburn, Henry (Lord Cockburn), 87
Collins, David, 42, 73–4, 166, 190
Colquhoun, Patrick, 36–7
competitive drinking, 166
Connell, Raewyn, 13, 217n44
Constitution Act (1842), 57
convicts: alcohol denied to, 26–7, 31, 35–6, 41; convict stain, 58, 108, 114, 117, 175; drinking practices and drunkenness, 67, 68, 72, 73–5, 76, 166–7; gendered punishment for drunkenness, 173–4; in NSW, 46, 47, 48–9, 52; rebellion fears, 45; transportation, 41, 53–4, 58, 172. *See also* plebian drinking
Cooper, Daniel, 206
Cowan, Brian, 18
Crook, William Pascoe, 129
Cruickshank, George: *The Bottle*, *149*, 149–50
Cummings, William, 93
Cunningham, Peter, 67, 116, 164, 199–200
Curthoys, Ann, 186, 193, 203

Damousi, Joy, 172
Darling, Elizabeth, 175, 176
Darling, Ralph: authoritarian governance under, 52–3; King's birthday celebration and, 104; on public dinners, 116; toasting of, 3–5, 9–10, 61, 79, 96–7, 107, 119, 121–2
Darvall, John, 206
Davis, Ann, 171
Davis, Benjamin, 166
Defour, Judith, 40
democratic political imaginary: introduction, 10–13, 19–20; Aboriginal people and, 184–5, 187–8, 203; alcohol and, 8–9, 9–10, 13, 15, 33–4, 211–13; drinking styles and, 71–3; feminine exemplars and, 156–7; gender and, 157–8, 180; masculinity and, 14; public dinners and, 211; temperance and, 18, 138–9, 147; toasting and, 108
Dickens, Charles, 91–2, 96
Dickinson, John, 156, 177, 206
Dietler, Michael, 90
dinners. *See* political dinners; public dinners; toasting
Dogherty, Edward, 99–100
domesticity, 14, 56, 81, 158, 161, 171. *See also* respectability

domestic violence, 14, 167–8, 180
Donaldson, Stuart, 204, 210, 211, 245n21
Dortins, Emma, 189, 190
Douglas, Mary, 15
Douglass, Dr, 4, 5, 104
drinking. *See* alcohol
drunken comportment: introduction, 16, 71–2; drunken savage trope, 51, 72, 182, 186, 187, 188–92, 193–7, *194*, *195*, 199–200, 202, 239n2; female stigma, 8, 27, 35–6, 40–1, 72, 158–9, 172–3; and flirting and sexual conduct, 31–2; idle drunkard trope, 36; plebian drinking and, 73–7, 166; vs restrained comportment, 7–8, 72–3, 158, 210
drunkenness: arrests for, 69, 199, 201; as deviance, 8, 15; First Fleet and, 30–1; gendered punishment, 173–4; governing Aboriginal drunkenness, 198–202; moral panic, 36–7, 40–2, 57; violence and, 76, 84, 166–8
Dudgeon, Elizabeth, 32
Duff, James, 167
Duffy, Charles Gavan, 244n4
Dumaresq, Henry, 104
Dunlop, John, 29, 33, 82, 94, 110, 230n10
Dunlop, Mary, 167
Duthille, Rémy, 87, 88, 91, 98, 99, 156, 160, 161

Earle, Augustus: *Natives of N.S. Wales as Seen in the Streets of Sydney* (1830), 193, *194*
Easty, John, 30, 31
Edgerton, Robert, 16, 71
education, 140–1, 142
egalitarianism: binge (spree) drinking and, 81–2; democratic political imaginary and, 13, 63–4; plebian drinking and, 75, 76–7, 78, 158; public houses and, 19; reciprocal treating and, 82–4; toasting and, 7–8, 9, 112–13
elections: "Australian Ballot" and manhood suffrage, 59; in NSW, 12, 55, 57; opposition to electoral reform, 210; political dinners and, 95–7; treating and, 33, 79–80
Electoral Act (1851), 58
Electoral Reform League, 154–5
emancipists, 5, 50, 51, 52, 105–6, 107–8, 114–16, 230n23
Empire, The (newspaper), 80, 153, 244n4
England. *See* Britain
Epstein, James, 98, 235n9
Evans, Catherine, 174
Evans, Julie, 186
exclusives (landowning elite), 50, 51, 52, 55, 108, 229n7
exclusivity, 108, 113–18

Faddy, William, 34
Fairfax, John, 146
feasting, 90. *See also* public dinners
Female Friendly Society, 175, 176
First Fleet, 24–7, 28–9, 30–1, 34–6, 41–2
Fitzgerald, Richard, 230n24
Forbes, Francis, 52, 129, 177
Ford, Lisa, 185, 192, 202
Fowler, Frank, 83
fraternity. *See* egalitarianism
Freeland, J.M., 69
free trade, 49, 65, 67
Friendship (First Fleet), 31, 34–5
Fulton, Henry, 230n24

Garcia, Lluís, 90
Garling, Mr, 4
Garth, Susannah, 32
Gazette, The (newspaper): on Aboriginal people, 191, 192, 198; Bennelong's obituary, 190–1; on female philanthropy, 176; on public dinners, 6, 93, 106, 111, 115, 116, 119, 120–1, 165; on Sydney Total Abstinence Society, 143
Geertz, Clifford, 9
gender: introduction, 22–3; alcohol consumption and, 27; domestic violence, 14, 167–8, 180; mixed-gender drinking, 158, 171; Mother Gin and, 40–1; NSW demographics, 47, 50, 52, 159; political imaginary and, 157–8, 180; public drinking and, 180; punishment for drunkenness and, 173–4; toasting and, 159–60, 160–3, 165–6. *See also* masculinity; women
Gill, Samuel: *Digger's Wedding in Melbourne* (1852), *209*, 209–10; *Old Colonists' Festival* (1853), 207, *207*; *Old Colonists' Festival Dinner* (1851), *208*, 208–9, 210
gin, 37, 40–1
Gipps, Elizabeth, 177
Gipps, George: on Aboriginal people, 197; governorship of, 54, 55; monarchs' birthday celebrations and, 104, 165; temperance and, 123–5, 126, 130, 132, 145, 147, 152, 177–8
Goffman, Erving, 9
Good Templars, 135
Gooseberry, Cora, 200–1
Goulburn, Major, 116
Great Britain. *See* Britain
Greenway, Francis, 230n24
grog, 67. *See also* sly grog shops
Grose, Major, 47–8, 102

Habermas, Jürgen, 11
Hall, E.S., 4–5, 93–4, 107, 112, 119–20, 121, 172, 215n11
Harbouring Act (1825), 225n17
Hard Labour Act (1777), 26
Harris, Alexander, 68, 69, 75, 76–7, 82; *The Emigrant Family*, 83
Harrison, Brian, 128, 138; *Drink and the Victorians*, 17
Hashemy (convict ship), 58
health-drinking, 86–7, 124
hegemonic masculinity, 13–14, 159–60. *See also* masculinity
Henry, Ellen, 173
Herald, The (newspaper): on Aboriginal people, 183–5, 201; on Donaldson's electoral loss, 210; on gendered nature of public drinking, 180; on liquor laws, 153; on public dinners, 154–5, 206, 244n4; on temperance, 133–4, 143, 146, 147–8
hierarchy. *See* exclusivity; patronage
Hill, George, 80
Hill, John, 74
Hogarth, William: *Beer Street and Gin Lane* (1751), *38*, *39*, 40–1, 149, 173; *A Rake's Progress* (1735), 149–50
Holt, Joseph, 163
homosociality, 7–8, 158, 159, 161–2
Howard, John, 26
Howe, Robert, 106, 107, 121
Howitt, William, 82
Hügel, Charles von, 193

humanitarian care, 51, 182–3, 185, 194–7
Hunt, Edward, 129
Hunter, John, 47, 48, 49, 191

identity politics, 22, 69–71, 91, 126
Ihde, Erin, 172
imaginaries. *See* democratic political imaginary
Indigenous people. *See* Aboriginal people
industrialization, 28, 30, 34
Ingram, James, 166
intoxication. *See* drunken comportment; drunkenness
Ireland, 45, 98
Irish, Paul, 187, 200, 201
Irving, Terry, 12, 57, 59, 97
Isakhan, Benjamin, 10–11, 12

Jeffrey, William, 142–3
Johnson, Richard, 41
Jones, William, 31
Joyce, Patrick, 11–12

Karskens, Grace, 47, 76
Kelly, Thomas, 31
Kemp, Anthony Fenn, 103–4, 146
King, Phillip Gidley, 42, 49, 61, 191

Ladies Total Abstinence Society, 134, 179
Lady Penrhyn (First Fleet), 31, 43
Lake, Marilyn, 14, 169, 212
Landes, Joan, 11
Lang, John Dunmore: on alcohol as problem substance, 151; on binge (spree) drinking, 81; on Brisbane's farewell dinner, 107–8, 229n7; democratic politics and, 58, 61–2, 210; National Banquet celebrating responsible government and, 206; temperance and, 129, 133, 140, 147
Langton, Marcia, 187, 189
Leddell, Mrs, 179
Lemon, Rebecca, 86, 87
Levine, Harry, 17, 139
Lewis, Mr, 143
Licensed Publicans Act (1826), 225n17
Licensed Publicans Act (1838), 68, 225n17
licensing, 65, 67, 68, 69, 225n17
Licensing Act (1830), 68
Licensing Act (1838), 185–6, 188, 199, 201, 244n108
Licensing Act (1882), 135, 240n17
Liston, Carol, 107
London Temperance Intelligencer (newspaper), 177
Lord, Simeon, 115, 230n23
loyal toasting, 86–8, 97–101, 103–4, 108, 118, 121–2, 126, 165
Ludington, Charles, 18, 94, 109–10, 112, 161
Lumsdaine, William, 133–4

MacAndrew, Craig, 16, 71
Macarthur, John, Jr, 108
Macarthur, John, Sr, 94, 111
Mackaness, John, 3, 5
Macquarie, Elizabeth, 103, 163–4
Macquarie, Lachlan: Aboriginal people and, 191–2, 199; emancipists and, 114–16; governorship of, 51; liquor laws and, 65, 67; public dinners and, 92, 163–4; toasting and, 102–3
Macquoid, Thomas, 111
Mahroot, 197–8, 203
Maine Law (1851), 133–4, 147–8, 153
Maine Law League, 134
Mancall, Peter C., 188

Mann, David, 74
Mansfield, Rev., 125
Mansfield, Robert, 111–12, 120–1
Marsden, Samuel, 172
masculinity: "Australian Legend," 13–14, 77, 81, 158, 211; competitive drinking, 166; drunken violence and, 75–6, 84, 166–8; hegemonic masculinity, 13–14, 159–60; and restraint and respectability, 157–8, 168–71; toasting and, 160–2, 164–6; Victoria Bitter adverts and, 212–13, 245n28. *See also* gender
Mason, Joseph, 80
Maxwell, James, 34
Maxwell-Stewart, Hamish, 47
McAllister, Anne Marie, 138–9
McCombie, Thomas: *Arabin*, 69–71
McCormack, Matthew, 97, 122
McEncroe, Rev., 147
McGrath, John, 167
McIntyre, Julie, 18, 66, 189
McKaeg, Rev., 143, 146
McKenna, Mark, 186
McLeay, Alexander, 104
McShane, Angela, 86, 113
media. *See* press
Meehan, James, 230n24
Meredith, Captain, 35
Meredith, Louisa, 164–5, 175–6
Miles, William Augustus, 168
military, 43, 45–6, 47–8, 50, 115–16, 118, 184
Mitchell, Jessie, 186, 193, 203
Moir, William, 168–9
Molesworth, William, 53–4
Molle, Colonel, 116
monarchy, toasts to, 100–4, 165
Monitor, The (newspaper): on Aboriginal people, 192, 198; on Darling's departure fete, 79; on female drunkenness, 172; on public dinners and social divisions, 117; public sphere and, 52; on toasting, 94, 112; on Turf Society's public dinner, 4–5, 6
moral enlightenment, 17, 56, 138, 141, 158
moral reform, 26–7, 37, 49, 123, 145, 159
Mudie, James, 78, 80
Muir, Thomas, 99
Mullen, Mrs, 179
Mundy, Godfrey, 82
mutinies, 99–100
mutual aid societies, 141–2
Myall Creek massacre and trials, 54, 181, 182, 184, 201, 203

Nagle, Jacob, 30
"National Banquet," 23, 156, 204–6, 210, 211
nationalism, settler-colonial, 184
Newman, Ian, 11, 88–9, 91, 161
New South Wales: introduction, 21, 44–5; alcohol supply, demand, and consumption in, 64–7; aspirations and purpose, 26–7, 41; authoritarian government (1788–1810), 45–50; colonial expansion, 47, 51, 54–5; democracy in, 12–13, 14; democratic government (1842–60), 56–60; demographics and gender, 47, 50, 52, 54, 159; drinking culture, 67–71, 163–6; drinking the health of during establishment, 42–3; drunken and sober political histories, 60–2; economic transformation, 77–8; elections in, 12, 55, 57; First Fleet, 24–7, 28–9, 30–1, 34–6, 41–2; gubernatorial government (1810–42), 50–6;

political dinners, 96–7; responsible government, 12, 58, 204, 211; Rum Rebellion, 17, 44, 49–50, 60, 151, 222n2; temperance movement, 59, 125–6, 128–35; transportation, 41, 53–4, 58, 172. *See also* Aboriginal people; alcohol; convicts; democratic political imaginary; gender; masculinity; plebian drinking; public dinners; temperance; toasting; women
New South Wales Act (1823), 51–2
New South Wales Alliance for the Suppression of Intemperance, 135
New South Wales Constitution Act (1855), 204
New South Wales Corps, 47–8, 102
New South Wales Temperance Society, 123–4, 129–30, 132, 139–40, 141, 143, 144–5, 146, 152, 177–8
newspapers. *See* press
Nicholls, James, 19, 139
Nichols (labouring man), 142
Nichols, Isaac, 92
Nichols, Robert, 119–20, 202–3

O'Connell, Daniel, 146
O'Dwyer, Michael, 100
O'Gorman, Frank, 33, 95, 96
O'Shaughnessy, Edward, 119–20, 230n38

Palmer, Thomas, 100
Palti, Elías José, 10
Parkinson, Naomi, 186
paternalism, 78, 128. *See also* exclusivity; patronage
patronage: Aboriginal people and, 192, 203; alcohol and, 26, 33, 67, 75, 78–9, 103; dining with the governor and, 114; electoral treating as, 33, 79–80; female philanthropy and, 175–6; *Old Colonists' Festival Dinner* (Gill) and, 208; "old corruption" politics and, 46, 51; reciprocal treating and, 82–3; temperance and, 123–4, 125, 127, 128, 129–30, 132, 139–40, 144–5, 152
People's Advocate (newspaper), 244n4
philanthropy, 127, 139, 175–6
Phillip, Arthur, 24, 25–6, 29, 41, 42, 47, 49, 101–2, 189
Pickering, Paul, 98–9
Place, Francis, 32, 69
Plato, 127
plebian, use of term, 73. *See also* convicts
plebian drinking: introduction, 21–2, 63–4; binge (spree) drinking, 67, 80–2; competitive drinking, 166; drunken comportment and, 73–7, 166; drunken violence, 75–6, 84, 166–8; female and mixed-gender drinking, 158, 171; as fraternal obligation, 82; patronage and, 78–80; public houses, 19, 31–2, 36–7, 67–8, 69, 76–7, 218n71, 225n15; reciprocal treating, 78, 82–4, 226n64; rural drinking, 29, 66–7, 68–9, 76, 78, 80–1; urban drinking, 66, 69, 76–7, 78, 80, 82
Plunkett, John Hubert, 124, 133, 165–6
Pocock, Robert, 110; *Pocock's Everlasting Songster* (1804), 88, 89
political dinners, 95–7, 156. *See also* public dinners
political imaginary. *See* democratic political imaginary

Pons, Enriqueta, 90
popular drinking. *See* plebian drinking
Port Orders (1810), 191
press (newspapers): public dinners and, 6, 90–1, 92–3, 96, 108, 118–22, 215n11; public sphere and, 52; temperance press, 178, 197; toasting and, 91, 121. *See also specific newspapers*
Proclamation Society, 41, 127, 145
Publicans Licensing Acts Consolidation (1830), 225n17
public dinners: introduction, 22, 86; alcohol and, 7–8, 94–5; anniversary dinner (1831), 118–21; banquets and feasting, 90; Brisbane's farewell dinner, 105–8, 116; "Commemoration Dinner" (1813), 92; commemorative artwork, 206–9, *207*, *208*, 210; democratic political imaginary and, 211; Dickens on, 91–2; for Duffy, 244n4; exclusivity and, 108, 113–18; Macquarie's dinners with emancipists, 114–16; mixed-gender dining, 163–4; National Banquet celebrating responsible government, 23, 156, 204–6, 210, 211; in NSW, 92–5; organization and rules, 6–7, 93–4, 109–12; politicization of, 103–4; press and, 6, 90–1, 92–3, 96, 108, 118–22, 215n11; radical dinners, 98–9; respectability and, 114, 117–18; St Andrew's Day dinner (1830), 231n40; St Patrick's Day dinner (1830), 111–12, 118, 231n40; ticket prices, 117; Turf Club dinner, 3–8, 9, 60, 72, 85, 93–4, 215n11. *See also* political dinners; toasting
public drinking. *See* alcohol
public houses, 19, 31–2, 36–7, 67–8, 69, 76–7, 218n71, 225n15
public sphere, 11, 52
pubs. *See* public houses

Quartly, Marian, 235n6
Quinlan, Michael, 47

radical politics, 45, 95, 98–100
Rechabites, 135
Redfern, William, 115, 230n23
Reid, Thomas, 172
respectability: public dinners and, 114, 117–18; temperance and, 17, 56, 59, 138, 139–42, 158; toasting and, 162–3, 164–5; women and, 50, 72, 73, 175–6. *See also* domesticity
responsible government, 12, 58, 204, 211
restrained comportment: introduction, 16; Aboriginal people and, 199, 203; masculinity and, 13, 163, 168–9, 170–1; as performance of citizenship, 7, 19, 72–3, 158, 171, 210, 212; temperance and, 124; toasting and, 109; wine and, 66
Roberts, Matthew, 95, 99
Robinson, Michael Massey, 60–1, 102, 107
Roe, Michael, 17, 138, 158
Roman Catholic Church. *See* Catholics and Catholic Church
Room, Robin, 15
Roseby, Mrs, 179
Ross, Robert, 25, 137
Rossi, Francis, 200
Rowcroft, Charles, 66
Rowe, William, 142, 143
Rowlandson, Thomas: *The Brilliants* (1801), *109*, 109–10
Royal Toast Master (1791), 88, 162

rum, 25, 28, 47, 49, 61, 64, 66
Rum Rebellion, 17, 44, 49–50, 60, 151, 222n2
rural drinking, 29, 66–7, 68–9, 76, 78, 80–1
Russell, Penny, 114
R v. Murrell (1836), 202, 244n101
Ryan, Thomas, 168–9

Sadlier, Richard, 134, 148, 241n39
Sands, Sarah, 154, 155, 157, 158, 180, 235nn6–7
Saunders, John: on Aboriginal people, 181–2, 184–5, 188, 194, 242n71; on alcohol regulation, 152–3; temperance and, 125, 129–30, 141, 147; temperance press and, 197; on women and temperance, 178
Savage, George, 3
Scarborough (First Fleet), 30, 31
Schofield, Samuel, 167
Scott, Joan, 157
Seditious Meetings Acts, 92, 95
Select Committee on Aborigines in British Settlements (1837), 183
Select Committee on Drunkenness (1834), 128
Select Committee on Intemperance (1854), 57, 134, 137, 148, 151–2, 153
Select Committee on the Condition of Aborigines (1845), 197–8
Select Committee on Transportation (1837), 53–4, 173
self-control. *See* restrained comportment
"Sheer Hulk" (sly grog shop), 68, 69, 76
Sirius (First Fleet), 30–1, 171
Skirving, William, 100
sly grog shops, 67–8, 80. *See also* public houses
Smith, Babette, 175
Smitley, Megan, 17
Smyth, Arthur Bowes, 31, 42–3
sober comportment: introduction, 30, 71, 73; feminine ideal and, 156, 175; masculinity and, 168–9, 171; respectability and, 138; temperance and, 124, 126, 131–2, 134, 136, 144, 212. *See also* temperance
social imaginaries, 10. *See also* democratic political imaginary
social mobility, 17–18, 56–7, 66, 126, 138, 139–42, 147
Sons and Daughters of Temperance, 135
spirits, 28, 49, 64–5, 66, 127–8. *See also* gin; rum
spree (binge) drinking, 67, 80–2
squatters, 54, 55, 57, 58, 182, 183, 184–5
Stanley, Lord, 197
Star, The (newspaper), 83–4
Starling, Nicole, 141
Steadman, Carolyn, 175
Stephen, Alfred, 137–8, 145, 169, 205–6
Stonhouse, James, 41
St Patrick's Total Abstinence Society, 132, 133, 141–2, 144, 146
Summers, Anne, 159, 177–8
Sweatman, John, 117–18
Sydney, Thomas Townshend, 1st Viscount, 24, 25, 26, 41
Sydney Aborigines Committee, 202, 203
Sydney Gazette and New South Wales Advertiser (newspaper). See *Gazette, The*
Sydney Journal (newspaper), 69
Sydney Monitor (newspaper). See *Monitor, The*

Sydney Morning Herald (newspaper). See *Herald, The*
Sydney Municipal Council, 55, 168
Sydney Total Abstinence Society, 124, 125, 131–2, 142–3, 144
Sydney Turf Club, 3–8, 9, 60, 72, 85, 93–4, 215n11

Tasmania. *See* Van Diemen's Land
tavern, use of term, 225n12. *See also* public houses
Taylor, Anya, 161
Taylor, Charles, 10
Teetotaller, The (newspaper), 132, 153, 177
temperance: introduction, 22, 56, 126–7, 136–9, 212; on alcohol as a problem substance, 137–8, 148–52; on alcohol regulation, 152–3; backlash against, 169–70; bands of hope, 134, 141; benefit and mutual aid societies, 141–2; democratic political imaginary and, 18, 138–9, 147; Gipps and, 123–5, 126, 130, 132, 145, 147, 152, 177–8; global movement and abstinence shift, 127–8; governmental perspective on drinking and, 15; Maine Law (1851), 133–4, 147–8, 153; in NSW, 59, 125–6, 128–35; patronizing temperance, 123–4, 125, 127, 128, 129–30, 132, 139–40, 144–5, 152; political participation and, 142–8; populist temperance, 128, 131–2, 139, 144; public processions, 143–4, 146; and respectability and social mobility, 17, 56, 59, 138, 139–42, 158; restraint vs sobriety, 73, 124–5; scholarship on, 17–18, 138–9; social elites and, 145–7; temperance histories of NSW, 61–2; women and, 17, 134, 135, 176–80. *See also* sober comportment
Temperance Advocate (newspaper), 80, 125, 130, 132
Tench, Watkin, 31
Terry, Samuel, 119, 121
Therry, Roger, 111
Thompson, Andrew, 115, 230n23
Thompson, E.P., 34, 73
Threlkeld, Lawrence, 195–6, 242n71
toasting: introduction, 22, 85–6, 108; Dickens on, 91–2; egalitarianism and, 7–8, 9, 112–13; health-drinking, 86–7, 124; loyal toasting, 86–8, 97–101, 103–4, 108, 118, 121–2, 126, 165; masculinity and, 160–2, 164–6; to the monarch's health, 100–4, 165; mutinies and, 99–100; at political dinners, 96; political hierarchy and, 102–3; as political performance, 9, 121–2; to political sentiments, 87–9; press reportage of, 91, 121; radical toasting, 98–9; respectability and, 162–3, 164–5; rules and standard features, 89–90, 109–12, 161; scholarship on, 18; at Turf Club dinner, 3–4; use of term, 227n1; women and, 87, 113, 155–6, 159–60, 160–1, 162–3, 165–6. *See also* public dinners
Toast Master (1789), 88
Tocqueville, Alexis de, 11
Tosh, John, 158
Total Abstinence Benefit Society, 144
transportation, 41, 53–4, 58, 172
treating: electoral, 33, 79–80; reciprocal, 78, 82–4, 226n64
Trotter, Thomas, 33
Trusler, John, 162

Turf Club, 3–8, 9, 60, 72, 85, 93–4, 215n11
Turnbull, John, 190, 241n42
Tyrrell, Ian, 234n35

United Kingdom. *See* Britain
United Kingdom Alliance for the Suppression of the Trade in Alcohol, 133
urban drinking, 66, 69, 76–7, 78, 80, 82

Vallance, Patrick, 31
Valverde, Marianna, 139
Van Diemen's Land, 52, 103, 129
Veracini, Lorenzo, 14
Vernon, James, 11, 12
Victoria Bitter adverts, 212–13, 245n28
Vidal, Mary: *Bengala*, 165; "Susan's Dream," 151
violence: domestic violence, 14, 167–8, 180; drunken violence, 75–6, 84, 166–8; vs gentlemanly code of conduct, 169; toasting as substitute, 160, 161

Wakefield, Edmund Gibbon, 55
Walker, George, 129, 196
Walton (blacksmith), 142
Ward, Catherine, 173
Ward, Russel, 13, 77, 80–1, 158
Wardell, Robert, 5, 7, 106, 116, 121–2, 215n11
Warrell, William, 201
Waterhouse, William, 32
Wentworth, D'Arcy, 105, 115, 230n23
Wentworth, William, 3–5, 7, 51, 53, 58, 60–1, 79, 105–7
Whiley, Henry, 76
White, John, 29, 30–1, 144
Wilkes, John, 91, 95, 98
Wilson, Colonel, 200
Wilson, Thomas, 40
Wiltshire, Alderman, 168
Windeyer, Richard, 198
Windschuttle, Elizabeth, 175, 178
wine, 18, 29, 65–6, 72, 124
Withington, Phil, 18
Wolin, Sheldon, 12, 212
women: introduction, 22–3; Aboriginal women, 200–1; democratic political imaginary and, 156–7; domestic violence, 14, 167–8, 180; drunkenness stigma, 8, 27, 35–6, 40–1, 72, 158–9, 172–3; Electoral Reform League public dinner and, 154–5; gendered punishment for drunkenness, 173–4; mixed-gender drinking, 158, 171; at National Banquet celebrating responsible government, 156, 204–5, 210, 211; in NSW, 47, 50, 52, 159; philanthropy and, 175–6; public voice, 56; respectability and, 50, 72, 73, 175–6; restrained drinking and sober comportment, 72, 73; temperance and, 17, 134, 135, 176–80; toasting and, 87, 113, 159–60, 162–3, 165–6; toasting the ladies, 155–6, 160–1. *See also* gender
Women's Christian Temperance Union, 135
Wood, Rebecca, 184
Wood, Thomas, 167
Woollacott, Angela, 186
Worgan, George, 101

Yeomans, Harry, 139